DONNE'S POETRY

DONNE'S POETRY

ESSAYS IN LITERARY ANALYSIS

BY CLAY HUNT

ARCHON BOOKS 1969

Copyright, 1954 by Yale University Press
Reprinted 1969 with permission
in an unaltered and unabridged edition

SBN: 208 00804 7
Library of Congress Catalog Card Number: 69-19227
Printed in the United States of America

Contents

Preface

ONE OF Dr. Samuel Johnson's best jibes was aimed at Donne's poetry. In the passage in the *Life of Cowley* in which he expressed his general distaste for the literary antics of the Metaphysical Poets, he quoted a particularly knotty passage from one of Donne's poems and made only this dead-pan observation: "If the lines are not easily understood, they may be read again." This book is for those who have found that Donne's lines are not easily understood and would like some help in reading them again carefully, or for those who are reading them for the first time. It is not, then, primarily a book for experts on Donne or on the literature of the English Renaissance—though I hope there are things in it which some experts will find interesting—but rather for that uncommon Common Reader who has a serious enough interest in poetry as demanding as Donne's to want to study it closely.

My scheme is to take a few poems and scrutinize them in detail, and then to proceed from these particularities to some general conclusions and speculations about Donne's work and about Donne himself. I have chosen poems that seem both good enough and difficult enough to make this kind of study worth while, and I have tried to make my selection fairly representative of the range of both thought and literary method in Donne's verse. Inevitably, I have leaned toward poems that are difficult, and I have passed up fine poems, like some of the "Holy Sonnets" and "A Hymn to God the Father," simply because they put up very little resistance to a modern reader. I have also passed up "The Ecstasy," for much the same reason, though it is a document of central importance for anybody who wants to understand Donne. It is very explicit, however, in technique; Grierson's explanatory notes clear up most of its difficulties; and it has recently been analyzed in detail by other critics. Nevertheless, I think it is generally true—though with exceptions and qualifications—that Donne's poetry is best when it is difficult, when the thought is subtle and intricate and the imaginative structure is complex; and my choice of poems reflects pretty much my personal taste on the matter of quality in Donne's work. Donne is one of the most uneven performers among major English poets, and I find more than half of his poems either not very impressive, or, like the two Anniversaries, impressive only in parts and unsuccessful as a whole. And a few of them, like that lurid poem "A Nocturnal upon Saint Lucy's Day," seem to me downright grotesque. I have made some concession to the claims of "significance" in deciding to analyze "Love's Alchemy," which is a powerful but rather unkempt poem, but otherwise the poems that I have chosen represent the kinds of Donne's verse which I most thoroughly enjoy.

My readings of these poems necessarily run to a good deal of explication, but I am not interested in explication as an end in itself. I am interested, rather, in how Donne makes the bits and pieces interact to evolve the organism of a poem, to give it continuity and the emergent qualities of form and dramatic vitality. The business of explaining the meaning of a few hard lines is incidental to my purpose of trying to define by analysis the distinctive character of the strong and individual artistic life which I find in each of these poems.

The critical method that I am using has occasioned a good deal of methodological squabbling in recent years, and this is not the place to squabble further. I am afraid, however, that those who resonate with fervor and solemnity to Oscar Wilde's intelligent witticism, "There are two ways of disliking art: one is to dislike it: the other is to like it rationally," will not find this book to their taste. I am well aware of the limits of this analytical method of criticism, but I still think it is a good way to go at the study of poetry. The kind of criticism that I find most useful is the kind which first tries to show me specifically what goes on in a poem, approaching it as an ordered sequence of literary events and endeavoring to define the course and the artistic consequences of its progress, and which does not proceed to generalities about a poem, or about the body of a poet's work, until it has first examined the evidence of that work in its full particularity. The method of close literary analysis, moreover, happens to be particularly useful in dealing with poetry like Donne's, which is intricately made and highly conceptualized. For poetry like this, detailed textual

study can articulate a much larger part of the aesthetic experience
than it can for poetry of other kinds. Of course it cannot define
it all, any more than any other critical method can, and like all
criticism which accepts its modest function and is content to be
primarily criticism and not literature in its own right, its aim is
finally to efface itself, to persuade the reader, eventually, to lay
the criticism aside and read the poems—reading them for the first
time if he does not already know them, or reading them again with
greater pleasure if he does.

In analyzing these poems, however, I have combined the method
of close critical analysis with some of the techniques of historical
literary scholarship. I realize that neither I nor any other modern
reader can succeed beyond a certain point in projecting himself
back into the mentality of Renaissance England and reading
Donne's poems exactly as his contemporaries read them. But the
attempt must be made if we want to see these poems as hard facts
of life existing independent of our individual subjectivities, and if
we want to understand what Donne was doing when he wrote them
with the expectation that they would be read by Renaissance Englishmen. Otherwise we see them out of focus and out of shape,
so that what Donne and his contemporaries thought of as conventional may strike us as original or strange, and what they saw
as fresh or daring may seem commonplace. I have drawn on what
I know about Renaissance thought and literature to supply some
basic information about the intellectual background against which
these poems were written and about the literary traditions and
conventions of Donne's time, in order to try to distinguish what
in them is purely conventional, from what is basically conventional
but treated in a novel way, and from what is essentially original.
Information of this sort is important for understanding any poet's
work, but it is especially important for understanding the verse of
Donne. To read Donne without some knowledge of the commonplaces of belief and poetic style against which he was playing his
poems is often to miss a major impulse behind those poems and
to miss much of their essential literary life, of the theatrical effects
of surprise and novelty which he often worked for in his verse
and which his contemporaries found there. I cannot have been
more than partly successful in defining that nebulous entity "the
average Renaissance reader," but Donne so clearly had that per-

sonage before his mind as he conceived some of these poems that
we must try to re-create this composite figure in order to understand why Donne wrote them as he did.

And I hope that, for readers not particularly conversant with
Renaissance literature, my attempt to place Donne's poetry in its
historical context will give this book a wider usefulness in accli-
matizing them to the Renaissance literary imagination. A mind as
clean and definite as Donne's registers the characteristic ideas and
mental processes of his age with unusual clarity. A careful study,
first of the way in which Donne's mind operates through several of
his best poems, and then of the ways in which the workings of his
imagination are like and unlike those of the imaginations of some
of his literary contemporaries, should make a modern reader very
much at home in the mind of the English Renaissance and should
habituate him to those of its typical concepts, mental attitudes,
and patterns of imaginative association from which the modern
mentality has become estranged. I hope he will find that the ad-
ventitious effect of oddness which three and a half centuries of
cultural change have given to some of these modes of belief and
literary expression will gradually drop away, and that they will
stand clear to him, finally, as normal and natural articulations of
human experience.

Since I am concerned with the poems which I have examined not
only as separate, self-contained works of art but also as a collective body of evidence for general conclusions about Donne's personality and about the ways in which the circumstances of his life
affected his work, I have frequently introduced, in my analyses
of individual poems, conjectures about the events in Donne's personal life which may have impelled him to write them. Except for
the "Hymn to God, My God, in My Sickness," we have no external
evidence, either certain or dubious, about the biographical circumstances under which any of these poems were written, nor do
we have any external evidence which would establish even an ap-
proximate date for them. My theorizing about the biographical
background of individual poems is therefore speculation, and I
have presented it as such, as a possible or probable causal relationship between the facts of Donne's life, insofar as we know them,
and the ideas and psychological attitudes which are embodied in
his poetry. In no case have I allowed these biographical conjec-

tures to modify my reading of the text of a poem, and those who find speculations of this kind uninteresting or critically irrelevant may neglect them.

But I find them both interesting and—within certain limits—significant for literary criticism. I realize that art is not life, in a one-to-one relationship, but it is an aspect of it, motivated in part by the circumstances of the life of a particular human being living in a certain place and time. Poems like "The Blossom," which was obviously written for a specific social occasion, or like "The Good-Morrow" and "The Canonization," which treat of a love affair that Donne presents as a personal revelation, as something unique in his own experience and radically different from the love affairs of other men, certainly set one to wondering what the social occasion was, or who it was that Donne was in love with. These questions arise in the mind of everyone who reads these poems with real interest. To exclude conjecture about them from literary criticism—either on the grounds that conjecture can never become certainty, or on the grounds that something which we all speculate about when we read a poem is not relevant to our understanding of it—seems to me scholarly or critical Puritanism.

Many passages in the poems which I have analyzed are not fully clear from the text of the poem alone, and I have cited in my notes a good many parallel passages in Donne's other work as corroborative evidence for some of my readings. The whole body of any writer's work provides a record of the characteristic tracks which his imagination follows and of the special, personal meanings which he may assign to some of his favorite literary materials. This is particularly true of Donne, whose mind shows a remarkable consistency in following certain associative patterns and whose artistic vocabulary is sometimes idiosyncratic. At those points in my analyses where I think my reading of a passage is questionable, the cross references to Donne's other work in the notes stand as support for my interpretations. The notes also explore minor subtleties of implication and refinements of interpretation which would have complicated the analyses unduly if I had discussed them in the text. And they present, further, a number of parallels between passages in Donne's verse and in the writings of his contemporaries. Parallels of this sort are critically significant because they bear on the question of the extent to which Donne's contemporaries would have found his verse private or obscure. Many passages in his poetry which seem recondite or private to a modern reader would have been readily intelligible to most readers of the Renaissance, but many others which present difficulties today would have seemed equally obscure in his own time. That intelligent and learned literary man, Ben Jonson, who was a friend of Donne's and who esteemed him "the first poet of the world in some things," would not have said that Donne "for not being understood, would perish" if he had not frequently had his troubles in trying to find out what Donne was saying in certain passages of his poems. The cross references to other Renaissance literature in my notes provide some basis, then, for defining the extent of Donne's poetic idiosyncracy. Since these notes are bulky, I have placed them at the back of the book, where they may be read as a commentary on the text.

In critical scrutiny as detailed as this, minutiae of text can sometimes be important, especially for poetry as precisely made as Donne's. In general my texts of these poems follow the authoritative modern editions of Sir Herbert Grierson and of John Hayward, but I have introduced a few variant readings and made a few emendations where I think the accepted modern text is almost certainly wrong. On the problem of spelling I have made a rough compromise. The vagaries of a Renaissance poet's spelling, and the further vagaries often introduced by the Renaissance copyist or typesetter, can present a minor but troublesome barrier to the reader who is not accustomed to them. I have therefore modernized the spelling in all but a few places where the original spelling points to a difference between Renaissance and modern pronunciation which is clearly important for the proper musical effect of a line. Texts in the original spelling are readily available for those who prefer them. I have preserved Donne's punctuation, however—or at least as much of his original punctuation as Grierson and Hayward have been able to recapture by collating the early editions of these poems, all of which were first published after Donne's death, with contemporary manuscript copies. Donne took punctuation seriously and was concerned over the mistakes in punctuation in the editions of his prose works published during his lifetime. His system of punctuation looks odd until one realizes that it is more rhetorical than syntactical: its purpose is often to indicate the kinds of pauses that he wanted in the reading of his verse. One can get the feel of his punctuation easily, and it is sometimes a help in indicating how he wanted the rhythms of a poem to fall. Donne also took capitalization seriously, but I have overridden him on this point and modernized most of the capitalization to keep from bastardizing the text any further. His capitalization is not indicative of metrical stress, and he seems generally to have followed the practice of tossing in a capital when a word had a particular intellectual significance for him; but most of the capitalization of this kind is not interpretively important and some of it seems merely whimsical. There is good evidence, however, from the 1633 edition of his poems, that Donne occasionally capitalized a word to point to the fact that he was using it in a special sense or that it carried an ambiguity or pun which the reader might otherwise miss, and I have preserved a few capitals where I think they have this kind of significance.

The various friends with whom I have discussed parts of this book, as well as a number of scholars who have written about the English Renaissance, will recognize where I have picked their brains. But I feel especially indebted to George Peck and Robert J. Allen, who have worked over the whole manuscript with friendly severity, and to Louis Martz, who, as editorial advisor for the Yale University Press, has suggested a number of changes which have made this a better book than it originally was. Williams College has assisted in the publication of the book by a generous grant from the 1900 Fund. And I owe a particular debt to Fred Stocking, who got me into this in the first place and who has helped out at every turn.

Williams College, 1953

THE INDIFFERENT

I can love both fair and brown,
Her whom abundance melts, and her whom want betrays,
Her who loves loneness best, and her who masks and plays,
Her whom the country formed, and whom the town,
Her who believes, and her who tries,   5
Her who still weeps with spongy eyes,
And her who is dry cork, and never cries;
I can love her, and her, and you and you,
I can love any, so she be not true.

Will no other vice content you?   10
Will it not serve your turn to do, as did your mothers?
Or have you all old vices spent, and now would find out others?
Or doth a fear, that men are true, torment you?
Oh we are not, be not you so,
Let me, and do you, twenty know.   15
Rob me, but bind me not, and let me go.
Must I, who came to travail thorough you,
Grow your fixed subject, because you are true?

Venus heard me sigh this song,
And by Love's sweetest part, Variety, she swore,   20
She heard not this till now; and that it should be so no more.
She went, examined, and returned ere long,
And said, Alas, some two or three
Poor heretics in love there be,
Which think to stablish dangerous constancy.   25
But I have told them, since you will be true,
You shall be true to them, who'are false to you.

Chapter 1

SOME MINOR POEMS:
"The Indifferent," "Elegy 19,"
"Love's Alchemy," "The Blossom"

I HAVE called these poems "minor" simply because they are slighter pieces than the poems which I will consider in later chapters. All of them are work of some distinction, and "The Blossom" is one of Donne's most delightful poems, but they are verse of less density and smaller reach than "The Good-Morrow," "The Canonization," and the "Hymn to God, My God, in My Sickness." They express attitudes peripheral to those with which most of Donne's mature poetry is concerned but important for an understanding of the complexity of Donne's temperament. Together, they will serve to suggest the range and variety of the verse one finds in the "Songs and Sonnets."

"The Indifferent"

"The Indifferent" is a poem in which Donne is having fun, and to pull a long face and settle down to the solemn analysis of fun seems a little heavy handed. But though the poem certainly does not require exhaustive analysis, it is worth some scrutiny. One does need some particular knowledge of current fashions in Elizabethan love poetry to enjoy the fun, and to see the precise point in some of Donne's spoofing of those fashions. And "The Indifferent" illustrates also some characteristic aspects of Donne's literary technique.

It is probably quite an early poem.[1] The simplicity and obviousness of its literary methods, its untroubled gaiety, and its pose

of libertinism all suggest that Donne wrote it when he was a
young man about town in Elizabethan London—a young man
known, as Sir Richard Baker later remembered him, as "not
dissolute but very neat; a great visitor of ladies, a great frequenter
of plays, a great writer of conceited verses." The poem is a piece of
light social verse, a work not for all time but definitely of an age
and of a particular social environment. It was written for an audience of would-be sophisticates who were splurging, with a *nouvel-
arrivé* abandon, in the varied and exciting new fashions belatedly
reaching England from the European Renaissance. To this audience love was one of the most interesting of these new fashions, and
the writing of love poetry was a requisite activity for anyone who
wished to be thought a cultivated gentleman. The enterprise of
being in love, and writing poems about it, might be undertaken
with full humanistic seriousness, as an experience which entailed
valuable intellectual and spiritual consequences; but it might also
be undertaken simply as one of the most diverting of social games.
In the first act of *As You Like It,* when Shakespeare is characterizing
Rosalind and Celia as sophisticated ladies of the court, Rosalind
finds herself in the dumps and Celia is urging her to be merry.
"From henceforth I will, coz," says Rosalind, "and devise sports.
Let me see; what think you of falling in love?" Donne wrote "The
Indifferent" for readers who knew the sport and had a practitioner's
familiarity with its techniques, who would expect of a love poet
not that he unlock his heart but rather that he take the stock materials of contemporary love poetry and display his skill and invention—his "artificiality," they might have said, and would have
meant the word as a compliment—by manipulating those conventions in a way which was new.

A good part of the comedy of "The Indifferent" depends on the
reader's familiarity with the literary fashion of Petrarchism, which
had its great vogue in England in the early 1590's—in fact, the
poem is conceived essentially as a spoofing of the Petrarchan stereotypes. Glancing back and forth between the text of the poem and
the mass of Elizabethan love sonnets, we can reconstruct easily the
sort of quintessential Petrarchan love sonnet which Donne had in
mind as he wrote "The Indifferent." The sonnets written in this
tradition elaborated the stock situation of the lover's worship of a
disdainful lady, normally blonde. Though she did not return his

love, he was constant in his devotion: he accepted the role of faithful though unrewarded subject of the tyrannical mistress, and the
poems in which he told of his love were most often love complaints
which analyzed his emotional frustrations. Their prevailing mode
was that of a gracefully artificial love woe, of "tear-floods" and
"sigh-tempests." Since they usually dealt with a love affair which
was not consummated and which might even be entirely imaginary,
they tended to treat love as more spiritual than physical and to
express that impulse to chivalric idealization of woman which
found a parallel manifestation in Renaissance Platonism. One of
their stock metaphors presented the love affair as high-minded religious worship, with the lover as devotee of a faith in which the
lady was a saint, and Venus and Cupid functioned as deities who
enforced the elaborate ritual of devotion.

It is against some such archetypal Petrarchan sonnet as this that
Donne directs the impudent wit of "The Indifferent" and of many
of his other early love poems. A contemporary reader would probably have caught on to what Donne was doing from the opening
line, in which the speaker announces that he can "love *both* fair
and brown," since the typical Petrarchan mistress was fair; but he
would certainly have recognized the particular target of Donne's
satire from the rest of the poem.

"The Indifferent" presents a poem within a poem: the first two
stanzas, which are followed by a concluding stanza of commentary.
Line 19, which describes the first two stanzas as a "song" that the
lover has "sighed," points the reader to the poem's central ironic
device. As the Petrarchan tag of the word "sighed" suggests,
stanzas 1 and 2 are cast in the traditional sonneteering mode of
the love complaint: they constitute a poem in which the distressed
lover bemoans the frustrations he suffers as a result of his mistress'
unreasonableness and inhumanity. But the resemblance stops
there: in all other respects the kind of love which this poem deals
with is the precise opposite of the standard situation in Petrarchan
verse. By simply inverting the stock attitudes and values of the
Petrarchan lover, Donne presents a lover who regards constancy as
a "vice" and promiscuity as the path of virtue and good sense, who
sees love simply as lust, and who views women unromantically, as
creatures who are normally as promiscuous as he is unless they are
perverted from this condition of moral health by the fashionable

new vice of constancy. Donne's poem inverts also the conventional relationship between the lover and his mistress. The lover addresses his complaint not to the one mistress of his heart but to *all* his mistresses, actual and potential, and he sighs, not because they are unresponsive or fickle, but because their egregious responsiveness and fidelity make them expect from him the devotion of a "fixed subject."

Now this is a clever enough trick, but it is a pretty obvious and mechanical device of perverse wit, hardly enough by itself to carry a poem. What brings the poem to life is the fresh comic ingenuity and the technical skill with which Donne dramatizes this slick, ready-made cynicism.

Donne makes the speaker of his poem a sharp dramatic character, and the personality is not at all the one we might expect—the flippant and breezy cavalier who is the obvious *persona* for stock, man-of-the-world cynicism about women. Instead, he is a serious man—in fact, in the last analysis, a moral man, though he is tolerant of normal vices—and he speaks as someone who is troubled and concerned. Donne maintains the dead-pan comedy of his plaintive earnestness throughout the poem. The speaker sees himself as eminently reasonable, scrupulous, and accommodating, and he therefore feels a mounting annoyance as he contemplates the way in which his own civilized tolerance is imposed on by the unreasonableness of women. The title of the poem means "The Impartial," and the speaker presents his plea to women in the manner of a man who regards himself as free of prejudice and accessible to any justifiable demand. He begins his complaint in a tone of weary and patient entreaty—an effect suggested by the slack syntax of the interminable string of coordinate clauses ("her . . . and her . . . and her . . .")—and works to a climax of irritation at the end of the first stanza:

> I can love her, and her, and you and you,
> I can love *any*, so she be not *true*.

This stanza seems so casually written and so free of stylistic manipulation that one may easily overlook its artifices: the formal devices of logical disposition, of rhetoric, and of prosodic variation which Donne has used to shape his material for an effect of gradual dramatic intensification. This effect is achieved, first, by

the climactic logical development of the stanza—the progression
from the catalogue of particular character types, to the more general "her, and her, and you and you," and then to the comprehensive "any" just before Donne springs the shock statement of
the last half line. And the rhetorical devices in the single sentence
which runs the entire length of the stanza are similarly climactic:
the cumulative development of the motifs "I can love" and "her
who"; and the repetition of the antithetic pattern, which is continued unchanged through five single lines, then varied in the
two-line antithesis of lines 6–7, repeated with a difference in the
"her, and her, and you and you" of line 8, and finally broken for
the logical climax in the last line. The rhythmic effects also assist
in this gradual stepping-up of the voltage. There is a rhythmic
progression from the even, steady movement and moderate stresses
of the opening lines to the slower pace, the stronger stresses, and
sharply defined metrical pattern of "her, and her, and you and
you," and finally to the very heavy accents on "any" and "true" in
line 9. The powerful thrust of these two words springs the final
line entirely free of the trochaic rhythmic pattern and gives it the
straining cadences of a groan of frayed patience.

Donne pushes his climax further in stanza 2, where the speaker
finally opens up on the unreasonableness of women with frank
exasperation. And here the expression of his annoyance acquires
a sharper satiric bite from the bluntness of his references to sex.
This tone has been suggested near the end of stanza 1 in the anti-
romantic details of "spongy eyes" and "dry cork." In stanza 2 it is
intensified by the connotations of the word "know" in line 15,
which is strong talk in Donne's vocabulary; by the reference to the
physically debilitating effect of intercourse ("rob me") in the high-
wayman conceit in line 16; and by the indelicate sexual pun on
the word "travail" in the following line.[2]

The irregular rhythms and heavy accents of the end of the first
stanza also carry over into the second. Donne is still using the
elaborate verse form of stanza 1, but here the metrical scheme
breaks down almost entirely from the numerous shifts in pace and
the exceptionally heavy stresses in many of the lines:

Will no *other* vice content you? . . .

Or doth a fear, that *men* are true, torment you?
Oh we are *not*, be not *you* so,
Let me, and do you, *twenty* know. . . .

Grow your fixed subject, because *you* are true?

The trochaic beat is heard only occasionally (lines 16–17), and most of the stanza does not have the metrical quality of verse at all but rather the shifting rhythms and uneven dynamics of urgent, impassioned speech.

After the theatrical climax of the second stanza, stanza 3 returns to the more even rhythms and the relaxed manner of the start of the poem; and here Donne shifts his metrical pattern to iambic in order to break away from the insistent rhythmic onset of the trochaic beat of stanzas 1 and 2. The opening line, "Venus heard me sigh this song," serves to tip off the reader, if he needs it, to the comedy of the dead-pan clowning which Donne has put his actor through in stanza 2. And after the ragged and dynamic rhythms of that stanza the word "song" is particularly ludicrous. It makes clear that Donne's failure to keep normal verse accent in stanza 2 —that poetic crime for which Ben Jonson said he deserved hanging—has been purposeful: it is intended as an element in the literary comedy of the poem. Metrically, the speaker's love complaint is virtually an anti-song: its rhythmic roughness and vigor are as sharply opposed to the smooth numbers of conventional love poetry as its attitudes toward love are opposed to the conventional attitudes of the Petrarchan lover. And since the whole poem has been built on the device of inverting the values and the literary effects of the conventional love poem, Venus' observation that "she heard not this till now" is almost certainly meant to carry, as an overtone, a sly reference to the poem's central purpose.

The method of turning Petrarchism upside down continues through the rest of stanza 3. Donne stands the stock analogy between love and religion on its head in his reference to the "heretics in love" in line 24, and he presents Venus as a hard-headed worldling who will stand for no nonsense about fidelity. But even the goddess can make no headway against the bull-headed irrationality of faithful women, and the closing lines return to the tone of weary resignation with which the poem began.

"The Indifferent" is not a poem for critical ponderosities. It is an amusing piece of light verse. But its informal, anti-poetic manner conceals a good deal of stylistic artifice. And the energy, the colloquial realism, and the dramatic vividness of the first two stanzas go far beyond any similar effects in the love poetry of Donne's contemporaries. Only Sidney, among Donne's predecessors, had shown a comparable ability to make live drama out of a short love poem, but no poem of Sidney's is so sharply theatrical as this or calls so strongly for an acting performance. The poem is the work of a man whose imagination operates in dramatic terms.

The satiric attitude toward Petrarchism which one sees in "The Indifferent" raises, however, a more general critical question which is important for an understanding of all Donne's poetry—the question of Donne's attitude toward literary conventions. Even in his early verse Donne was far from a die-hard opponent of the conventions of the Petrarchan tradition—in fact, he used almost all of the Petrarchan machinery at one time or another in his love poems, and sometimes used it without any suggestion of ridicule. He once observed breezily that "whilom, before this age of wit, and wearing black broke in upon us, there was no way known to win a lady, but by tilting, tourneying, and riding through forests"; [3] and he was not averse to the handiness of these new methods, particularly to their artistic handiness for a bright young man who saw that writing love poems was a good way to make one's mark in Elizabethan London. Nor, on the other hand, was Donne by any means the first Elizabethan poet to see the literary possibilities in satirizing the conventions of Petrarchism. No Elizabethan love poet was unaffected by these conventions, but no poet of any consequence devoted himself merely to rehearsing slavishly and uncritically "poor Petrarch's long-deceased woes." A critical attitude toward the Petrarchan stereotypes was well established in Elizabethan love poetry before Donne began writing—it is pervasive, for instance, in the sonnets of Sidney, which seem to have been a major influence in starting the vogue of Petrarchism in England. In fact, by the time Donne began his literary career, the tendency to poke fun at the artificiality of the Petrarchan conventions had already become simply another of the Petrarchan conventions.

In a sense, then, all of Donne's early love poetry is merely an exploitation of the elaborate stock of literary commonplaces in Elizabethan love poetry of the 1590's. But he exploited them with a difference. Even in the poems where he seems to be trying to play them straight—to say without a snicker that his mistress is the sun, or that her eyes are; that she is an angel; that love is religious worship, or that it is warfare with the "loved foe"; that he is tormented by sighs and tears and will surely die from her scorn, and so on—what comes out looks different from the numbers Petrarch flowed in, and from the verse of most of the Elizabethan love poets. Pieces of this sort—a poem like "Air and Angels," for instance—have a way of spinning off either into pyrotechnics of wit or into lively enterprises of metaphysical speculation in which analytic intellectuality chills the warm lifeblood out of romantic hyperbole. Donne was incapable of that evocative, myth-making power of the imagination which is the spirit behind the letter of Petrarchan verse, or of any other mode of romantic love poetry, and without which its conventions of extravagant statement become mere absurdities or fantastic intellectual jugglery. He was temperamentally too skeptical, and also too arrogant, to be able to project himself with any wholehearted imaginative commitment into that knightly role of humble and courteous servant of an idealized mistress which was so congenial to the romanticizing imagination of Spenser and many other Elizabethans. Nor could he, like Sidney, set free his critical intellect to make game of the absurdities of romantic love and of the Petrarchan love conventions only in order that he might finally call it to heel, as Sidney does again and again in such closing lines as "True, and yet true that I must Stella love," thus conceding with dramatic effectiveness to everything in those conventions which is emotionally valid.

But it was not only Donne's temperamental insensitivity to the spirit of romance which made his Petrarchan poems either unsuccessful, or successful in a brilliant, tensely intellectualized way which places them in a different aesthetic category from the best of Petrarchan love poetry. He was too restless, too individualistic, and too ruthless of mind to have any essential taste for the formal artifices of courtly behavior. Let us look for a minute at "The Apparition," a poem which derives from one of the Petrarchan stereotypes:

When by thy scorn, O murderess, I am dead,
And that thou think'st thee free
From all solicitation from me,
Then shall my ghost come to thy bed,
And thee, feigned vestal, in worse arms shall see;
Then thy sick taper will begin to wink,
And he, whose thou art then, being tired before,
Will, if thou stir, or pinch to wake him, think
    Thou call'st for more,
And in false sleep will from thee shrink,
And then poor aspen wretch, neglected thou
Bathed in a cold quicksilver sweat wilt lie
    A verier ghost than I . . .

One may have to look twice at this piece of brutal sexual realism to recognize that its point of departure is one of the most prettily artificial of the Petrarchan clichés: that the lover will die from his mistress' scorn. Donne is not satirizing the convention here, though he is clearly trying to do something new with it. But the convention is entirely out of its element in this poem. After all, as Rosalind pointed out, men have died from time to time, and worms have eaten them, but not for love; and they have no business doing so in such a coldly realistic poem as this. The hard violence of the poem tears the pretty artifice of the conceit to tatters. If Donne had ever given much sympathetic attention to the Petrarchan hyperboles, or had ever felt any solid appreciation for those elegant and semi-playful extravagances of the code of sophisticated courtship which the tradition embodied, he would have known better than to introduce any of them into this poem. Donne simply had no habitual feel for this sort of thing. That urbane temper which makes one at home within the conventions of formal society, which allows one to find aesthetic pleasure in the grace of the artifices of polite social intercourse while being fully aware of their artificiality—the aristocrat's balance of mind which Sidney maintains so beautifully in his love sonnets—was something which Donne rarely achieved and perhaps never tried very hard to achieve. For all his familiarity with the cultivated society of Elizabethan London, he seems to have remained at heart a good deal of a maverick.

So, though Donne evidently tried on occasions to be a courtly poet of romantic love according to the standard Elizabethan pattern, it was not only humor which kept breaking in, but also ugly realism, and bare sexual passion, and abstract intellectual excitement. And he functioned best when he was trying not to be a courtly love poet. The most successful of his early love poems are those which either ridicule Petrarchism or break through that tradition into love poetry of a different kind. Moreover, Donne's ridicule of the Petrarchan stereotypes is often of a more serious kind than the playful, essentially conventional anti-Petrarchism of Sidney's sonnets and of Shakespeare's "My mistress' eyes are nothing like the sun." Donne is having his fun in poems like "The Indifferent" and "Go, and catch a falling star," but it is rowdy fun, of a tough and muscular kind. Though the intent of these poems is clearly comic and though the role of cynical realist is obviously an assumed literary pose, they have an energy and dramatic force which shoves them toward the borderline between merely entertaining light verse and serious poetry.

It was something more fundamental, then, than a desire for the mere flash of literary novelty which impelled Donne to make game of the commonplaces of contemporary love poetry. And I think the psychological roots of that impulse lay deeper than the merely intellectual biases of that skeptical, hard-headed cast of mind which estranged Donne from the courtly grace, the myth-making romanticism, and the moral idealism that are the dominant qualities of Elizabethan poetry in the early 1590's. There is, in fact, something a little peculiar about the sharpness with which Donne's imagination actualized the contemporary literary patterns which he manhandled in his early love poetry. Renaissance poets in general were more conscious of the conventions of literary artifice than most later poets have been, but no Elizabethan poet seems to have been so acutely and constantly conscious of them as Donne. With a clear objective perception of those set patterns in expression and behavior which gave manageable form to the lives of others—and which a young man with his way to make and large plans for himself must get to know—and with an equally clear subjective perception of all in his inner life which was lively and recalcitrant and which kept breaking out of these patterns to which others adapted themselves more readily, Donne seems at times to have an almost physical apprehension of literary conventions, as though he felt them as external forms pressing uncomfortably against his haughty sense of personal separateness. Those forms represented to his mind The Reader, the normal member of a society from which Donne seems early to have regarded himself as somewhat alienated. In poems like "The Indifferent," which are essentially maneuvers with poetic commonplaces and which seem more procedural than substantive, Donne is manipulating those conventions—either handling them in a fresh way or kicking them rudely aside—as a means of manipulating that reader's mind, and thereby startling or shocking him into an awareness of what is John Donne.

No other Elizabethan poet shows so constant a sense of what the average reader will expect from a certain kind of poem or seems so persistently concerned to disappoint or to exceed those expectations. For all that scholars have shown of the contributory influences on Donne's literary style and of the many similarities between his work and that of his contemporaries, his poetry— even some of his earliest poetry—was a new thing under the sun. From the start of his literary career Donne seems to have wanted to make it just that, and to make his reader sharply aware that, like Venus in "The Indifferent," he "heard not this till now." Playing fast and loose with well-established literary convention was one of the simplest and most dramatic ways by which this effect could be produced.

Dr. Johnson, in his censure of the Metaphysical Poets in the "Life of Cowley," responded to the effect, but at least for Donne misunderstood its cause: "as they were wholly employed on something unexpected or surprising, . . . they never inquired what, on any occasion, they should have said or done." [4] Clearly on many occasions Donne inquired very carefully what ordinary people would have said or done—because he wanted to dramatize the fact that John Donne did not do things that way.

In his later verse Donne's sense of alienation from his society hardened into a stern condescension which inclined him to look on normal men as "the laity," an image which recurs throughout his love poetry, and to think of his personal experience as something which they could never understand:

> And if this love, though placed so,
>   From profane men you hide,
> Which will no faith on this bestow,
>   Or, if they do, deride:
>
> Then you have done a braver thing
>   Than all the Worthies did;
> And a braver thence will spring,
>   Which is, to keep that hid.[5]

But in his early poems, written before he had ruined his chances for advancement by his marriage and while he was still hoping for a career in the great world of Elizabethan London, he seems still concerned to work out a modus vivendi with that world. Even there, however, he enjoys taking up positions which place him somewhat at odds with his audience, writing poems which seem to be calculated assaults on their normal literary expectations.

All this may sound like an account of the way in which any good poet operates. But this procedure was much less characteristic of the Elizabethan poets than it has been of many poets of the nineteenth and twentieth centuries. The poet who is primarily concerned to assert his distinctive individuality in his work has been the norm in modern literature until very recently, but he is one of our legacies from the Romantic movement and, ultimately, from the Renaissance, when modern man first began to sanctify his individuality and to believe, as Donne was naturally one of the first to notice, that

>   he hath got
> To be a Phoenix, and that then can be
> None of that kind, of which he is, but he.[6]

But that concern was much less primary to most of the good poets in England in the 1580's and 1590's. Humbly conscious that their nation had come up behind in the cultural advance of the European Renaissance, and patriotically desirous of producing a literature in English which might take its place in the great tradition that derived from "insolent Greece" and "haughty Rome"[7] and might challenge comparison with the new national literatures of

Italy and France, most poets of that time were not only content but eager to begin by writing within some pre-existent and reputable literary tradition, and were willing to manifest their originality merely by working creatively within that tradition's literary patterns.

When one recognizes how general was this deliberate acceptance of convention among Elizabethan poets, Donne's rejection of this approach to the writing of verse becomes more dramatic.[8] It was only rarely, for instance, that he seems to have made any attempt to formulate that concept of *genre* which was so normal an initial step in the creative process for most Elizabethan poets, to ask himself as he began a poem, "What literary kind am I using here, and what effects of style are required by the rules of 'decorum' in that genre?" [9] And it cannot be mere happenstance that, though he started his career as a love poet at the height of the vogue for writing sonnets, and though he experimented busily with other intricate verse forms, he never used the sonnet form for a love poem. Unlike Jonson—and unlike Spenser, and Sidney, and Shakespeare, and that strong individualist John Milton—Donne seems generally to have been unwilling to surrender his personal individuality to the set patterns of a literary tradition and to undertake to operate, however creatively, within that tradition throughout a poem. Even Marlowe, who seems quite as intransigent, as energetic, and as individualistic as Donne—and quite as disposed to jolt the complacent—was content to channel his great original talents through traditional literary modes in "Hero and Leander" and "Come live with me and be my love." When Donne participated in the contemporary literary game of writing answers to Marlowe's pastoral lyric—that refined essence of the ideality of pastoral which seems to express so little of what Marlowe was personally—his approach was characteristic: instead of writing a "reply" to Marlowe's poem, he set himself the task of taking Marlowe's literary material and giving it a new and distinctive twist of his own:

> Come live with me, and be my love,
> And we will some *new* pleasures prove
> Of golden sands, and crystal brooks,
> With silken lines, and silver hooks.[10]

Like Ezra Pound, with whose temperament he had certain affinities, Donne's concern in his early poetry was to "Make It New," and to make it distinctively Donne.

Essentially, then, what Donne is endeavoring to startle his reader with in poems like "The Indifferent" is a sense of the author's singularity. I think the desire to make a splash as a wit is only a superficial motive behind these early love poems, and behind the "Paradoxes and Problems" which Donne was writing at the same time: his basic drive in these works seems to be the desire to dramatize the fact that everything is more complicated than most people think, and that John Donne is more complicated than most people think they are. One of his favorite strategic maneuvers in many of these poems—a trick of theater which reminds one, at its most playful, of Bernard Shaw, and at its most serious, of Yeats, in some of his late lyrics—is to reverse his course suddenly in the middle or at the end of a poem, so that just as soon as the reader is sure that he knows what Donne is saying, or what the tone of a poem is, and has begun to settle comfortably into understanding where this poem is headed, Donne jerks him around and heads off in the opposite direction.[11] This was not what he meant at all, it seems, and he really means just the opposite, and you mustn't think that conventional people like yourself can understand John Donne so easily.

This tendency to explore paradox and to engage in Jesuitical disputation in the role of Devil's Advocate reflects, to be sure, a general taste of Donne's age for wit of this kind, as anyone can see from the wit combats in Elizabethan plays. It was an age in which civilization could be defined, as Sidney defined it in *An Apology for Poetry,* as a capacity "to find a pleasure in the exercises of the mind," and in which training in formal logical disputation, a normal part of a university education, disposed men to find a particular pleasure in the intellectual game of debating logical opposites. But no Elizabethan poet devoted himself as relentlessly as Donne to investigating whether the opposite of what was normally believed might not also be true. And the paradoxical wit of his early light verse finds a parallel in his more serious poems in that persistent pattern of argument which maintains that flesh is actually like spirit, or that west is really east, or that death is life. This tendency of mind can have come, I think, only from strong psychological disjunctions in Donne's inner life and from a vivid sense that his personal experience fitted none of the conventional patterns. As one follows it through his later poems and his sermons, this impulse seems at times almost a neurotic compulsion. But in his early work it led him to find in the role of cavalier image breaker one of the most comfortable of his literary masks.

ELEGY 19: TO HIS MISTRESS GOING TO BED

Come, Madam, come, all rest my powers defy,
Until I labour, I in labour lie.
The foe oft-times having the foe in sight,
Is tired with standing though he never fight.
Off with that girdle, like heaven's Zone glistering,   5
But a far fairer world encompassing.
Unpin that spangled breastplate which you wear,
That th'eyes of busy fools may be stopped there.
Unlace yourself, for that harmonious chime,
Tells me from you, that now it is bed time.   10
Off with that happy busk, which I envy,
That still can be, and still can stand so nigh.
Your gown going off, such beauteous state reveals,
As when from flow'ry meads th'hill's shadow steals.
Off with that wyerie coronet and show   15
The haiery diadem which on you doth grow:
Now off with those shoes, and then safely tread
In this love's hallowed temple, this soft bed.
In such white robes, heaven's angels used to be
Received by men; thou angel bring'st with thee   20
A heaven like Mahomet's Paradise; and though
Ill spirits walk in white, we eas'ly know
By this these angels from an evil sprite,
Those set our hairs, but these our flesh upright.

License my roving hands, and let them go, 25
Before, behind, between, above, below.
O my America! my new-found-land,
My kingdom, safeliest when with one man manned,
My Mine of precious stones, my empery,
How blest am I in this discovering thee! 30
To enter in these bonds, is to be free;
Then where my hand is set, my seal shall be.

Full nakedness! All joys are due to thee,
As souls unbodied, bodies unclothed must be,
To taste whole joys. Gems which you women use 35
Are like Atlanta's balls, cast in men's views,
That when a fool's eye lighteth on a gem,
His earthly soul may covet theirs, not them.
Like pictures, or like books' gay coverings made
For laymen, are all women thus arrayed; 40
Themselves are mystic books, which only we
(Whom their imputed grace will dignify)
Must see revealed. Then since that I may know;
As liberally, as to a midwife, show
Thy self: cast all, yea, this white linen hence, 45
Here is no penance, much less innocence.

To teach thee, I am naked first; why then
What need'st thou have more covering than a man?

Elegy 19: "To His Mistress Going To Bed"

The nineteenth Elegy is the most astonishing performance of Donne's early phase as a brilliant young practitioner in the verse of wit and impudence. It is an easy poem to enjoy and to understand in general, and much of it needs no explanation to anyone past the age of twelve. But after a loosely written and relatively conventional beginning, the poem suddenly rises to verse of passion and power, and it concludes with a closely contrived passage of perverse philosophic ingenuity which is one of Donne's most intricate and exciting pieces of intellectual virtuosity. It is this latter half of the poem, especially the concluding section, which is worth our attention. These are the passages which make the Elegy something more than a piece of mere clever indecency.

The Elegy belongs almost certainly to the early or middle 1590's, to the period when Donne was writing poems like "The Indifferent," and it was clearly written against the particular social and literary background which I have described in discussing that poem. Donne expects his reader to be familiar with some of the stock imagery of Petrarchan love poetry and to be struck by the novelty in his treatment of the standard poetic propositions that a love affair is a war and the mistress the "loved foe," that the mistress is an angel, that love is religious devotion, and that the mistress's beauties are the treasures of the Indies. He is writing also against the background of the general Debate between the Body and the Soul which was the dominant intellectual issue in the literary treatment of love in the 1590's. The two most sharply opposed points of view in this debate can be roughly identified, in their literary manifestations, with the Ovidian and the Platonic traditions in Elizabethan love poetry. Those theorists on love who espoused the doctrines of Renaissance Platonism looked on the body as inessential temporal clothing for the eternal reality of soul; and they believed, if they carried their doctrine to its ultimate conclusion, that the rational lover not only should aspire to rise above sensuality but might hope to advance beyond even a purely spiritual union with the soul of a woman, progressing up the steps of the Stair of Love until his love was finally consummated by the union of his soul with God in the Mystic Experience. Standing against the Platonists was a group of philosophic opponents who thought this conception of the essential nature of love absurd. To this school, who found their chief literary ancestor in Ovid, love was bodily passion unhampered by reason—where both deliberated, the love was slight.[12] True love, in their view, was the irrational and satisfying experience of mere lust.

An Elizabethan reader would have had some hint of what to expect of Elegy 19 from the verse form itself. As a poem about love, written in heroic couplets and entitled an "elegy," it is cast in the currently fashionable literary form derived from Ovid's *Amores*. It was to be expected that a poem in this form would adhere to the Ovidian tradition, that the author would align himself with the proponents of the Body and celebrate the techniques of seduction from the sophisticated point of view of a man about town, and that his literary style would display his ingenuity and wit in elaborate conceits. Donne does not disappoint these expectations.

The Elegy seems to present an actual dramatic situation. The poem is apparently spoken by a lover who is lying in bed waiting for his mistress to join him. It is cast in the form of an argument urging her to undress and get into bed, and it maintains a certain argumentative character throughout. But the latter part of the poem evolves into what is less a direct address to the mistress than a transcript of the private workings of the lover's excited imagination as he anticipates the successive stages of his love-making. At the end of the poem the mistress is still undressing and her lover is still waiting for her. When we have finished the poem, the dramatic situation which it presents appears to be less an actuality than a vividly imagined fiction. The Elegy is a dramatized love letter, an Ovidian verse epistle to an only moderately coy mistress.

Donne starts the poem powerfully, with one of the explosive, theatrical openings which are among the distinctive effects of his love poetry. The first four lines derive from one of the most common of the Petrarchan conventions, the comparison of love to warfare, but Donne freshens this stale conceit by exploiting its latent dramatic possibilities. He makes the beginning of the poem a call to battle, a vigorous challenge delivered in a tone of swagger and arrogance. And the sexual puns which he scatters through these lines produce a tough, anti-romantic quality that accentuates the brusque tone suggested by the call-to-battle image.

After this promising beginning, the rest of the opening section

(lines 5–24) offers little more than an exercise in the mannerisms
of the genre. This passage is jaunty and conventionally indelicate,
but it has very little dramatic continuity and no central artistic
structure. It presents merely a string of disconnected, flashy, and far-
fetched conceits, enlivened by sexual innuendoes.[13] Donne is straining to be novel and clever, but what he writes in these lines is
simply a routine performance in the conventional manner of Ovidian erotic verse.

But the poem comes to life again, after the slackness of these
lines, in the dramatic power of the following section. The ex-
uberant exploration conceit of this passage has become a *locus
classicus* to illustrate the passion and imaginative excitement which
the Elizabethans found in geographic exploration and in the discovery of the New World, but the emotional power of Donne's
image is the counterpart of a lively intellectual elaboration which
explores the analogy in precise detail. The basic metaphor—a
comparison of the physical beauties of the mistress to the material
riches which the Indies offered to the Renaissance voyagers—is
one of the commonplaces of Elizabethan love poetry,[14] but Donne's
dramatizing imagination works this routine material to sharp concreteness in the treatment of both the metaphor itself and the sexual experience that it describes, which is presented with an almost
anatomical precision. The lover addresses the mistress in the specific role of an explorer who is requesting a royal patent ("license")
which will permit him to discover a new land, explore its unknown
riches, conquer it, and, having established himself as its autocratic
monarch, bring it under the firm mastery of his civil authority.
The political implications of the conceit are sharpened by allusions
to some of the commonplaces of Renaissance political thought, to
the view that an autocratic monarchy is the most stable form of
government (line 28), and to the doctrine that the ruler's freedom
in exercising his power is offset by the responsibilities ("bonds")
which that power entails (line 31).[15] This development of the
conceit comes to a dramatic climax in the final line of the passage,
which presents the lover's assumption of full command over his
mistress in terms of the authoritative conclusion to a legal document or proclamation: "To this I have set my hand and seal." The
pun on "seal" in this line, like the other sexual ambiguities
throughout the passage, parallels the particularity of the metaphor

with an equally concrete realism in presenting the experience to which the metaphor refers.[16]

These lines present, then, a splurge of virtuoso wit in Donne's elaboration of a detailed parallel between the lover's sexual advances and the discovery and political subjugation of a new land. The exploration image dramatizes vividly not only the lover's passionate excitement but also his exultant sense of power in his sexual mastery of his mistress. And the cadences of the verse—the slow, powerful surge of rhythms through "Before, behind, between, above, below" to the outburst of "O my America! my new-found-land"—underscore the metaphoric suggestion of rapt physical passion. The effect of the emotional climax of the passage in line 32, like that of the opening of the poem, is one of bold, swaggering theatricality.

This effect of cumulative intensity carries over into the exclamatory opening of the following section and is sustained throughout the passage as the lover excitedly imagines the "whole joys" of sexual consummation. And the intellectual ingenuity which has been operating in the preceding section drives to a climax of virtuosity in lines 33–45 as Donne launches into an intricate and detailed analogy between the ecstatic physical consummation of this *affaire de corps* and the consummation of a purely spiritual love in the religious ecstasy of the Beatific Vision. The link which relates this piece of breezy blasphemy to the general subject of the mistress's undressing is the conventional clothing metaphor suggested in lines 34–5, an image which Donne often used in his later serious treatments of spiritual love and of the Mystic Experience.[17] Since those who regarded love as essentially an impulse of the soul thought of the body as mere evanescent "clothing" for the eternal reality of spirit, the Mystic Ecstasy might be thought of as an experience in which the soul divested itself of its temporal clothes and went naked to immediate contact with God.[18] The basic intellectual maneuver which Donne performs at this point in the poem is simply to turn this stock metaphor upside down. The fanciful argument which this section of the poem develops reduces, then, to the following logical proposition, which is implied in lines 34–5: since the Beatific Vision is like taking off your clothes to experience full joy, then taking off your clothes to experience full joy is like the Beatific Vision. This argument is expanded in the passage as a pseudo-theological validation for nakedness and lust.

Before examining the details with which Donne develops the conceit, we might pause to reflect on how a Renaissance reader would react to this analogy. It is certainly the most startling of all Donne's paradoxes. The basic conceit not only equates the sinful pleasures of the flesh with the pure bliss of heaven, but in effect it also equates the soul with the body, since it identifies the full intellectual "joys" of the naked soul with the full sensual joys of the naked body. Donne thus obliterates, by a single stroke of wit, that sharp dichotomy between Sense and Reason, body and soul, temporal matter and eternal spirit, "things visible" and "things invisible," which was not only the central organizing concept in his own thought but also one of the fundamental conceptual antitheses in the thought of the whole Renaissance. The bright young man who set himself up, at the start of his literary career, as a special practitioner in the shock effect of witty paradox never devised a more shocking paradox than this.

But the perverse wit of this passage would have had a further and more specific point for the Elizabethan reader. When one reads the poem in the context of the love debate which runs through Elizabethan love poetry, it seems certain that Donne's irreverent allusions to spiritual love and to the Beatific Vision in the climactic section of a poem celebrating the pleasures of purely physical sex could be intended only as ridicule of the school of Platonic Love. The clothing metaphor on which the conceit is based was a conventional analogy not only in Christian mysticism but also in Renaissance Platonism. Though the details of Donne's phrasing and some of the analogies which he uses suggest that his actual source for the doctrines on which the conceit is based was Christian mystical literature rather than the writings of the Renaissance Platonists, the logical progression which is suggested by the analogies in these lines is nevertheless that of the Platonic progression up the Stair of Love. In fact, the details of the conceit in this passage take on logical continuity only when one supplies the theory of Platonic Love as an implied philosophic context. The poetic proposition of this section of the Elegy asserts, in effect, that loving a woman's naked body is philosophically equivalent to loving her soul, and that consummation in sexual intercourse and consummation in the Mystic Experience add up to pretty much the same thing. And that, one might think, would dispose of the Platonists once and for all.

But this passage of the poem needs closer scrutiny, because the powerful shock of Donne's conceit derives chiefly from the rich philosophic and theological implications of the precise details with which he elaborates the basic analogy.[19] The technique of the passage is extremely compressed: Donne throws out, in quick succession, a series of literary or philosophic commonplaces which are intended to call up to the reader's mind a whole systematic body of thought. In order to make clear the logical pattern which gives continuity to the suggestions of each of these details, I will confine my commentary at this point purely to the imaginative implications of the passage, without pausing to point out what each of the details of Donne's conceit actually refers to, in terms of the facts of the situation which the poem presents. It may be useful, therefore, to set out at the start the basic imaginative equations on which Donne builds the entire structure of metaphor in these lines:

(a) As the fundamental equations:
    the body = clothes.
    the soul (or spiritual essence) = the naked body.

(b) Therefore:
    ordinary, sensual lovers = lovers who are content with women who keep their clothes on.
    enlightened, Platonic lovers = enlightened lovers like the speaker, who want women naked.

(c) Finally (lines 42–5):
    God = the mistress's naked body.
    The Beatific Vision = the sexual orgasm.

The pseudo-logical premise for this fanciful argument is laid down at the start in lines 34–5:

> As souls unbodied, bodies unclothed must be,
> To taste whole joys.

These lines refer to the intellectual joys which the soul can experience fully only by direct contact with God in heaven. The joys of mortal life, by contrast, are partial, since the soul, while it is imprisoned in the earthly body, can know God only mediately,

through the distorting veil of sense experience. The soul's yearn-
ing for the "whole joys" of immediate, intellectual apprehension
of God's Essence can therefore be satisfied only when it strips
off the fleshly clothing of the body, when the soul is "unbodied."
For most men the soul can be unbodied only after death, but a
few chosen spirits are privileged to know this bliss at certain moments during mortal life, when their souls are temporarily withdrawn from their bodies in the Mystic Experience—or, to use
Donne's normal terminology, in an "ecstasy."

These are the full doctrinal implications of the first two lines
of the conceit. My rather specific expansion of their philosophic
suggestion is based on Donne's development of these ideas in the
lines which follow, and particularly on the implicit reference to
the soul's apprehension of God's Essence in lines 43–5, but the
doctrines are so much a commonplace in the formal thought of
the Renaissance that an alert and philosophically sophisticated
contemporary reader might have guessed what Donne was doing
from these lines alone.[20]

In the following lines the imagery defines more fully the implications of lines 34–5 and outlines the process by which a mortal may
attain "whole joys." If one responds only to the suggestions of
Donne's structure of metaphor and neglects the factual reference
of these lines, the following ordered philosophic argument plays
above this section of the poem like a continuous, discordant obbligato, clashing violently at every note with what Donne is actually saying. The process of attaining "whole joys" will start (lines
35–8) with the love of earthly women. But this love must not be
sensual. Women's bodies ("gems" in line 35 = clothes [21]) appeal,
to be sure, to men's physical senses ("views" = the sense of sight),
but this sexual appeal is superficial and will attract only the unen-
lightened lovers ("fools"). These lovers misdirect their love into
sensuality because that is all which their minds can comprehend:
they have "earthly souls," which give them the faculties of physical sensation, but they lack the higher faculty of reason, which
should distinguish man from the beasts.[22] Therefore their love is
distracted (the Atalanta analogy [23]) from its proper object: it is spent
in physical desire for the inessential temporal bodies of women
("theirs") instead of being rationally directed toward women's
metaphysical essences, their eternal souls ("them").[24] But (lines

39–40) these sensual lovers misunderstand God's purpose in creating physical beauty if they believe that beautiful women are intended to serve no further end than physical satisfaction. God
created the beautiful bodies of women for a purpose analogous to
the church's use of religious "pictures" to instill faith in the layman. The church does not intend these pictures to be enjoyed
simply in themselves and to provide mere pleasure for the senses.
They are intended, rather, to give to ordinary men, who acquire
knowledge solely through their senses, a visual experience of
beauty which should lead them to the higher, suprasensory understanding which comes from reason and faith.[25] And, on the same
grounds, those men who are intellectually incapable of a direct,
rational response to the content of a sacred book may be drawn
indirectly to the knowledge which it offers through their sensory
responses to its beautiful binding.[26] For the same reason, God has
"arrayed" a woman's soul, her essence, in a physically beautiful
body. He has done this in order that ordinary men ("laymen"),
after responding to the initial sensory attraction, may be led beyond
this physical experience to a rational response to the beauty of
her soul and thus to an awareness of the eternal reality of spirit,
of which the beautiful body is merely a transitory physical manifestation.

The superior lovers ("we"), on the other hand, neither desire
nor need this intermediate sensory step to attain the intellectual
enlightenment which is the proper end of love. Having renounced
sensuality, they feel only a rational attraction to the intellectual
beauty of women's souls ("themselves," "them," as distinguished
from "theirs").[27] They desire to apprehend their souls directly by
seeing the souls divested of their fleshly clothing ("themselves . . .
we . . . must see revealed").

At this point in the poem (lines 42–3) Donne's language takes
on a specifically theological reference. This shift in the connotative suggestions of his diction produces a quick imaginative transition. It suggests that, in the metaphoric structure of his conceit,
Donne is no longer thinking merely of women's souls as an example
of the kind of metaphysical essence which may be apprehended by
the enlightened lover, but has turned his thoughts instead to the
Essence of God. What actually happens here, as Donne elaborates
the logic of his conceit, is that his imagination suddenly takes a

quick skip up several steps of the Platonic Stair. According to the
doctrine of the Platonists, the lover who has learned to love the
beauty of his mistress' soul and to rise above the attraction of her
bodily beauty has reached only the first step in the Stair of Love.
As he progresses up the logical steps of the stair he proceeds, next,
to a love of the beauty of all women; then to the formulation of a
universal concept of beauty "that is generally spread over all the
nature of man"; and finally to an awareness of God as "the fountain
of the sovereign and right beauty." He sees then that the consummation which his amorous soul desires is that of being "haled from
the body" and "coupled" with God in the Mystic Experience.[28]

Donne's imagination jumps to this final stage of the Platonic
progression in lines 42–3 as he elaborates the hint contained in the
word "mystic." "See revealed" carries strong theological overtones.
It suggests a desire for a supernatural "revelation" of God rather
than for a mere apprehension of a woman's soul.[29] That this transition has been accomplished—that, in the imaginative structure of
the conceit, the concept of the spiritual essence of a woman ("themselves") has shaded over into the logically analogous concept of
the Essence of God, and that the Platonic lover is now desiring to
see God "revealed" in the Beatific Vision—is made clear by line
42, which implies that the revelation will come through the lover's
receiving "imputed grace." Donne here uses a technical term from
theology [30] to imply a specific theological doctrine—a doctrine
which would not need to be introduced into the poem if the erotic
experience to which the conceit alludes at this point were nothing
beyond the Platonic lover's rational apprehension of the intellectual beauty of a woman's soul. For this kind of intellectual apprehension, the imputation of Grace would not be required. But God's
Grace would have to be imputed before a mortal could enjoy the
Mystic Ecstasy. The Mystic Experience was not regarded by Christian theologians as in any way an automatic reward for the Platonic
lover, or for the Christian mystic, who mortified the flesh and followed a prescribed regimen of devotion. It was a privilege granted
to few men in this life, and they did not receive it by virtue of
any inherent right or any righteousness to which they could attain
as mortals. Moreover, from the standpoint of Christian theology,
the apprehension of God's Essence which resulted from the experience did not come through any natural powers that their

souls possessed. The Beatific Vision was granted to the soul, and the soul was enabled to experience it, only through God's special "imputation" of Grace to a being who was inherently neither worthy nor capable of the experience.[31] Donne's reference to this doctrine, then, in lines 42–3, in conjunction with the word "mystic" in the preceding line, implies that the lover seeks this special dispensation which will enable him to pass beyond a union of soul with an earthly woman to the consummation of his love through the union of his naked soul with God.[32]

The following lines (43–5) climax Donne's development of the basic conceit and finally define specifically the philosophic implications of the reference to the "whole joys" of "souls unbodied" at the beginning of the passage. If one responds merely to their imaginative implication and neglects their factual reference, these lines suggest the lover's prayer to God to impute to him the Grace which will permit him to experience the Mystic Ecstasy.[33] They are a plea to God to manifest His Essence so fully ("liberally . . . show thy self") that the desires of the lover's soul may be completely satisfied.[34] This satisfaction is the experiencing of the "whole joys" referred to in line 35: it will consist in "knowing" (line 43)—and at this point Donne alludes to one of the key biblical texts which provide authority for the concept of the Beatific Vision in Christian theology.[35] The soul's joy in the Mystic Ecstasy will consist in the satisfaction of its thirst for knowledge through a complete comprehension of metaphysical reality, which, since the soul is "unbodied," will be revealed without the distortions of the veil of sense and can thus be apprehended by the soul directly and intellectually.

It may be necessary at this point to issue a reminder that this elaborate structure of philosophic idealism, in the specialized forms of the doctrines of Platonic Love and Christian mysticism, exists in the poem merely as an imaginative analogue to the factual implications of Donne's conceit in these lines. Considered in terms of its denotation, the passage is actually a pseudo-logical presentation of the metaphysic of lust, and Donne's real subject is the sheer physical pleasure of sexual intercourse. Donne brings his reader down to earth, and drives home the shock of his general conceit, by sprinkling the prayer in lines 43–5 with sexual puns. He puns, first, on the sexual meaning of "know," then on "liberally," which carries its Renaissance ambiguity of "lewdly," [36] and on "show,"

which is an indecent Renaissance colloquialism for sexual expo-
sure.[37] These ambiguities give the lines a tonal quality which is far
from delicate, but Donne's final thrust is reserved for the word
"self" in line 45. In line 41 "selves" refers—on the poem's factual
level—to a woman's naked body; but the ambiguity on "show" and
the precise anatomical suggestions of the phrase "as liberally, as to a
midwife" limit the reference of the word in line 45 and make clear
that "self" in that line refers not to the woman's body as a whole
but rather to her genitals. This twist in the reference of the word
is enforced also by the suggestion of the imagery of these lines: this
imagery equates the mystic's passionate desire to see the innermost
depths of God's Essence with the lustful lover's desire to see the
sexually essential part of the mistress' naked body.[38] The modern,
secularized reader might pause, at this point, to consider the effect
of these lines for the reader of a theologically religious age: they
do nothing less than identify a woman's genitals with the Essence
of God.

The lover's imagination has now returned from metaphysical
acrobatics to concrete fact, and he thinks of the moment when the
mistress, in the sequence of events that he anticipates, will have removed all her clothes except her shift. The theological preoccupation of the preceding lines carries over into his final command to
her, as he ironically compares her white linen to the ecclesiastical
garb of virgins and religious penitents:

> Cast all, yea, this white linen hence,
> Here is no penance, much less innocence.[39]

And the poem's argument for the desirability of undressing concludes, in a summary point of wit, as the lover puns on the sexual
meaning of "covering."

The Elegy shows Donne as a brilliant apprentice who is still
short of technical mastery. It is an uneven performance, ordinary
in some passages and dazzling in others. Though it shows more
sense of form than most of Donne's Elegies, the poem as a whole
lacks the clear imaginative organization and precise formal definition of his mature work. And the closing section (lines 33 ff.)
certainly makes extraordinary demands on the reader. Donne's
conception in these lines is brilliant, but it is only partly realized

in the execution. In this passage he certainly pays heavily in loss of clarity for what he gains through compression, and I wonder how many of his contemporaries could have followed the skittering of his speculative imagination through these lines. In fact, I wonder how many of them would have noticed at all the high-powered intellectual activity which goes on, at this point, beneath the bright, slick surface of the poem.[40] On the other hand, in its dramatic power, in the adventurousness of its imaginative conjunctions, and in the vividness of its shock effects, the Elegy belongs with Donne's finest work.

The final tone of the poem, and the precise state of mind behind it, are a little hard to define. In many ways the Elegy seems simply a poem of juice and high spirits. It is verse of flash and glitter, the display piece of a young virtuoso who is showing what he can do with the themes of Ovidian poetry by playing them on his own instrument. But, though I think this was probably Donne's initial intention in the poem, there is a good deal left over when one tries to define the temper of the poem in this way. For one thing, the formal rhetoric of the Elegy gives it qualities of weight and dignity which are lacking in most of the Renaissance erotic verse in the Ovidian tradition.[41] And certain parts of the poem carry a voltage which is far beyond the potential of the conventional Ovidian verse of witty and sophisticated indecency. The evocative power of the exploration metaphor in lines 25–32, and the climactic effect in lines 33–45, as Donne drives the logical implications of his conceit with utter ruthlessness to a culminating intellectual shock, are of the order of intensity of serious poetry. This final section of the poem seems, in the last analysis, much more than a piece of outrageous intellectual impudence on Donne's part. When one turns back to this poem after having read "The Ecstasy," "The Canonization," "A Valediction: Forbidding Mourning," and "The Good-Morrow," the concluding section takes on a different character. One of the peculiar characteristics of those later love poems is Donne's use of extravagant intellectual ingenuity as a mode of expression for strong feeling. In these poems the florid virtuosity of wit is not, as the eighteenth century and Romantic critics thought, a force in artistic conflict with emotion —it is simply Donne's poetic vehicle for emotion. When read in the context of Donne's later work, these lines in Elegy 19 appear

as some of his most passionate love poetry; and the tonal pattern
of the last half of the poem seems not that of an impassioned climax
in lines 25–32, followed by a passage of virtuoso cleverness, but
rather that of a continuous crescendo of emotion to a point of
incandescent intensity.

Moreover, when one looks back at the Elegy with an awareness
of Donne's lifelong effort to find a philosophic reconciliation for
the conflicting claims of the soul and of the body in his personal
experience, this section has the effect of suddenly adding a new
dimension to Donne's treatment of sexual experience in the poem,
a dimension which is entirely lacking in Donne's assumption of
the poetic role of sexual libertine in "The Indifferent." Up to this
point the Elegy has presented unreflecting passion unreflectingly.
The play of Donne's intellect over this material has been directed
into elaborating conceits which have little or no philosophic im-
port. But the sustained philosophic overtones of the concluding
section finally place the sexual act in a metaphysical context. Here
Donne's mind seems suddenly to pierce through the flesh to see
what this act means. The shock of these lines is the intellectual
shock of what he sees. In effect, they present the wholehearted
acceptance of sensual satisfaction as an act which entails taking
up a philosophic option, which forces one to embrace a philosophic
materialism and to reject completely the doctrines of philosophic
idealism—to reject, in fact, the fundamental doctrines of Christianity. In these lines Donne's celebration of lust becomes literally
and substantially metaphysical.

Furthermore, the rough treatment which Donne gives to the
Mystic Experience in this passage shows a remarkable conceptual
accuracy and reflects an interest in the subject which is clearly
more than casual. And this poem's identification of sexual experience with religious mysticism echoes throughout the serious
love poetry and religious poetry of Donne's maturity, as well as
in some of the great prose passages in his sermons. It reappears
most strikingly in "The Ecstasy," where the same comparison is
presented in a different key—this time with essential seriousness,
as an analogy which has a genuine psychological and metaphysical
validity.

I think it would be forcing a point to insist that these portentous
emotional and intellectual implications are of primary importance

in the effect of the last section of this Elegy. They are present in the passage only as over- and undertones. But they give to the lines a fullness of resonance which is not the tonal quality of verse that is just wittily indecent. What seems to have happened in the writing of Elegy 19 is like what evidently happened in "The Apparition," that piece of mordant realism which takes off from one of the most artificial conventions of Petrarchan *vers de société*. I think when Donne started to write the Elegy he probably planned to write a piece of clever erotic verse in the Ovidian manner. But some of what came out, after this material was processed by a powerful literary imagination, was, for all its high-spirited gaiety, not light verse at all.

I think, then, that the artistic paradox of the Elegy—its mixture of bumptious, perverse wit with excited philosophic speculation and strong emotion—is never fully resolved in the poem. Probably the poem as a whole was never brought to complete definition in Donne's mind; it grew on him as he wrote. And I think that, for all its brilliance, the poem never quite assumes shape as an artistic whole. But for the student of Donne's poetry the Elegy provides one of the earliest glimpses of the major poet latent in the bright young man who was "a great visitor of ladies, a great frequenter of plays, a great writer of conceited verses." And the poem reveals also the identity of mind and temperament which lies beneath the surface contrast between Donne's secular verse in the "Elegies" and the "Songs and Sonnets," and his religious verse in the "Divine Poems." In his later years, when he was Dean of St. Paul's and the most powerful and sensational preacher of his day, Donne sometimes dramatized his assumption of a new role in life by thinking of his career as divided between two lives: "Jack Donne," who had written the witty and paradoxical work of his early career, and "Doctor Donne," who was writing the sermons. But that sharp dichotomy was a theatricality of Donne's imagination. It is not surprising that in trying to elucidate the difficulties of Jack Donne's poem I have found some of the most helpful commentary in Doctor Donne's sermons.

Some that have deeper digged love's Mine than I,
Say, where his centric happiness doth lie:
    I have loved, and got, and told,
But should I love, get, tell, till I were old,
I should not find that hidden mystery;   5
    Oh, 'tis imposture all:
And as no chemic yet th'Elixir got,
    But glorifies his pregnant pot,
    If by the way to him befall
Some odoriferous thing, or medicinall,   10
    So, lovers dream a rich and long delight,
    But get a winter-seeming summer's night.

Our ease, our thrift, our honor, and our day,
Shall we, for this vain bubble's shadow pay?
    Ends love in this, that my man,   15
Can be as happy'as I can; if he can
Endure the short scorn of a bridegroom's play?
    That loving wretch that swears,
'Tis not the bodies marry, but the minds,
    Which he in her angelic finds,
    Would swear as justly, that he hears,   20
In that day's rude hoarse minstrelsy, the spheres.
    Hope not for mind in women; at their best,
    Sweetness, and wit they'are; but, Mummy, possessed.

"Love's Alchemy"

In "Love's Alchemy," as in the two poems we have just examined, Donne is again taking a heterodox position: he is operating as a skillful debater who is attacking a lofty and widely accepted view of love. But here the role is a serious one, and more is involved than the mere game of playing Devil's Advocate. Wit is turned into sarcasm, and there is no time for comedy. The poem is a tense and bitter expression of disillusionment.

The subject of "Love's Alchemy" is the same as that which lies behind both the facetious antics of "The Indifferent" and the metaphysical acrobatics of the conclusion of Elegy 19: the problem of the nature of love; and the poem is another document in that Debate between the Body and the Soul, between two philosophically antithetic conceptions of love, which was centered on the doctrines of Renaissance Platonism. But "Love's Alchemy" reflects a so much stronger emotional engagement with Platonic doctrine than we see in the Elegy that it may be well to pause for a moment to investigate why the question of the essential nature of love could seem a matter of such consequence to a thoughtful man of the Renaissance, with implications which extended beyond mere problems of psychology or of a code of personal behavior.

In the loosely integrated body of ideas from classical metaphysics, the Neo-Platonic Schools, and patristic and scholastic theology which made up the intellectual heritage of the Renaissance, the experience of human love was regarded, among other things, as an analogue of that act by which God had reconciled the warring elements in Chaos and created the order and beauty of the cosmos. Earthly love was conceived also as an analogue of religious experience. Since love was thought of in scholastic theology as the proper expression of the faculty of Will in the soul, human love could be seen as simply a lower manifestation of that latent impulse which impelled every soul to seek a direct relation with its Maker, an impulse which, in its higher, more spiritualized forms, shaded over

33

into religious devotion and into transcendental intuition. To feel the spiritualizing influence of love was therefore, according to the Platonists and the Christian mystics, to undergo an experience by which man might penetrate into the hidden mysteries of the universe and arrive at his proper orientation in it. Not only the general doctrines of Platonic metaphysics but also the particular theory of Platonic Love—with its emphasis on the longing of the soul to escape the fleshly prison house of this world and enter into the eternal realm of spirit—had been built into the structure of Christian doctrine, and they had been integrated with a great systematic world view in a way in which no modern theories of love have ever been.

When these other-worldly doctrines from medieval Christianity came in conflict during the Renaissance with the crosscurrents of the paganism and materialism which flowed from the rediscovery of classical civilization, the question of the essential nature of love took on new urgency as a live philosophic issue. Donne's busy, speculative intellect, trained from childhood in the doctrines of Catholic theology, could not long have failed to explore the outer metaphysical reaches of the Renaissance philosophizing on this subject. And the doctrines of Christianized Platonism could not have failed to appeal to that strong strain of other-worldliness and idealism in his temperament which was always in conflict with an almost equally strong realism and skepticism.

"Love's Alchemy" was written for readers who were familiar with the contemporary discussion of the pros and cons of Platonic doctrine and who would recognize that doctrine as the most widely held and most philosophically respectable contemporary theory of love. The whole pattern of thought in the poem, as well as much of its imagery, derives from the literature of Renaissance Platonism, and Donne expects his readers to understand the significance which these literary materials would have in their original context. He enters the debate in rebuttal against the Platonists, and his tactics are to seize on some devices in the opposing argument, turn them in his hands, and fling them back in his opponents' faces. The argumentative maneuver which forms the basis for his poetic strategy is that of giving a new twist to the metaphor from alchemy which he uses as a central conceit for the poem. This metaphor was a Platonic tag, since the analogy between alchemic research and spiritual love was a commonplace of Renaissance Platonism.[42] In this poem Donne starts his attack by accepting, for purposes of argument, the validity of this analogy; and he proceeds, then, to explore still further aspects of the parallel between alchemy and Platonic theory, driving the analogy with a relentless imaginative logic which beats Platonic theory into the ground.

The logical points of departure for Donne's rebuttal are the normal implications which the Platonists had developed from this conceit. We can see those implications from the orthodox, essentially conventional treatment of the analogy in Sir John Davies' "Orchestra":

> [Love] first extracted from th'earth-mingled mind
> That heavenly fire, or quintessence divine,
> Which doth such sympathy in beauty find
> As is between the elm and fruitful vine;
> And so to beauty ever doth incline:
> Life's life it is, and cordial to the heart,
> And of our better part, the better part.
>
> This is true Love, by that true Cupid got . . .[43]

Here love is likened to alchemy, first, because it is a process of spiritualization. Since the power of "true love" enables lovers to pass beyond sensuality to spirituality and thus to release the pure essence of their souls ("our better part") from the gross material encumbrance of their bodies ("th'earth-mingled mind"), love is analogous to the process by which the alchemist extracts the "quintessence"—the essence of gold, or "soul" of matter—from the base elements of "earth." But the phrase "cordial to the heart" in Davies' lines glances at another stock implication of the alchemy conceit in Platonic literature, an implication drawn from alchemic medicine. In the "New Physic" of Paracelsus, which was enjoying a vogue in England around 1600, the alchemist's quintessence, the *Elixir Vitae,* was supposed to be a medicine (a "cordial") which was a panacea for all the ills of the flesh.[44] Since poets writing in the Platonic tradition often used the stock metaphor of a fever to suggest the restless inquietude of lust, and presented rational or spiritual love as a balm or sovereign remedy for the fleshly disease of sensuality,[45] the medicinal powers attributed to the alchemist's Elixir provided them a basis for a further analogy between alchemy and spiritual love.

Donne suggests both of these conventional implications of the alchemy conceit in lines 7–10 of the poem, where he refers to the "chemic's" search for "th'Elixir" and to the "medicinall" values of the products of the alchemist's "pot," assuming that his reader will be familiar enough with the stock metaphor to supply the logical connections between the references to alchemy and the allusions to Platonic doctrine in the rest of the poem. But he drives the analogy back on the Platonists by pointing out a further parallel which they seem to have overlooked: the pursuit of spiritual love is like the practice of alchemy not only in these ways but also in another: both are swindle games for the naïve and soft-minded: "Oh, 'tis imposture all." And before the poem is finished he has nailed the opposition with another parallel or two which they have neglected to point out.

The poem opens with two tight-packed lines which lay the imaginative groundwork for the analogy between spiritual love and alchemy that emerges later, and which also set the ugly, savage tone that Donne maintains throughout the poem. The lines are addressed to the Platonists: they are a sarcastic appeal for some convincing evidence from those more profound thinkers who maintain that from long experience of love they have passed beyond the early stage of sensuality and have penetrated "deeper" into love's "hidden mystery" until they have at last found its "centric," or philosophically essential, "happiness"—and that word carries not only its modern meaning but also its Renaissance sense of "good fortune." [46] The technical philosophic sense in which Donne regularly uses the word "centric"—to refer to "essence," to something spiritual rather than physical in nature—implies that the goal of this philosophic quest is the ultimate spiritual reality underlying ordinary physical love. And the religious implication of "mystery" in line 5, a word which Donne always uses as a philosophic term to refer to spiritual truths that lie beyond the normal laws of the physical world and beyond the grasp of Natural Reason, serves to define further the philosophic reference of "centric." [47] The image of digging for gold [48] in a mine suggests the arduous endeavor of the philosophic quest for a love whose essence is

spiritual, and it implies also the conventional Renaissance identification between gold and the human soul which forms the doctrinal basis for the central alchemy conceit.[49] But from his image
of a gold mine Donne develops further suggestions which jar rudely
against the reference to the Platonists' spiritual quest in these lines.
"Dig" is a standard sexual term in Renaissance slang, and the coarse
physical concreteness of that image is developed further by a pun
on "centric," which refers also to a woman's genitals.[50] The Platonists maintained, to be sure, that the spiritual progression up the
Stair of Love to a love based on the soul rather than on the body
must usually begin, in youth, with an initial phase of sensuality,
but Donne's picture of these lofty moral idealists seeking after
spiritual essence by busily digging deep in the "centric" mine of
a woman's body grinds down that doctrine with savage irony.

The sarcastic intensity of this opening drives on through the
following lines of the poem to the climactic burst of scorn in "Oh,
'tis imposture all." And the effect of hard disgust at sexuality is
sustained by the tough connotations of the word "got," which is
tonally equivalent, in Donne's vocabulary, to the sexual term "had"
in modern slang.[51] Donne also exploits the alchemy metaphor to
support this effect of grossness in his treatment of the physical aspects of love by insisting on the sexual concepts which were common in the theory and terminology of the alchemists. He drives an
ugly analogy between the alchemist's pot and the woman's womb,
impregnated by the lover who "glorifies" (brags about) the satisfactions and the "medicinall" power of spiritualized love, and who
believes that he is near to discovering the pure "Elixir" of a love
based solely on the mind.[52] And after the naked directness of statement and the anti-metrical rhythmic violence of the middle lines,
Donne brings the stanza to rhythmic balance and to a formal
rhetorical close in the ironic term-by-term antithesis of the last two
lines, which play off the would-be Platonists' sentimental "dream"
of an emotionally satisfying and enduring spiritual love against
the hard fact of the coldness and ephemerality of a single short
night of lust.[53]

In the second stanza Donne seems at first to have discarded the
alchemy conceit. He returns to the direct mode of statement used
in the middle of stanza 1 and in the slow, insistent climactic series
of the opening lines strikes out at the moral degradation and

comprehensive destructiveness of lust.[54] The double intensive of "vain bubble's shadow" is a specific thrust at the Platonists, since the images of a bubble and of shadow (in contrast to the metaphysical "substance" of spirit) are stock metaphors in Platonic literature to suggest the transience and insubstantiality of fleshly love. Donne now turns back those metaphors against the "imposture" of the Platonists' concept of a spiritual love. And the invective of the rest of the stanza strikes with a similar specific point at characteristic attitudes and arguments in Platonic literature. Donne brushes aside the Platonists' priestly sense of exclusiveness, their aristocratic pride in having found a love beyond the reach of common men and attainable only to the cultivated intellects and refined sensibilities of gentlemen. He himself can discover nothing in love beyond the momentary animal pleasure available to any common servant who is willing to degrade further his already humble condition in order to "endure the short scorn of a bridegroom's play." He ridicules, next, the Platonic doctrine that, through the love of women whose minds are literally "angelic" (i.e., purely intellectual, without any taint of fleshly desire [55]), one can rise above fleshly pleasure to a direct rational apprehension of other forms of spiritual beauty. Donne disposes of this fantasy in lines 21–2 by simply repeating, with heavy sarcasm, one of the stock Platonic arguments for this theory. These lines allude to one of the commonplaces of Renaissance Platonism, the contention that an initial sensory response to even so crude a sensuous embodiment of the Idea of Beauty as the music of a cheap, popular song might lead a man to an intellectual apprehension of the nonphysical beauty of the "intelligible world," typified by the Music of the Spheres. To the Platonist, this analogy served as evidence that one might progress from an initial physical desire for a woman's bodily beauty to a rational apprehension of the Idea of Beauty which resides in the Mind of God.[56] Donne simply lays this piece of idiocy on the table for all to see.

He finally sums up his case against Platonism in the disgusted "Hope not for mind in women." And at this point he suddenly turns back to the alchemy analogy. That conceit had apparently dropped out of the poem after stanza 1. But it makes a dramatic re-entrance at the end of the last line in a sharp stroke of wit which draws the poem together formally and provides a fierce thrust of

irony for the conclusion. For the final countertwist on the Platonists' own analogy, Donne returns to their contention that "true
love," like the "medicinall" Elixir, is a sovereign medicine for the
fever of fleshly desire. There is something in this argument,
Donne implies, but the Platonists haven't got it right. Since true
love can never be anything but lust, because women in the act of
love are mere mindless flesh, the only available cure for the fever
of lust lies in the degrading act of animal sexuality. This *is* a medicine of a sort, but the proper analogy for this remedy is not the
pure spiritual essence of the Elixir Vitae, which does not exist and
which is as much an "imposture" as the concept of spiritual love;
rather it is *another* of the panaceas of alchemic medicine—
Mummy.[57] This, it seems, is a logically sound analogy, because the
powder made by grinding up mummies provides a medicine which
is physical rather than spiritual in nature; [58] and the stuff of dead
bodies is exactly analogous to women in love, because then they
lose such intellectuality as they are sometimes capable of and
become mere flesh without soul. The final image of the sexual
"possession" of dead bodies, with its suggestion of strong physical
revulsion, ends the poem with a climactic burst of disgust. And the
metrical suspension in the middle of the last line makes the two
final words fall like the strokes of a bludgeon.[59]

This is a taut, brutal poem. But its hard, illusionless realism is
an unhappy realism, and the bitterness with which it discards
Platonism is the bitterness of a disillusioned Platonist. All of the
ideas about love which the poem deals with lie within the conceptual frame of Christian Platonism, and Donne's spurning of
those idealist concepts certainly reveals no attraction to what he
sees as their inevitable philosophic alternative. "Love's Alchemy"
suggests, in fact, one of the standard genres in the poetry of Renaissance Platonism, the Renunciation Sonnet, in which the lover expresses his revulsion against lust and his resolve to abandon a love
that reaches but to dust and to make his mind aspire to higher
things. But in this poem those higher things, on which one has
placed so considerable an emotional stake, cannot be found, and
lust cannot be denied. The only answer is a sensualism and a materialism which is far from heart whole.

"Love's Alchemy" seems a frankly personal poem. There is

none of the calculated dramatization of an attitude through an assumed literary role which one sees in "The Indifferent" or in the
nineteenth Elegy; instead Donne seems to be trying for the raw
directness of personal statement. When one compares the rhetoric
and generality of Shakespeare's "Th'expense of spirit is a waste
of shame"—the only contemporary invective against lust which
has a comparable dramatic power—with the colloquial liveliness
of phrase, the touches of personal realism, and the artistic roughness around the edges of "Love's Alchemy," it seems that, for all
the devices of literary artifice in the poem, Donne is working for
an effect of immediacy of utterance, of a man speaking clear his
own private mind. And to place the other two poems that we have
examined alongside "Love's Alchemy" is to see both how much
of Donne's private mind had gone into those poems and how much
had not. The attitude of cheerful abandon to mindless sexuality
reflected in "The Indifferent" and the Elegy is certainly merely a
dramatization of something which Donne knew. But "Love's Alchemy" reveals what had been excluded by that dramatization,
or what, in the Elegy, had been allowed to enter only in order that
it might be cast roughly aside: the activity of a mind busy to tell
up the data of loving and getting, and curious to search out the
hidden mystery not only of love but of a whole category of "centric"
reality beyond the physical world. And "Love's Alchemy" reveals
also the revulsion of that mind against sex and the flesh—the strong
asceticism that breaks out in Donne's sermons in those passages of
grisly satisfaction in the corruption of the body—which was always,
throughout Donne's life, at grips with his strong sensuality.

The tension of "Love's Alchemy" is the tension of the conflict
of the body and the soul in Donne himself, and it is no accident
that both the thought and imagery of the poem organize cleanly
around that logical antithesis between matter and spirit, between
"things visible" and "things invisible," which forms the central
structural concept in most of Donne's later work. A poem like this
enables one to understand better the attitude which finds recurrent
expression in some of Donne's other love poems: the sense of ecstatic emotional release and joyous intellectual revelation in the
discovery of a kind of love which could admit the demands of sex
and still rest inviolable in the soul, that we encounter in poems
like "The Ecstasy," "The Good-Morrow," "The Canonization,"

and "A Valediction: Forbidding Mourning"—the poems which are probably based on Donne's love for his wife.

But there is another fact about "Love's Alchemy"—a fact incidental to the essential statement of the poem—which offers some justification for considering it in relation to the poems which Donne wrote to Anne More. It looks as though the particular personal motivation behind Donne's bitterness toward women in this poem may have been his concern over the problem of marriage. The marriage image in " 'Tis not the bodies marry, but the minds" was a conventional enough metaphor, and I would hesitate to insist, from this line alone, that Donne is using "marry" in any exact sense. But "the short scorn of a *bridegroom's* play" is particularized beyond any of the internal logical or artistic necessities of a poem which deals with the reflections of a man who has "loved, and got, and told" in a variety of ways and on numerous occasions. I see no reason why Donne should have used "bridegroom" here unless he had been thinking about placing himself in that situation, and had backed off from the prospect. I think it is likely that the bitterness of this poem, though it appears in the form of a general commentary on a theory of love and a general attack on women, probably arose in part from the conflict between Donne's desire to marry and his sense of the constant frustration to all his idealism which he had encountered in his own sexual experience.

The idealism which is balked and baffled in the poem is, however, an idealism of a peculiarly intellectualized kind. It is not the warm, romantic spirituality of Edmund Spenser, idolizing woman for the qualities of gentleness and grace which inhere in her soul, but an idealism whose temper is much more austere. "Sweetness and wit" women had—"at their best"—but to Donne those qualities were still not the "mind": they did not offer a companionship above the fury and the mire of human veins in that firm, clean realm of ideas where so much of his own life lay.

THE BLOSSOM

Little think'st thou, poor flower,
  Whom I have watch'd six or seven days,
And seen thy birth, and seen what every hour
Gave to thy growth, thee to this height to raise,
And now dost laugh and triumph on this bough,   5
        Little think'st thou
That it will freeze anon, and that I shall
To morrow find thee fall'n, or not at all.

Little think'st thou poor heart
  That labour'st yet to nestle thee,   10
And think'st by hovering here to get a part
In a forbidden or forbidding tree,
And hop'st her stiffness by long siege to bow:
        Little think'st thou,
That thou to morrow, ere that sun doth wake,   15
Must with this sun, and me a journey take.

But thou which lov'st to be
  Subtle to plague thyself, wilt say,
Alas, if you must go, what's that to me?
Here lies my business, and here I will stay: 20
You go to friends, whose love and means present
        Various content
To your eyes, ears, and tongue, and every part.
If then your body go, what need you a heart?

Well then, stay here; but know,   25
    When thou hast stayed and done thy most;
A naked thinking heart, that makes no show,
Is to a woman, but a kind of ghost;
How shall she know my heart; or having none,
    Know thee for one?   30
Practise may make her know some other part,
But take my word, she doth not know a heart.

    Meet me at London, then,
    Twenty days hence, and thou shalt see
Me fresher, and more fat, by being with men,   35
Than if I had stayed still with her and thee.
For God's sake, if you can, be you so too:
    I would give you
There, to another friend, whom we shall find
As glad to have my body, as my mind.   40

"The Blossom"

To turn from "Love's Alchemy" to "The Blossom" is to enter another world, that of the graceful artifices of polite society, where wit is happily at play and gentled by the warmth of affectionate social intimacy. But the subjects of the two poems are very similar, and the qualities of the personal temperament which they reflect are much the same; the difference is merely one of key. In "The Blossom" all is high comedy. It is that rare phenomenon in Donne's work, a truly successful piece of vers de société.

"The Blossom" was evidently written as a personal poem, an address by Donne himself to a particular lady, and it was obviously written on a particular occasion. The last two lines of the second stanza indicate that Donne wrote the poem at the end of a visit with the lady: he is expecting to depart for London early the next morning. He has been spending a week with her (lines 1–2), possibly at her country house, and lines 33–4 may imply, though this is less certain, that he expects to see her again when she comes to London "twenty days hence." The poem was evidently written to her as a gesture of good-by on this occasion, a sort of dramatized bread-and-butter letter.

We do not need to identify the lady to understand or enjoy the poem, but I think it is likely that she was Donne's friend and patron Mrs. Magdalen Herbert, and that the poem may have been written after one of Donne's visits with her at Montgomery Castle.[60] Donne's friendship with Mrs. Herbert seems to have been easy and affectionate, one of the few close personal friendships of his life; and some of the other poems which he wrote to her—the verse letter "Mad paper stay," and "The Relic," which is almost certainly addressed to her—are distinguished by a quality which is rare in Donne's work—the quality of humor, of gentle, sympathetic spoofing of her, of himself, and of their fondness for one another.[61] In this respect they contrast sharply with the chilly, intellectualized adulation of Donne's poems to the Countess of Bedford and to other noble ladies who were, or who might be persuaded to become, his patrons. In the funeral sermon Donne preached after Mrs. Herbert's death, which is the most personal of all his sermons, he described her "inclination and conversation" as "naturally cheerful and merry, and loving facetiousness and sharpness of wit." [62] It was clearly to a lady of this sort, at least, that "The Blossom" was written; and whether or not the poem was actually written to Mrs. Herbert, a few of the other poems which were certainly or probably addressed to her are so like "The Blossom" in their imaginative dramatization of Donne's relationship with the lady that they are worth looking at as an introduction to the kind of poetic game which Donne is playing in this poem.

"Friendship" and "love" were overlapping terms to the Renaissance mind, and a Renaissance poet, contemplating a friendship of this sort—a friendship with a married woman, based on affection, respect, and intellectual sympathy—would inevitably think of it as a Platonic love affair. Donne presents it in this guise, half seriously, in "The Relic." And if the poet had a dramatic imagination and wanted to play the situation for comedy, the related conventions of Petrarchan courtship lay ready to hand: the miserable lover could worship the lady hopelessly from afar, forced to solace himself with the thin satisfactions of a spiritual love because her coldness frustrated his sexual desires. Donne plays out this little social comedy, with various modifications, in "The Relic," "The Funeral," and "Mad paper stay," and it perhaps lies behind the Pythagorean ingenuities of "The Primrose," which may also have been written to Mrs. Herbert. In some of these poems the lady's husband shows briefly off stage as the villain of the piece: because of her marriage vow she must reject Donne's love and condemn him to the suffering of unrequited passion. But, as Donne hints in a few bawdy passages in these poems, this excuse is pretty thin, the pretense at respectability of a sentimental and silly woman; at heart she is just as promiscuous as all women, as she herself will learn in time, or as her other lovers (and there's hardly any secret about them) may have already discovered.[63]

This same comedy is played again in "The Blossom." Donne casts the first two stanzas in the conventional mode of the Petrarchan love complaint, in order to dramatize himself in the traditional role of the courtly lover. He begins with an address to his "heart," or soul—and the word "heart" throughout the poem is roughly equivalent to "soul" or "mind." [64] His heart is a Petrarchan lover's heart: devoted, idealistic, and naïvely unaware of the hopelessness of its love, it is content to be near the mistress and is temporarily happy in a purely spiritual communion with her, taking no thought of the suffering or death which a parting from her will bring. Donne speaks to it in these stanzas with tenderness and sympathy, gently advising it of the folly of this sentimentality. The end-of-summer imagery and the dying-fall music of these two stanzas, with the rhythmic inflections of the refrain operating as subtly and skillfully as the rhythms of one of Wyatt's songs, surround these Petrarchan attitudes with a mood of gentle melancholy and elegantly reticent romantic sentiment. All of the literary machinery of these stanzas is drawn from the stock of Renaissance love poetry. The flower metaphor of stanza 1 may have been suggested to Donne by its traditional place in poems appealing to the coy mistress, but his use of it as an image for transient joy is completely conventional. And the other conceits in the stanzas are equally commonplace: the images of the soul as a bird (stanza 2), of sorrow in love as freezing cold (line 7), of parting as death (line 8), of the mistress' eyes as the sun (line 15), and of courtship as a "long siege" laid to the fortress of the mistress' chastity (line 13).[65] Donne introduces a minor effect of novelty only in the special twist that he gives to the tree image, which is probably intended as an oblique reference to the lady's marriage. "Forbidding" refers merely to the traditionally unresponsive character of the Petrarchan mistress, whose moral "stiffness" makes her deny her lover's passion; but "forbidden tree," with its suggestions of sin, evidently alludes to the sin of marital infidelity. There is nothing in the two stanzas, however, which should lead the reader to expect anything novel in the poem: they are a graceful exercise in a conventional courtly mode.

This pretty structure of courtly artifice is brusquely shattered in stanza 3. The opening of the stanza seems at first to be in the same key of gentle, pathetic meditation; but in the third line Donne brings the reader up with a sharp jolt, and the poem makes one of those dramatic reversals of course which are a characteristic trick of Donne's poetic strategy, and heads off suddenly in a very different literary direction. As the soul starts to talk back in stanza 3, Donne discards the literary mode of the Petrarchan love complaint and turns to another Renaissance genre, the Debate between the Body and the Soul. Part of the fun of the last three stanzas lies in the highly unconventional way in which Donne handles this standard literary form, which in the Middle Ages and the Renaissance was normally a genre of religious poetry.

The logical point of departure for this new tack which the poem takes is the stock conceit that the lover leaves his soul with his mistress when he parts from her. The proper literary habitat for this convention is the sentimental atmosphere of the first two stanzas, but Donne hauls it into the hard light of day, treats it as literal fact, and evolves from this pretty convention of courtly verse a little scene of dramatic realism in which the body and the soul are sharply actualized as dramatic personalities and set to haggling with one another with all the racy vividness of colloquial speech.

Donne's soul, it seems, is not the green innocent he had thought it. It is a hard-headed and willful brat, given to back talk and to perverse resistance to the worldly wisdom of the body. As it begins to assert its independence Donne's attitude toward it changes from sympathy to annoyance, and the rest of the poem develops as an acrimonious squabble between Donne and his soul.[66]

Despite its impractical spiritual devotion to the lady, the soul is a tough and skillful debater. It not only stands firm on its legal rights under the lovers'-parting convention, but puts up a strong practical argument for separating from the body and staying with the lady. Spiritual love is *its* "business," and that business, which is no concern of the body anyhow, must be pursued in the vicinity of the lady. Moreover, the soul knows the body's tastes only too well. In the fleshpots of London the soul would be simply an encumbrance—"what need you a heart?" And the body will find there all that *it* desires: "friends" (and that word includes the meaning of "lovers") who offer not only love but also "means." The body will be fully satisfied with the luxuries and sophistications of the World. These things don't appeal to the soul, of course, but it is happy to allow the body the "various" pleasures of "eyes, ears, and tongue," and (with something of a leer) *"every part."*

In reply, Donne, who now speaks in the role of the body, wearily concedes the point: "Well then, stay here." He has been through this before and knows the futility of talking sense to a soul that loves to be subtle to plague itself. But he wryly explains to the soul a few of the facts of life. With the practical wisdom which comes from the flesh, he knows all about women and he can see that the soul won't get anywhere with the lady. This particular lady is not only heartless and therefore unable to recognize a heart; [67] she is also a woman and therefore interested only in "show" (outward

physical display), and she is incapable of responding to the purely
intellectual attractions of a disembodied soul ("a naked thinking
heart").[68] With a little more experience she may come off her high
horse and discover the pleasures of lust (and "practise," "know,"
and "part" in line 31 function as bawdy sexual puns), but certainly
—"take my word"—never the pleasures of spiritual love. However,
since the soul is impervious to such practical sense, it can go its
obstinate way and hover around the lady for another twenty days.
Moreover, Donne reflects, the separation is probably a good idea.
It will be good for the body to get away from sentimental women
for a while and live in the clear-headed, practical world of men.
If it is free from the bothersome folly of the soul, it won't be continually getting dragged into the pointless enterprise of unrequited
love; it will grow "fresher and more fat," and will have a chance
to recover from the lean cheek and blue eye which are the marks
of the frustrated Petrarchan lover, as it certainly never could if it
"stayed still with her and thee." His parting advice to the soul is
an exasperated expression of the not-too-sanguine hope that it will
perk up too and snap out of this sentimental love woe: "For God's
sake, *if you can,* be you so too." And this advice has a very practical reason behind it. When the soul finally comes up to London
after its twenty-day vacation,[69] he wants to use it in another love
affair ("another friend" = another mistress). But that will be a
very different business from all this nonsense that he has just been
through, and he doesn't want any of the soul's sentimental idealiz-
ing of sexual frustration to get in his way on that occasion. He has
learned his lesson: this time it will be a different kind of mistress,
the sensible, worldly type whom one finds in London—"as glad
to have my body, as my mind."

I have outlined the last three stanzas by this novelistic method
because it is the only way in which I can suggest the full dramatic
life and the richness and subtlety of the comedy which Donne
creates out of the perfectly stock materials he is working with. But
the effect of his clowning in this concluding piece of realistic theater
is, in the final analysis, not that of destructive satire but rather
that of high comedy. The turnabout in the middle of the poem
makes fun of the conventionalized emotion of the first two stanzas,
but the ridicule is so engagingly playful that it does not actually
obliterate the romantic sentiment of the opening. Its effect is rather

to sophisticate that sentiment by criticism and thus to give to it a suggestion of essential genuineness which it originally lacked.

The trick of this poem is something which Donne never quite pulled off again. Though the poem is more vividly theatrical and richer in its comedy than any of Sidney's sonnets, it is Donne's nearest approach to the civility of *Astrophel and Stella*. When he tries this sort of thing in other poems passion breaks through, or the energetic dialectical wit gets out of hand and destroys the relaxed, subtly modulated tone of humor.[70] The closest he came to it elsewhere was in "The Relic," but there the emotional power of the closing lines, and the bite of "a bracelet of bright hair about the bone," give the poem qualities of tension and seriousness beneath the vers de société surface. In "The Blossom" everything is wit, sentiment, and charm. It is Donne's most humane poem, the poem in which he gets most successfully outside himself and into the urbane world, from which he can look on all his peculiarities of temperament with mere amusement.

But those peculiarities are reflected in the poem, and not merely in the explicit self-criticism of the reference to his mind as one which loves to be subtle to plague itself. What the poem dramatizes, after all, is not just a love affair but also Donne's own analysis of himself. Other Renaissance poets dramatized in their love poems the psychological conflict of the body and the soul, but none of them discovered in himself two such fully developed personalities at odds with one another as the two dramatic characters which Donne presents in this poem. These characters seem to rise readily to his imagination, each with a clearly defined set of values and a separate life of its own, enjoying a very unstable association. The personality which speaks as Donne, as the "I" of the poem in the last three stanzas, and which is roughly identified with the body, is not a mere sensualist but rather a realist, a hearty practical worldling, fond of luxury and of all the sophisticated pleasures of London life, including the pleasures of sex. And the other personality, the soul, is disposed to the ideality of spiritual love, to busy, subtle, and sometimes pointless intellectual analysis, and to moods of despondency. To the realist, the unworldliness and impracticality of this other personality are a continual source of annoyance. But the soul is not nearly as soft and naïve as Donne would like to think when he regards its activities from the pragmatic point of view of the man of the world. It is vigorous and tough, and it enforces its claims. The result of this uneasy partnership is the continual inner dialectic which the poem dramatizes, the mercurial shifts in beliefs and emotional attitudes which are reflected in the intellectual tensions of its argument and in its sharp contrasts of tone.

"The Blossom" is an engaging piece of social comedy; but it is also, if one reads between the lines, one of the most candid pieces of self-revelation that Donne ever wrote. I have conjectured that the four poems which I have discussed in this chapter were written several years apart, and written, perhaps, in the order in which I have discussed them. But it is clear from "The Blossom" that Donne could have written all of them on the same day.

THE GOOD-MORROW

I wonder by my troth, what thou, and I
Did, till we loved? were we not weaned till then?
But sucked on country pleasures, childishly?
Or snorted we in the Seven Sleepers' den?
T'was so; but this, all pleasures fancies be.   5
If ever any beauty I did see,
Which I desired, and got, t'was but a dream of thee.

And now good morrow to our waking souls,
Which watch not one another out of fear;
For love, all love of other sights controls,   10
And makes one little room, an every where.
Let sea-discoverers to new worlds have gone,
Let maps to others, worlds on worlds have shown,
Let us possess one world, each hath one, and is one.

My face in thine eye, thine in mine appears,   15
And true plain hearts do in the faces rest,
Where can we find two better hemispheres
Without sharp North, without declining West?
Whatever dies, was not mixed equally;
If our two loves be one, or, thou and I   20
Love so alike, that none do slacken, none can die.

Chapter 2

"The Good-Morrow"

AT FIRST GLANCE, "The Good-Morrow" might appear to be one of Donne's minor poems, in the sense in which I have used that term in the preceding chapter. On a quick reading it seems a lucid and fairly simple poem which presents difficulties only in the closing lines. But to read it closely against the background of Renaissance literature and of Donne's own work is a literary revelation: the poem starts into focus with a sharpness of definition and a richness of implication which are astonishing. It is actually the densest and most tightly organized of Donne's major love poems.

Like the other love poems we have examined, "The Good-Morrow" is in part a fresh handling of some of the standard materials of Elizabethan love poetry. For its doctrinal content the poem draws heavily on the ideas of Renaissance Platonism, and here Donne is presenting this theory of love with seriousness and whole conviction. Furthermore, some of the imagery and also the form of the poem derive from conventional patterns in contemporary verse. But, though Donne seems at times to be consciously trying to treat some of these standard literary materials in a new way, the business of ringing new changes on conventional ideas and literary devices is a much smaller part of his purpose in this poem than it was in the four poems which I have discussed in Chapter 1. "The Good-Morrow" is primarily substantive and only superficially procedural. Here Donne is only incidentally concerned with producing effects of surprise by playing off his originality against the expectations of the conventional reader. The poem seems to arise from a state of mind removed and withdrawn, and Donne's real concern is to analyze and articulate a personal experience in his fully developed personal style.

Donne begins the poem by procedural maneuvering with the reader's reactions, but he works away from those tactics after the first stanza. The form of the poem derives from two related genres in Renaissance love poetry: the *aubade,* a morning serenade of a lover to his mistress; and a similar popular literary form, the *aube,* a love poem which presents a conversation between two lovers as they awaken at dawn after a night of love.[1] This latter genre was one which Donne used on other occasions, in "Break of Day" and in "The Sun Rising," where he worked for somewhat different effects in his handling of it. The standard dramatic situation for this literary form is established in "The Good-Morrow" by the implications of the title and by the rather oblique indications of lines 8–11 and 15–16: the poem presents a bedroom scene in which two lovers lie at morning peacefully gazing at one another. The title, furthermore, suggests a stock literary form,[2] and Donne evidently wants his reader to be aware that he is reshaping conventional materials. The normal tone for this literary form is one of relaxed, tender eroticism,[3] but Donne breaks this pattern in "The Good-Morrow" as he did in "The Sun Rising" by giving the poem an explosive, dramatic opening. The opening here does not have the brusque violence of "Busy old fool, unruly Sun," but the first line presents, nevertheless, an oath and a burst of emotion to start the poem with a *coup de théâtre:*

> I wonder by my troth, what thou, and I
> Did, till we loved?

The colloquial phrasing, and the heavy stresses and broken rhythms of impassioned speech continue into line 5. The lover seems to be dramatizing, in a rangy, somewhat sardonic manner, the excitement of his first discovery of love. The energy of the verse movement, the vivid, antiromantic quality of "weaned," "sucked" (= suckled), and "snorted," and the extravagance of metaphor in these lines produce an effect of mildly comic exaggeration.[4] The lover is astonished to discover what he and his mistress have been missing: they have been simple-minded babies; they have wasted their time on naïve diversions ("country pleasures") when they might have been enjoying the sophisticated sport of sex; they have been dead asleep and out of the world in all of their life up to now.[5]

This is the effect of a first reading of the opening lines. They seem a vigorous and straightforward piece of theatrics, and they apparently deal with the eye-opening effect, on two hitherto innocent young lovers, of their first encounter with sexual experience. But this is not what the lines refer to, and it is the reader whose eyes are opened as he proceeds further into the poem. As one reads beyond line 5 and discovers what the over-all tone of the poem is and what kind of love affair it really deals with, the first five lines not only take on more precise connotations but undergo an actual change in meaning. I think this false lead at the start is deliberate tactical maneuver on Donne's part, a calculated dramatic effect similar to the turnabout in the middle of "The Blossom." It brings his reader up short with the surprise of what would be described, in the language of the theater, as a "double-take" on these opening lines.[6]

The lover's dramatized excitement comes to conclusion in the exclamatory "T'was so." It seems at first to be continuing in the rest of line 5, as he explains that, in comparison with the vivid actuality of the pleasure of love, all the other pleasures which he has known seem insubstantial and imaginary ("fancies").[7] But the last half of line 5 actually begins a tonal modulation from the dramatic vigor of the opening lines to the quieter, more reflective, and more emotionally harmonious treatment of love in the rest of the poem. And the last two lines of the stanza,

> If ever any beauty I did see,
> Which I desired, and got, t'was but a dream of thee,

produce a sharp intellectual surprise. They reveal that "pleasures" in line 5 does not refer, as one had thought, to nonsexual pleasures: it refers to the lover's earlier sexual conquests. The words "beauty," "desired," and "got" all have a specific usage in Donne's vocabulary. Donne regularly uses "beauty" in a sense roughly equivalent to the modern slang use of "babe": it refers to a woman whose charms are purely physical.[8] And "desired" and "got" have a specifically sexual implication.[9] Similarly, the word "pleasure" often has, both in Donne's vocabulary and in general Renaissance usage, the restricted meaning of "sensual pleasure," and Donne sometimes uses the word in a limited sense to refer to sexual satisfaction.[10] All of these words in lines 5–7 have, therefore, a definite reference to sensuality. They are also rather tough talk in Donne's vocabulary, and he often uses them with connotations of distaste.

The punch word "got" in the final line, then, throws an entirely new light on the kind of love affair which the poem deals with. The two lovers, especially the speaker, are not young innocents who have just discovered sex: they are old hands at the game. But heretofore they had thought that love was nothing more than lust. Hence the present love affair assumes for them the character of a revelation: they realize that until now they have not "loved." Under the back-pressure of the closing lines of the stanza, this word in line 2 undergoes a semantic shift and takes on a limited and precise meaning. It is now clear that Donne is using "love" in a sharply proscriptive sense to refer to a relationship which is not primarily sensual. He has been playing with the ambiguity of the word, manipulating the reader's mind by suggesting to him first the more normal meaning, only to bring him to later with the dawning realization that this is not what "love" means at all, and that true love is actually the revelatory experience which is the subject of the poem.[11] The speaker in the poem has not only made this discovery, but he feels also that his present mistress has revealed to him a hitherto unknown category of reality. He now sees that the pleasures of purely sensual love are "fancies," and that the "beauties" which he has "got" physically are not real: they seem merely a "dream" of her, a shadowy physical manifestation of the ultimate reality which she embodies.

Though Donne does not push this statement to the philosophic extreme of explicitly equating the mistress with the Idea of Beauty, which has been temporarily shadowed forth in the physical beauty of other women, some approximation of this Platonic concept evidently lies behind lines 5–7. The generally Platonic cast of Donne's thought appears also in his use of the stock metaphor of a "dream" to characterize sensual love, in the exclusive meaning which the poem assigns to the word "love," and in the implied antithesis between love and lust, as two sharply differentiated categories of erotic experience. And it is further revealed by the opening of the second stanza, "And now good morrow to our waking souls." This line performs several functions in the imaginative structure of the poem and operates on more than one level of significance; but the philosophic implications of the first stanza—and the development of those suggestions in the rest of the poem—make clear that on one level of meaning this line implies that the present love affair, unlike the lovers' earlier fleshly liaisons, has brought about an awakening of their souls, and that their souls have now entered as active agents into their experience of love.

Line 8 carries this implication, however, only as an overtone. On its primary level of meaning the line establishes the particular circumstances in which the lover is speaking, and it establishes also the poem's central symbol. Taken literally, the line refers to the fact that the lovers had just waked up: their souls, or minds, have awakened after sleep, and they greet one another with "Good morrow." But Donne uses this concrete situation to generate a powerful symbol for the whole poem. The morning bedroom scene is merely the physical setting for the poem. Donne's actual subject is not this waking-up situation but rather the nature of a love which has been, for both the lovers, a psychological and intellectual awakening as well. To the two lovers this revelation has the eye-opening quality of an awakening after sleep; and the speaker's "Good morrow," which is actually addressed to the newly aroused souls of himself and his mistress, is loaded with much more than its conventional meaning. What Donne does here, then, is to take the poetic form itself, the literary type of a love poem dealing with awakening at dawn, and treat it symbolically as a rich metaphor which objectifies in concrete terms the subjective experience that is his real subject. All the evocative suggestions of peace and quiet joy in a scene of lovers awakening at dawn are concentrated in the radiant serenity of the line in which the lover expresses his sense of intellectual revelation:

> And now good morrow to our waking souls.

But the effect of full and final emotional release with which this line is charged ("and now") derives also from the fact that the waking-up image has been building up through the last part of stanza 1. The last four lines of that stanza have presented the lovers' earlier adventures in lust partly through the imagery of sleep: they seem to have been in "the Seven Sleepers' den," [12] and the other women whom the lover has enjoyed seem "fancies" and "dreams" in contrast to the clear actuality to which he has now awakened. After the surge of energy at the opening, the first stanza has come to rest in the wondering peace of "t'was but a dream of thee." This effect pours on into the smooth, sure flow of "And now good morrow to our waking souls," and into the quiet, even verse movement of the rest of stanza 2.

Other details in the imagery of the first stanza now take on either a different or a more precise significance in the light of the reader's awakening to the kind of love affair which this poem presents. "Sucked on country pleasures" acquires, as its primary meaning, a specific implication of lust. The sexual reference of the word "pleasures" has been established by line 5, and "country" is a Renaissance colloquialism for gross sensuality.[13] The imagery of lines 2–3, moreover, has presented lust as infantile. In view of the general Platonic pattern of Donne's thought in the poem, I think this suggestion is meant to carry a scornful moralistic implication: it implies that a conception of love as merely lust is one of the naïvetés of youth and intellectual immaturity, an attitude which the mature and enlightened lover looks down on as childish.

Lines 6–8, then, accomplish a dramatic refocusing of the first stanza and give it a new and sharp definition. Stanza 1, together with the opening of stanza 2, not only establishes the fact of the lovers' intellectual awakening but also lays down a contrast between this love and the common, sensual variety of love which they had known before. This antithesis between two kinds of erotic experience—between "love" and lust—is elaborated throughout stanzas 2 and 3. It functions as the organizing concept for the thought and imagery of the entire poem.

Stanza 2 develops this contrast by suggesting the difference in emotional temper between this love affair and the sensuality which is the only erotic experience that "others" know. Here Donne focuses on some of the concrete details of the scene and treats them symbolically, just as he has treated the details of awaking and of the lovers' "Good morrow" to each other, to define the distinctive quality of this love. The small bedroom and the contented gaze with which the lovers contemplate one another are treated as outward and visible symbols of the withdrawn peace, the security, and the full satisfaction which they have discovered in their love. The special significance which Donne assigns to the fixed gaze of the lovers derives from the importance given to the sense of sight in Renaissance theories about love. As Shakespeare pointed out in the song in *The Merchant of Venice,* love was "engendered in the eyes, with gazing fed." Hence the fixity with which the lovers look at one another dramatizes their constancy; and the contrast between their steady eyes and the roving glance of the sensual lover, who is continually drawn by what the Bible describes as "the lust of the eyes" to "love of other sights," suggests the difference between their mutual fidelity and the promiscuity which characterizes sensual love affairs.[14]

As the lovers lie gazing serenely at one another they are not watching each other "out of fear"—they are not subject, that is, to the suspicions and to the fear of infidelity which trouble ordinary lovers—because this love is so strong a force that it overpowers ("controls") any desire which either might have to look at anyone else.[15] And the small bedroom, which shuts out the world, serves as a symbol for the entire contentment of a love that enables them to renounce not only other loves but also all of the normal activities of life in the world. They need seek no further in love because the transforming power of their love for one another has converted "one little room" into the entire world ("an every where").[16]

In the following lines the imagery of exploration and discovery expands the intellectual and emotional suggestions of "makes one little room, an every where" in a dramatically powerful and richly significant conceit:

> Let sea-discoverers to new worlds have gone,
> Let maps to others,[17] worlds on worlds have shown,[18]
> Let us possess one world, each hath one, and is one.

This imagery functions on several levels of implication. In the first place it develops, as a central theme for the poem, the suggestion latent in line 11 that the world is well lost for love. Donne sharpens this stock theme by giving it a precise logical basis in one of the philosophic commonplaces of his age: the concept that man is a microcosm, or a "little world." The world is well lost because, since each of the lovers is, from a philosophic standpoint, a complete world, each has gained an entire world merely in possessing the other. And the emotional suggestion of the exploration imagery in these lines expands vividly the connotations of wonder and revelation in stanza 1. By paralleling the experience

of the two lovers with all which the geographical discoveries of
new lands had meant to the Renaissance imagination, Donne com-
municates the sense of exciting discovery and enlargement of the
horizons of experience which they have found in this love affair. Since Donne elaborates this microcosm-exploration conceit
throughout the final stanza of the poem, the symbol of geographical discovery hovers over all the last half of the poem, as the symbol
of awakening dominates the first half. The similar evocative suggestions of these two rich symbols give emotional order to the
whole poem.

But the reference to the "sea-discoverers" functions also as
a powerfully dramatic statement of the utter happiness and satisfaction which the lovers have found in each other. Donne measures
their love against the greatest and most exciting events in the life
of his age, the discovery of new worlds. The world which is well
lost is not a drab affair of getting and spending; it is a magnificent
world of romantic adventure and heroic enterprise, in which man's
imagination is continually fired with revelations of the fresh wonders of the earth. But from the vantage of the secure and peaceful
joy of this love, of *this* discovery and revelation, all the adventurous
curiosity, the heroism, and the romance of the life of the Renaissance seem of small account, the trivial and restless scurrying of
foolish men who do not know what the heart desires. With lofty
equanimity the lover can say, "Let them . . . Let us possess one
world."

The contrast between the lovers and the "sea-discoverers" and
eager map readers carries, however, more than this literal, surface
meaning. Donne gives a further symbolic significance to these
details, which suggest what ordinary people are doing with their
lives, by using them to develop his theme of the contrast between
this love and that of ordinary lovers. This contrast has been established (in lines 1–11) as the method by which the speaker is defining the distinctive quality of his own experience; and the
imaginative transition from "love of other sights" to "let sea-discoverers . . . ," a transition which makes these two statements logically parallel, suggests that the "sea-discoverers" and the map readers of lines 12–13 are intended as images for sensual lovers. This implication is not fully established until the final stanza; but the development of Donne's thought in the rest of the poem, which makes

clear that all the details of the poem are organized around the antithesis between spiritual and sensual love, finally forces this metaphoric significance on lines 12–13.[19] On this symbolic level of meaning, these lines carry several implications about the precise nature of this love affair. In the first place, the exploration imagery carries a general suggestion of the two lovers' sense of the exclusiveness in their experience: theirs is not the love of other men. And, more specifically, by its reference to the eager curiosity of Renaissance men to discover and explore new worlds, it suggests the restlessness and instability which characterize sensual love.[20] Finally, the imagery of these lines implies that spiritualized love leads to a completeness of satisfaction which is beyond anything that ordinary lovers can attain to. The word "possess" in line 14 is emphatic and stands in contrast to "have gone" and "have shown." Those phrases suggest the inadequate and merely partial acquaintance which is all that other lovers can experience, as distinguished from the entire possession of one another which these lovers enjoy.[21]

In the final stanza Donne expands the exploration conceit of stanza 2 into a rich and intricate imaginative maneuver, an elaborate piece of analogical philosophic thinking in which his imagination drives all the literary materials of the poem into final shape and full intellectual definition in the realm of metaphysics. In this stanza the poem loses much of its emotional drama, and its analysis of the character of the love affair becomes increasingly abstract and conceptualized. But the point of departure for Donne's progress into philosophic abstraction is startlingly concrete. He returns to the fixed gaze of the two lovers, which he had treated symbolically in stanza 2, and develops a further symbolism from this detail of the actual scene by probing into the physical phenomenon of the lovers' stare with minute sensory precision:

> My face in thine eye, thine in mine appears,
> And true plain hearts do in the faces rest,
> Where can we find two better hemispheres . . . ?

As the lovers lie gazing fixedly at each other, each sees his image reflected in the other's eyes. Spread across the eyeball, each image takes the form of a hemisphere; and Donne treats the congruence of these two hemispheres as a symbol of the sympathetic fusion of the lovers into a single self-contained entity, which is like a perfect

sphere made up of two matching halves. By analogizing this sphere
to the "one world" which the lovers possess, in contrast to the different "worlds on worlds" which other men seek, Donne progresses
to a final metaphysical definition of the contrast between spiritual
and physical love in terms of the Christian world view which
dominated the thought of the Renaissance.[22]

The startling concreteness of this eyeball conceit would certainly
have been a striking literary effect for a Renaissance reader. But
the conceit would have seemed far less fantastic to Donne's contemporaries than it does to the modern reader, because they would
have recognized its factual basis in contemporary scientific theory
about love. Donne's treatment of the image in the eyeball as a
concrete object, and as an object which has some functional importance in the experience of love, derives from a general Renaissance epistemological doctrine which provided a theory of sensation and an explanation of how the soul received knowledge from
sense experience, and it derives also from a specialization of this
doctrine into a theory that explained the process by which the soul
entered into the experience of love. These doctrines, which came
from classical thought through scholastic theology, were commonplace in the thought of the Renaissance and underlie a good deal
of Renaissance love poetry, particularly the love poems in the
Platonic tradition.[23] According to the general epistemological
theory the senses, from which the soul's knowledge is derived, do
not apprehend the philosophic essences of external objects but
receive only images from them. In the special form of the theory
which Donne normally uses, the experience of sight is initiated by
the following process: the eyes emit beams which strike on external
objects; when the eyebeam impinges on an object it picks up one
of the "phantasms," or images of itself, which the object emits;
and this image is carried back along the eyebeam to the eye of the
beholder.[24] This theory conceives of the image, then, as something
existing apart from the body which is looked at, and Donne obviously visualizes the image as a more or less concrete object which
comes from outside and impinges on the eyeball.[25] Since the particular experience of love was thought to be "engendered in the
eyes," this conception of the process of visual sensation was fundamental to Renaissance scientific accounts of what took place when
one fell in love. According to a standard theory [26] the experience

of love begins with the physical sensation of the sight of a beautiful woman, and the arrival of the image of the woman at the eye of the lover initiates a specific psychobiological process which results in love. After the image strikes the lover's eye it is conveyed to the heart. As it lodges there, it heats the heart and releases the "spirits" in the blood, which mediate between the body and the soul. This release of the spirits activates the soul, which is seated in the heart, and conveys to it the apprehension of the woman which the senses have received; and thus the rational faculties of the soul become involved in an experience which began with bodily sensation. The resultant motion of the soul opens the pores of the body and allows the spirits and the soul to "transpire." [27] In this way the love experienced by the soul is manifested in the lover's face.[28]

At least some of this theory lies behind lines 15–16 of "The Good-Morrow." Donne is not expounding these doctrines in the poem, however, and I have summarized them only to account for the concreteness with which he visualizes the images in the eyes and to explain the logical continuity between line 15 and line 16. As the lovers lie gazing at one another, the images enter their eyes and activate their awakened souls, and thus their souls ("hearts") [29] are manifested in their faces. Line 16 suggests also the distinctive moral and psychological character of their relationship. It is faithful and constant ("true"), frank and without guile ("plain"). And the connotations of "plain" and "rest" suggest also its evenness of temper and emotional stability. These qualities stand in contrast to the restlessness, the suspicions, and the desire for novelty and for change which stanza 2 has presented as characteristic of the sensual love of "others."

But this is only the factual meaning of lines 15–17. In terms of the imaginative logic of the poem, Donne's minutely physical treatment of the images in the lover's eyes is merely a function of his development of the microcosm analogy presented in the final line of stanza 2, a device which gives that analogy a concrete basis in the details of the actual scene the poem presents. Donne exploits the concrete detail of the two hemispheres in the eyes symbolically as a means for expanding his parallel between the lovers and a world, and for evolving from that analogy further reaches of significance. As he elaborates the microcosm conceit in stanza 3, the form of the analogy changes. At the end of stanza 2 he had presented

each of the lovers as a complete world, in absolute possession of
the separate world of the other ("each hath one, and is one").
But at the start of stanza 3 he presents these two worlds as a single
globe made up of two congruent hemispheres. This shift in the
analogy implies a different statement about the nature of the relationship between the lovers: it implies that their love has produced a union of their souls so complete that their separate identi-
ties (their souls, or "hearts," which are reflected in the hemispheric
images in the eyes) have merged into one another so that the lovers
have become a single personality. What happens at this point in
the poem, then, is that Donne makes a logical transition from a
conception of the love relationship as the lovers' complete possession of one another to a conception of the love as a fusion of the
lovers' souls into a single new identity. And this intellectual progression is involved with an imaginative transition from a metaphor of the two lovers as two discrete worlds to a metaphor which
presents them as fused into a single globe.

As Donne develops this metaphor he presents the globe formed
by the two hemispheres as characterized by the same qualities of
permanence and peace which were implied by his characterization
of the love in the statement, "true plain hearts do in the faces
rest": it is "without sharp North, without declining West." This
perfect sphere (the complete and satisfying spiritual union of the
lovers) is therefore "better" than any other sphere, or world, which
they can find.[30] But the comparative value judgment in "better,"
and the suggestion of seeking to find new and better worlds in
"where can we find two better hemispheres," point back to stanza
2, to the contrast between the one private "world" which the lovers
have discovered and the "worlds on worlds" which "others" are
continually and restlessly seeking. These "worlds on worlds" belong to the physical realm of earthly things, while the new world
which the lovers have discovered belongs to the philosophic category of spirit. In the three tight-packed, elliptical lines with which
the poem ends, Donne develops this philosophic implication latent
in his contrast between the search for two different kinds of worlds.
And the complex conceit from astrophics which is concentrated
into these three lines also operates to make clear that the references
to the "sea-discoverers" and the map readers in stanza 2 are to
be read not only literally, as a suggestion of the normal, busy

activities of the world which the lovers have renounced, but also symbolically, as images for the restless promiscuity of lust.

The astrophysical conceit of these lines is essentially the same as the one which Donne develops more fully in stanzas 3-5 of "A Valediction: Forbidding Mourning," and that poem provides the most useful commentary on the difficulties in the closing lines of "The Good-Morrow." [31] The basic concept behind these lines is that of the contrast between the two different substances of which the earth and the heavenly spheres are composed: between matter, the heterogeneous substance of the earth, which belongs to the category of "things visible" and is gross, mutable, and mortal; and the fifth essence, the homogeneous substance of the spheres, which belongs to the category of "things invisible" and is pure, stable, and eternal. The conclusion of "The Good-Morrow," like the "Valediction," draws a parallel between this structural dichotomy in the universe and the contrast, in both emotional temper and metaphysical nature, between the two kinds of human love. Sensual love, since it is a gross union of the unstable fleshly matter of lovers' bodies, is analogized to the earth; and spiritual love, since it is a pure union of the eternal substance of lovers' souls, to the heavenly spheres.

This analogy to the principles of Renaissance physics and metaphysics is first suggested by lines 17–18. The essentially spiritual love which the two lovers have discovered opens to them a world "better" than the sphere of the earth, which is the sphere subject to "sharp North" and to "declining West." The world of their love is, in other words, like a celestial sphere. The celestial sphere does not have the physical characteristics of the earth: it is immutable and eternal, free from painful seasonal change ("sharp North"), and not subject to decay and death ("declining West").[32] It is immortal because it is "mixed equally" (line 19)—it is composed, that is, of materials which are uniform and physically compatible, and it is therefore free from the internal physical stresses, produced by the combination of the heterogeneous qualities of the four elements, which the physics of the Renaissance regarded as the cause for the mutability of all material substance. Like this sphere their love will be permanent, because it also is "mixed equally" and is therefore not in the category of mortal things ("whatever dies").[33] This love is, in its nature, a mixture of two substances which are pure and inherently at rest (the "true plain hearts," or souls, of line 16).[34] And since their love is the product (lines 20–1) either of a complete fusion of their souls into a single identity or of a conjunction of two separate love experiences which are identical and inherently stable,[35] it is, in essence, a homogeneous mixture, and therefore, by the principles of physics, it cannot die. The astrophysical analogies of these lines provide, therefore, both an analogical philosophic argument to prove the enduring character of this love affair, and a suggestion of the metaphysical cause of its distinctive qualities—its purity, constancy, evenness of temper, and emotional peace.

The analogy also suggests, though more obliquely, the contrasting qualities of sensual love. Lines 9–14 have implied a comparison between lust and a desire for possession of the earth. And this imaginative identification between the flesh and the earth is further established by line 18, where in his allusion to the mutability of the earth Donne chooses particular details which will carry, as connotations, suggestions of the cruelty and coldness ("sharp North") and of the inconstancy ("declining West") which destroy ordinary love affairs.[36] These characteristics of sensual love are suggested also by the logical implications of the central conceit of stanza 3: if a love based on a union of souls is characterized by the physical properties of the fifth essence, then a love based on a union of the flesh is characterized by the physical properties of matter—it is restless, emotionally unstable, and impermanent.

This tightly compressed conceit of the closing lines operates, therefore, as a summarizing conclusion for all of the ideas in the poem. The intellectual implications of the contrast between the earth and the spheres elaborate and define more clearly the latent implications of the microcosm-exploration imagery of stanza 2, and they also sum up everything which the two preceding stanzas have said about the contrast between love and lust. But this conceit not only draws together the poem's analysis of love: it is also, like the same conceit in "A Valediction: Forbidding Mourning," an implicit philosophic statement, in terms of the method of reasoning through analogy which the Renaissance still regarded as a valid means for arriving at philosophic truth. This statement carries the process of analysis to full intellectual resolution by disposing the love in its cosmological context. "Where can we find two better hemispheres" implies that their love for one another has enabled the two lovers to discover at last their "sphere," their natural and proper mode of existence in the ordered scheme of the cosmos.[37] It is a mode different from the busy, materialistic concerns of other men—a life private and withdrawn from the world, in which their distinctive individualities attain peace through a love which leads them to contemplation of things of the spirit.

If I were to choose an epigraph for "The Good-Morrow" I would preface the poem with the opening of Ben Jonson's "Epitaph on Elizabeth, L. H.":

> Wouldst thou hear what man can say
> In a little? Reader, stay.

I know of no poem of comparable length in which so much goes on, nor of any poem which forms a more tightly organic entity. I think it is a superb performance, rich, vivid, and fully ordered. But it represents the extreme point of that tendency to concentration and to elliptical expression which appears throughout Donne's work, and it certainly demanded a great deal even of the readers of Donne's own time. It is possible, of course, that Donne wrote the poem with some such conscious literary purpose as that which Jonson had in writing the "Epitaph on Elizabeth, L. H.": to show how much could be packed into a short poem. Renaissance poets often set themselves literary problems of this kind, and Donne seems to have engaged in similar deliberate technical experiments in other poems.[38] But I think it is unlikely that Donne was consciously undertaking any such literary exercise in "The Good-Morrow." After the opening lines he seems little concerned with the reactions of his reader and much more occupied with the problem of defining and accounting for the specific and peculiar personal experience which the poem deals with. The increasing subtlety and complexity of the thought, and the progressive concentration of expression up to the tight-clenched final lines, appear to arise naturally from the state of mind which the poem is articulating. What we seem to be following as we trace the psychological progression of the poem, from the vigorous extroversion of the opening, through the serene withdrawal of stanza 2, to the intellectual intricacies and obscurities of the final stanza, are the steps by

which a mind turns in on itself to an ultimate introversion, with-
drawing gradually from the energetic restlessness of the outer world
of "sea-discoverers" and "others" who are busily seeking novelty
and change and worldly satisfactions, to the fastness of its own inner peace and personal philosophic resolution, to the one private
world which it is at last fully content to possess.

I think, then, that "The Good-Morrow" is a personal poem,
based directly on Donne's own experience, though I have analyzed
it as though it were not. It shows so many parallels, in both thought
and literary devices, with "A Valediction: Forbidding Mourning,"
"The Ecstasy," and "The Canonization" that it must derive from
the same experience which those poems almost certainly deal with
—Donne's love for his wife.[39] In most of those poems, as in "The
Good-Morrow," Donne discards the clowning and the antic poses
of his early love poetry and treats love with a gravity and a richness of thought and emotion which suggest his entire personal involvement with his subject. And the particular subject of "The
Good-Morrow"—the sense of joyous discovery and sudden intellectual revelation in finding that the long inner debate of body
and soul can be resolved in a wholly satisfying love which includes
physical sex but is essentially spiritual—suggests that the poem
may have been written soon after Donne's marriage to Anne More
and soon after he wrote "The Ecstasy." That poem is obviously
the record of Donne's attempt to account for this same revelatory
experience of a new kind of love. It records both his happiness
and his intellectual puzzlement in discovering a resolution for
the bitter dilemma of "Love's Alchemy," in finding that body
and soul can be fully compatible in love.

> This ecstasy doth unperplex
>   (We said) and tell us what we love,
> We see by this, it was not sex,
>   We see, we saw not what did move . . .

"The Ecstasy" is a detailed logical analysis of this intellectual
problem, oddly unlike Donne's other major love poems in its
naked explicitness and its expanded, expository technique. It is a
sort of verse essay in which Donne painstakingly examines the
experience and carefully and persuasively lays out his theory about
it for all to see. In "The Good-Morrow" that process of intellectual

accounting seems to be behind him. The experience has been comprehended by the mind and can now be wrought into poetry of concentrated dramatic power.

But Donne saw his love for Anne More not merely as the personal intellectual revelation, almost a metaphysical conversion, which he presents in "The Ecstasy." He saw his elopement with her also as an act of final moral choice by which he had probably cast aside all his hopes of worldly success. As we can see from the distress of his friend Izaak Walton over this act, marrying a gentlewoman without her father's consent was a far more serious matter in the Renaissance than it would be today. Donne went to prison for it, and it was from prison that he wrote his wife the letter that Walton records in which he implied that, because of their marriage, John Donne and Anne Donne were "undone" in all worldly terms. If one reads "The Good-Morrow" against the biographical background of Donne's marriage, much of what the poem has to say about the love affair takes on a richer significance from being placed in that personal context. When one remembers that Donne's love for Anne More was a love which drove him to wreck all the chances for the brilliant career in the world that had been promised by his talents and by the successes of his early life, the renunciation of the second stanza of this poem takes on a more vivid actuality:

> Let sea-discoverers to new worlds have gone,
> Let maps to others, worlds on worlds have shown,
> Let us possess one world . . .

This world which was well lost for love was, moreover, a world with which Donne had long felt somewhat at odds. That revulsion against its materialistic values which keeps cropping out in his earlier poems, and that proud sense of personal differentness from his contemporaries, and of the sanctity of his individuality, which is pervasive in all his verse, beat through Donne's impassioned commitment in "The Good-Morrow" to the enterprise of building out of his love a lofty, removed, private world which he can possess in security and in quiet.

THE CANONIZATION

For God's sake hold your tongue, and let me love,
    Or chide my palsy, or my gout,
My five gray hairs, or ruined fortune flout,
        With wealth your state, your mind with arts improve,
            Take you a course, get you a place,   5
            Observe his Honour, or his Grace,
Or the King's real, or his stampèd face
        Contemplate, what you will, approve,
        So you will let me love.

Alas, alas, who's injured by my love?   10
        What merchant's ships have my sighs drowned?
Who says my tears have overflowed his ground?
        When did my colds a forward spring remove?
            When did the heats which my veins fill
            Add one man to the plaguy bill?   15
Soldiers find wars, and lawyers find out still
        Litigious men, which quarrels move,
        Though she and I do love.

Call us what you will, we are made such by love;
        Call her one, me another fly,   20
We'are tapers too, and at our own cost die,
        And we in us find the'Eagle and the Dove.
            The Phoenix riddle hath more wit
            By us, we two being one, are it,
So to one neutral thing both sexes fit: 25
        We die and rise the same, and prove
        Mysterious by this love

We can die by it, if not live by love,
    And if unfit for tombs and hearse
Our legend be, it will be fit for verse;
    And if no piece of chronicle we prove,
        We'll build in sonnets pretty rooms;
        As well a well wrought urn becomes
The greatest ashes, as half-acre tombs,
        And by these hymns, all shall approve
        Us canonized for Love:

And thus invoke us; You whom reverend love
    Made one another's hermitage;
You, to whom love was peace, that now is rage;
    Who did the whole world's soul contract, and drove
        Into the glasses of your eyes
        (So made such mirrors, and such spies,
That they did All to you epitomize,)
        Countries, towns, courts: beg from above
        A pattern of your love!

Chapter 3

"The Canonization"

"The Canonization" looks in many ways like the bright and flashy poems of Donne's early career. The flaring theatricality and the splatter of realistic detail in the first two stanzas, as well as Donne's playing with the conventions of Petrarchan verse throughout the poem, suggest the poems which he wrote in the 1590's. And the trick of ending the first and last lines of each stanza with the word "love" is one of those merely ingenious devices of formal artifice which are typical of that period of self-conscious technical experiment in English poetry. But as the free-swinging energy of the opening tempers to gravity and philosophic seriousness in the closing stanzas, and as the elaborate intellectual and imaginative structure of the poem unfolds, it is clear that in "The Canonization" we have one of the major poems of Donne's literary maturity.[1]

I think it is almost certain that the poem derives from the personal circumstances of Donne's marriage. In fact, "The Canonization" seems to take up the job of analyzing and justifying Donne's love at the point where "The Good-Morrow" leaves off. It returns to the theme that the world has been well lost for love and explores again the philosophic implications of that decisive act. But the state of mind behind this poem is less secure than that behind "The Good-Morrow." The world which has been renounced is now obtruding its claims on the surety of the love: its voice is heard strongly in the poem, and its practical demands must be answered. The poem is a dramatization of this personal problem in a tough and hard-fought debate between John Donne and the World.

The technical device on which "The Canonization" is based is the poetic maneuver of giving a new twist to one of the most worn conventions of Elizabethan love poetry. The comparison of love to religious worship, and the complex of theological and ecclesiastical conceits which derived from this basic analogy, had had a long career in the medieval literature of the Courts of Love before it entered the Petrarchan tradition and became a commonplace in the love poetry of the Renaissance; and Renaissance poets had enriched its imaginative potentialities by exploring the further parallels between love and religious experience which they found in the doctrines of Christian Platonism. In Elizabethan England the general analogy between love and religion was a part of the stock in trade of every casual sonneteer, and the particular form of the analogy which Donne uses in "The Canonization"—the conceit that true lovers are saints or martyrs of the faith—was also completely commonplace in the love poetry of his time. This one can see from *Romeo and Juliet,* where Shakespeare uses this conceit, together with the verse form of the sonnet, to suggest the merely polite and socially conventional character of the love-making between Romeo and Juliet at Capulet's ball.

"The Canonization" is conceived partly as a fresh treatment of this convention. But in this poem, as in many of Donne's other poems, the game of literary surprise is the front for a more serious purpose. The comparison between love and religion manifests itself finally, when one has finished the poem, as an adventurous and seriously meant metaphysical speculation about the striking psychological similarities between erotic and religious experience; and as Donne's imagination expands the lover-saint conceit to full and precise definition in the scheme of Catholic theology, a shopworn literary cliché takes on a new and vivid artistic life.

But though the conceit of erotic sainthood is the imaginative base for the entire poem it does not begin to emerge until the end of stanza 3, and Donne does not really commit the poem to its central metaphor until he reaches the two closing stanzas. "The Canonization" starts in an artistic area which seems far removed from religious speculation; it bursts on the reader with a violent oath and hustles him straight into the busy, prosaic world of everyday fact: of palsy, gout, gray hairs; of getting ahead, making money, scrambling for favor at Court; of financial speculation in argosies; of crop failures, plagues, wars, and lawsuits. Once again, as in "The Blossom" and "The Good-Morrow," Donne's artistic strategy is that of the false-lead opening. The reversal of course which comes after the first stanzas is not so sharp as in the other two poems; rather it is a gradual modulation away from the anticipations set up by the opening. But one of the special excitements of all three poems comes from the dramatic surprise of following an emotional and intellectual progression which turns at some point to a conclusion that is wholly unexpected.

"The Canonization" is cast, ostensibly, in the form of a debate with a friend who is arguing, in terms of hard practicality, the folly of the speaker's love. The first two stanzas dramatize this debate vigorously. The explosion of the oath with which the poem opens, the highly theatricalized tone of exasperation in the first two stanzas, the sardonic comedy which Donne produces in stanza 2 by juxtaposing the stock hyperboles of Petrarchan love poetry with the practical concerns of the world of fact, and the accumulation of the details of life in the workaday world—all these devices operate to prepare the reader for anything but a serious ethical and metaphysical examination of an intensely romantic love. These opening stanzas seem deliberately anti-romantic; and the realistic subject matter, the truculence of the speaker's manner, and the rough colloquial vigor of the style suggest the genre of verse satire rather than that of serious love poetry.

These stanzas also suggest that the speaker's attitude toward his love is anything but intellectually serious. He seems to present himself in stanza 2 as the standard courtly lover: his love is a matter of sighs-and-tears, of colds-and-heats, of desire which is a burning fever, of concord as contrasted with wars and quarrels. In the comic context of this stanza these Petrarchan tags suggest the satirist's type figure of the foolish fashionable lover and seem to imply that the speaker looks on his own love with wry amusement. This implication fits perfectly with the general argument of both stanzas: he seems to concede, with cheerful exuberance, that his love affair is an act of headlong irrationality, something contrary to all standards of normal and sensible behavior, and that in pursuing it he has chosen to renounce all the promptings of good sense.

In short, if we consider the first two stanzas apart from the rest of the poem, there is little in them—except for their driving energy —to suggest that anything very serious is at stake here. The poem seems headed for being an entertaining and extroverted piece of light verse, uncomplicated by either romantic emotion or serious intellectual analysis, about the stock theme of the sweet folly of love.

But again Donne is deliberately maneuvering with his reader, setting the hook and playing him a while before he hauls him into the net. In the third stanza the poem starts to take a new turn. This stanza begins a literary progression which reveals, finally, that the two opening stanzas have had a more serious intellectual purpose than one had thought on first reading, so that one goes through the same kind of double-take on these stanzas that Donne worked for in the opening lines of "The Good-Morrow." The whole poem, in fact, seems designed to put the reader through the experience of a gradual awakening to the serious purpose at work beneath a surface texture of lively, flashy cleverness. This surface effect continues into the final stanza, but beneath it the dramatic character of the poem undergoes a gradual change. After the first line of stanza 3 the speaker seems to work away from a direct concern with his opponent and, as his mind turns inward to an examination of his love, the poem loses the lively conversational immediacy of an answer to an actual opponent and takes on instead the character of an analytic private meditation. But throughout the reverie of the last two stanzas, in which we seem to follow the operations of a mind working through to the resolution of a personal problem, the poem maintains the logical structure, if not the dramatic character, of a debate: it is an argument in which the speaker proceeds, by an ethical and metaphysical justification of his love, to a final rebuttal of the opponent with whom he was contending at the beginning of the poem. We discover, then, as the poem develops, that the first two stanzas were merely a debater's opening maneuver, a tactical device for disarming the opposition by recognizing and defining the opponent's point of view ("Call us what you will") and by seeming to concede to its reasonableness, only to make more dramatic the counterturn to the destruction of that position in the reply. And the speaker's calculated tactical assault on his opponent is also, in effect, John Donne's calculated tactical assault on his reader, who seems to be identified in Donne's mind with a personal opposition whose standards are those of conventional worldly values.

Actually Donne has laid the logical groundwork for the later progress of the argument by his picture of life in the World in stanza 2. This picture, with its details of the loss of argosies, of crop failures, of plagues, wars, and predatory lawsuits, has been colored to suggest the instability of fortune and the vanity of worldly enterprise.[2] And the intellectual basis for the speaker's dissociation from these concerns has been hinted at in stanza 1 by the ironic force of the imagery of religious worship in the lines:

> Or the King's real, or his stampèd face
> Contemplate . . .[3]

But these ethical implications are only faint overtones in the first two stanzas, and it is not until the end of stanza 3 that the poem begins to formulate the antithesis between material and spiritual values which is the organizing concept for its argument.

The real business of stanza 3, beneath the surface cleverness of its paradoxes, is to begin the rebuttal by arriving at a preliminary definition of the nature of the love affair. The stanza is constructed as a series of conceits which suggest first the physical and then the spiritual qualities of the love. This series forms a gradual imaginative progression which culminates in the religious imagery of the last two lines and thus prepares for the emergence of the central sainthood conceit in stanza 4. In lines 20–1 the speaker, still conceding to the objections of his opponent, admits that his love is an indulgence in sexual passion and that (according to Renaissance medical theory) it will waste him physically and hasten his death.[4] The image of the fly in line 20 carries implications not only of shortness of life but also of lust, since to the Renaissance mind the fly was a standard example of both ephemerality and unbridled sexuality.[5] The taper image in the following line—a particularization of the conventional metaphor of lust as fire—carries the same double implication. And Donne works the word "die" for a sexual ambiguity: it refers first, in its common Renaissance meaning as a sexual pun, to the sexual orgasm; and second, to the eventual death which will be hastened by the lovers' sexual indulgence. The statement that the lovers die "at our own cost" seems innocent enough at this point in the poem—a mere passive suggestion that "after all, we're not hurting anybody but ourselves." But in the light of the rest of the poem the word "cost" acquires a sharp

ironic force as an argumentative thrust at the opponent's materialistic standards of value.

In the next line the antithetic image of the eagle and the dove
provides a logical transition from the implications of the images
of the fly and the taper to those of the conceit of the phoenix in
lines 23–7. The contrast between the eagle and the dove—as types
of strength and sweetness, of activity and passivity, and hence, in
the primary significance which Donne gives it here, of masculine
and feminine sexuality—is one of the conventional antitheses in
Renaissance literary allusions to natural history.[6] Donne uses this
reference to suggest not only the physical union of the lovers,
which the preceding lines have referred to, but also the mysterious
character of a relationship in which polar opposites are harmonized
and united. This characteristic of the love is further suggested by
the initial meaning that Donne develops from the image of the
phoenix in lines 23–5, which implies that the sexual relationship
has resulted in the fusion of the two lovers into a single personality
—"we two being one." [7]

But if one looks more closely at the thought behind the witty
conceits of this stanza, these three lines, together with lines 26–7
in which the phoenix conceit is further developed, suddenly inject
into the poem a wholly new body of both doctrinal implication
and imaginative connotation, which contrasts sharply with the
suggestions of the first half of the stanza. Lines 20–2 have conceded
that the relationship between the lovers is that of a strongly physical
sexuality, and both the fly and the taper images carry the derogatory
suggestions of uncontrolled lust. But the statement that the two
lovers have become "one," that love has fused them into a single
personality or a single soul, belongs to a different category of doctrine: it derives from the Platonic tradition in the Renaissance
philosophy of love.[8] To Donne especially, but also to the Renaissance mind in general, this concept was associated either with
masculine friendship or with spiritual love between man and
woman, in contrast to a merely physical relationship. And the
word "neutral" (= sexless) in the line "So to one neutral thing
both sexes fit" sets up a similar doctrinal paradox: it implies that
the lovers have somehow been transfigured by their sexual union
so that their relationship has been purged of its specifically sexual
character.

By means of the religious overtones of the imagery, which become increasingly insistent from line 22 to the end of the third stanza, Donne enforces these hints of an essentially spiritual quality in the physical union of the two lovers. To the Renaissance mind the eagle and the dove were not only antithetic types from natural history: they were also symbols in Christian iconography for contrasting types of religious temperaments. Moreover, both the Middle Ages and the Renaissance saw in the phoenix—that unique bird which was periodically consumed by fire and then rose in new splendor from its own ashes—an emblem of Christ and of the doctrine of the resurrection. It is this further suggestion of the phoenix myth which Donne calls up by the phrase "we die and rise the same" in line 26.[9] Finally, the word "mysterious" in the last line of the stanza has, as it always does in Donne's work, a specific reference to religious "mysteries"—that is, to spiritual phenomena, like the Resurrection, which violate the laws governing the physical world and which are beyond the comprehension of Natural Reason. The actual meaning of "we die and rise the same" is apparently that, despite its component of fleshly desire, their love is faithful and not subject to change; it remains constant after repeated sexual experience. Its essential "mystery," therefore, is that it seems to violate the laws which normally govern sexual love: it manifests the characteristics of a spiritual union and is removed from the instability which usually characterizes fleshly love.

But one hesitates, at this point in the poem, to look for any very serious implications behind these brash paradoxes. One wonders, in fact, what the basic tone of the poem is. The paradoxical suggestions of this stanza, which are climaxed in the shock effect of equating sexual intercourse with Christian death and resurrection,[10] have set up in the poem a strong imaginative tension, and that tension is not finally resolved, nor is the essential tone of the poem established, until the closing stanza. The high spirits of stanzas 1 and 2 have appeared to carry over into stanza 3, and the colloquial phrasing, as well as the flip, jaunty rhythms of the verse,

> The Phoenix riddle hath more wit
> By us, we two being one, are it,

give the end of the stanza a quality of cockiness and bounce which suggests that the shock statement of the last two lines may be merely an outrageous piece of perverse wit without any serious philosophic significance.

Stanza 4 fails to resolve the paradox of fleshly spirituality set up in stanza 3; instead it steps up the imaginative tension of the poem by evolving out of the general analogy between love and religion the specific image of the passionately sexual lovers as saintly ascetics who have renounced the world and all things of the flesh. The essential tone of the poem remains still in question throughout this stanza. The shock effect of the conceit and Donne's display of ingenuity in elaborating it suggest that the basic attitude may be one of mere witty cynicism. But other effects in the stanza begin to pull against these suggestions of superficial cleverness. The connotations of serenity in the image of saintly death, and the change in verse movement, from the nervous energy and broken musical phrasing of the early stanzas to a broad, even flow throughout stanza 4, produce in these lines a countereffect of calm and sober meditation.

The thought of the poem also takes on a graver cast in stanza 4. Here, and in stanza 5, the poem turns to the contemplation of the actual death of the lovers and of the ways in which they will be remembered by posterity. At the beginning of the stanza the jarring suggestions of the sexuality of this spiritual love are firmly tuned out of the poem and do not appear again, except for the shadowy backward reference to the metaphors of the phoenix and the taper in the word "ashes." Donne makes this intellectual transition by modulating on the word "die" in the opening line of the stanza: here it has its normal meaning (in antithesis to "live" later in the line), and the sexual reference of the word, which had been its primary meaning in stanza 3, exists only as a faint connotative echo. From this point on to the end of the poem the love is presented simply as spiritual in nature. The speaker turns now to consider the actual death of the lovers as the consequence of a love which, he admits, is so impractical in any worldly terms that they cannot live by it. And at this point of apparent ultimate concession to his opponent's objections, he begins to exploit his analysis of the love as a spiritual "mystery" and suddenly turns boldly to justify the love and to demolish the opponent's argument. This argumentative maneuver consists simply in rejecting the opponent's premises—his standards of value. If the lovers are to die from this commitment of their lives to the spiritual values in their love, their

death will be like the martyrdom of saints who have deliberately
renounced all worldly values, and the rewards of martyrdom cannot be comprehended by those who think only in worldly terms.
As Donne begins to evolve his conceit of saintly martyrdom for
devotion to the faith ("we can die by it"), he organizes the stanza
sharply around the dichotomy between the ethical values of a
life devoted to Things of This World and those of a life devoted to
Things of the Spirit. This contrast is implied by the imaginative
pattern which places the tomb and the "chronicle" (the history of
worldly achievement) [11] in antithesis to the urn (the repository
for the relics of a saint) and the verse "legend" (the history of a
saint's life).[12] Turning to the reflection that the lovers will be
memorialized after death in those poems—among them "The Canonization"—in which they have recorded, as in religious hymns,
the spiritual satisfactions of their love, Donne draws on the classical-
Renaissance commonplace that poetry embodies a more lasting
and more ethically respectable memorial than the richest tomb—
the theme of Horace's "Exegi monumentum aere perennius" and of
Shakespeare's

> Not marble, nor the gilded monuments
> Of princes shall outlive this powerful rime.

In this context the tomb stood to the Renaissance mind as a symbol for the folly of worldly ambition, and Donne enforces that
ethical condemnation by the ironic contrast between the gross
pretentiousness of "half-acre tombs" or the lengthy "chronicle" [13]
and the modest and delicate beauty of the "well wrought urn" or
the "pretty" sonnet or hymn.[14]

In the climactic word "canonized" at the end of stanza 4, Donne
finally springs his central conceit of the sainthood of the lovers,
and then drives it to full imaginative definition in stanza 5. The
complex intellectual implications of this closing stanza give a
philosophic organization to the entire poem: they resolve the
paradoxes of flesh and spirit which have been set up by the preceding stanzas; they define the central thread of argument which gives
the poem its logical structure; and they reveal the serious philosophic basis for the imaginative equation between love and religious experience.

Drawing together the reference to martyrdom at the opening of stanza 4 and the resurrection motif from the end of stanza 3, Donne proceeds to elaborate the sainthood conceit with hard theological accuracy, pushing its imaginative logic to final conclusion. By the lover's testimony, in the "hymns" which they have left, of their self-less devotion to the faith, all the devout of later times will have evidence of the saintliness of their lives; and this general "approval" of their sanctity through the witnessing of the faithful will insure their canonization. As martyrs to the faith the saints will have achieved after death immediate resurrection into the Church Triumphant, and they will thus be able to perform the traditional saintly office of mediation, receiving prayers from the faithful and interceding for them with God ("beg from above") to seek special manifestations of Grace to men below. Moreover, as line 39 implies, there will be good cause for the faithful in later times to seek the intercession of these saints. Drawing on the currently popular doctrine of the Decay of Nature,[15] Donne implies that after the death of the two lovers the progressive decline of moral virtue in the world will eradicate the last remnants of spirituality in human affairs and will cause love to degenerate into mere lust. Therefore those lovers who still hold to the true faith of spiritual love will have need to appeal to God for a new manifestation on earth of a "pattern" of the ideal love which the two saints had embodied during their earthly lives. This line of argument also justifies the prediction of stanza 4; it is for this reason that the saintly lovers can be sure that their "legend" will be preserved after their death and that their "hymns" will continue to be read as documents of devotion.

But beneath this ingenious play of wit the last stanza carries effects of strong emotion—in its intensive diction, and in the rhythmic surge of the verse, the build and lift of its rhetoric from the quiet opening to the emotional climax and formal close of the last two lines. Moreover, the rich metaphysical implications and the effects of intense intellectual excitement which suddenly crowd on the reader in this stanza are much too heavy freightage for poetry that is merely clever.

This stanza returns to the analysis of the love begun in stanza 3 and presents the love affair not only as a renunciatory act of moral choice but also as an experience which has led the lovers to an ultimate metaphysical vision. It treats the love as essentially above sex, a conjunction of souls; and the doctrinal pattern of Donne's thought throughout the stanza is that of Christian Platonism. One sees this at the start from the contrast between the "peace" of this love and the "rage" of the love affairs of others, a contrast which reflects the Platonist's standard distinction between the serene temper of the spiritual love of the élite and the feverishness of the lustful love of common men. And the proscriptive force of the phrase "reverend love" has a similar suggestion: it implies not only that this love is spiritual but also that it is conceived of as a particular kind of love, in distinction from other forms of eroticism.[16] These suggestions of the exclusiveness of the lovers' experience were latent in stanza 3 in the image of the phoenix, which carries the implication of uniqueness, and in the description of the love as "mysterious," as something beyond the comprehension of normal men. And they are further defined in the opening lines of stanza 5 by the image of the hermitage, which carries connotations of separateness from the world, as well as suggestions of peace and of ascetic renunciation of the flesh.

These implications about the nature of the love affair are expanded through lines 40–4 in a complex conceit which seems to be a condensed reworking of the poetic materials of the final stanza of "The Good-Morrow." On the level of literal meaning, these lines present a visual picture of the two lovers staring fixedly into one another's eyes. This picture serves to suggest the intensity and the constancy of the love, but its most important function is to dramatize the renunciation of the world which has resulted from their love: the lovers devote themselves entirely to the serene contemplation of one another and never turn their eyes to "countries, towns, courts." And this renunciation is possible because each finds in the other the entire world. Each sees his image impinging on the mirror-like surface of the other's eyeballs;[17] and each finds in this image of the beloved a contracted picture of "the whole world's soul," of "All" epitomized, of "countries, towns, courts." The word "epitomize" hints at the submerged logical basis for the whole conceit: the concept of man as a microcosm, or, in the stock phrase which was used by Donne and other Renaissance writers, as the world "in epitome." And Donne regularly uses the word "All" in its special meaning as a technical term from theology to refer to the world, or sometimes, more generally, to the entire created uni-

verse, the "All" which God created *ex nihilo*.[18] Since "All" is
logically parallel in these lines to both "the whole world's soul"
and "countries, towns, courts," it is clear that Donne is using the
word here to denote the world, considered in its metaphysical
nature as matter informed by the spiritual essence of the World
Soul, or *Anima Mundi*.[19]

Each of the lovers, then, is able to renounce the world because
each sees in the microcosm of the beloved the world in epitome.
But the "world" which they find in each other is not physical in
nature. Here, as in "The Good-Morrow," the world of their love
is metaphysically "better" than the actual world which they have
renounced. The image which each receives is the result of a vision
which abstracts the soul from the body ("who did the whole world's
soul contract"),[20] so that the lovers are drawn together by a Platonic
contemplation of one another's souls rather than by a physical
attraction. And the dynamic connotations of "contract" and
"drove" suggest the intellectual intensity of their vision as well
as the passionate intensity of their love. The word "epitomize"
also acquires a further meaning in this intellectual context: the
lovers not only see the world epitomized in the microcosm of one
another; they have also epitomized the world philosophically, seeing through the illusion of materiality to its metaphysical essence,
to the ultimate reality of soul, which they have discovered in their
love for one another. The description of their eyes as "spies" sup-
ports the suggestion of the intellectual penetration of their metaphysical vision. And the connotations of the metaphor of the lovers'
eyes as "glasses" and "mirrors" enforce further the general metaphysical implications of these lines. This image is, of course, concretely descriptive of the reflecting surface of the eyeball, on which
the phantasm of the beloved impinges. But both of these words
suggest also one of the stock philosophic metaphors of the Renaissance, a metaphor which was used to define the way in which the
physical world manifests metaphysical essence and to suggest also
the merely mediate knowledge of ultimate reality which is all
that most mortals can attain during earthly life. It was a Renaissance commonplace to describe the material world, in St. Paul's
metaphor, as a "glass" through which mortals see darkly to the
hidden reality of divine spirit, or as a "mirror" in which God's
Essence is indirectly reflected to men—*per speculum creaturarum.*

In the poem these philosophically loaded metaphors parallel the general implications of the rest of the passage: in the experience of this love, in which the image of the physical body of the beloved, impinging on the eyeball, has initiated a process by which the lovers have attained to a love based not on the body but on the soul, the eyes have functioned as the instruments of a more comprehensive metaphysical vision: they are the "glasses" and "mirrors" by which the lovers have seen through to the spiritual reality ("the whole world's soul") which lies behind the veil of sense and thus have been led to renounce all the material satisfactions of the transitory and philosophically inessential world of "countries, towns, courts."

These suggestions of the metaphysics of Christian Platonism are pushed to philosophic conclusion in the two final lines. The word "pattern" is a technical term in Neo-Platonic thought for Ideas in the Mind of God; [21] and the fact that the saints are asked to beg the Pattern "from above" (i.e., from God, in Whom it reposes) indicates that Donne is using the word in this special philosophic sense. Therefore the concluding prayer, in which God is asked to re-embody the Pattern in the world of sense to serve as a model for other lovers, carries the philosophic implication that the experience of the lovers has been essentially religious, an experience through which they have approached or attained to the absolute ethical ideal for the souls of mortals, an ideal which exists beyond the physical world as an Idea in the Mind of God.[22] The word "pattern" in the final line of the poem stands, then, as a culminating intellectual shock, a powerfully dramatic logical climax to the paradoxical argument which began by conceding the passionately physical character of the love affair and which then proceeded to justify this love metaphysically as an act of ascetic renunciation and lofty spirituality.

This final metaphysical definition of the nature of the love resolves the doctrinal incongruities of stanza 3. It is clear that Donne is dealing in this poem with the puzzling experience of love which he analyzed in the "The Ecstasy," where he arrived at the conclusion that

> Love's mysteries in souls do grow,
> But yet the body is his book.[23]

It is a love which begins with physical desire and which involves sexual union. But this sexual union is merely the philosophically inessential but pragmatically necessary means by which the lovers attain to the end of a union of souls ("we two being one"), so that the physical relationship is "neutralized," ultimately, into a spiritual experience. It is this double "mystery" of the love—first that of the "mystical" union of lovers' souls, and second that of the transmutation of sexuality into spirituality—which Donne has suggested by the double implication that he developed from the phoenix myth at the end of stanza 3. And I believe that the resurrection analogy in "we die and rise the same" is intended to carry a more exact implication and to give precise definition to the second of these mysteries. Donne is not the man to use a major theological concept loosely, and the doctrine of the resurrection of the body held a particular fascination for him. In "we die and rise the same" I think he is implying an exact parallel between the rationally inexplicable phenomenon of the fleshly spirituality of this love and the specific theological mystery inherent in the doctrine of the resurrection. The mystery of the love is that the lovers are spiritualized through the bodily "death" of sexual intercourse. And the mystery of the resurrection of the body, as defined by St. Paul, is that the body does not die but is changed: it dies a carnal body, but it is reconstituted in the resurrection as a spiritual body. In the light of the final stanza, then, the resurrection conceit appears not as a mere cynical shocker but rather as a dramatic statement of one of the central concepts of the poem.

The closing stanza also throws into sharp relief the poem's central logical framework. By its statement of the theme of the poem and by the *da capo* effect of its reference back to the subject matter of stanzas 1 and 2 in the phrase "countries, towns, courts," it draws the opening stanzas into place as part of a logical development which has run through the whole poem and which has led to this conclusion. The theme, as in "The Good-Morrow," is that the world is well lost for love. And Donne gives this conventional piece of romantic sentiment a metaphysical basis by the argumentative progression of stanzas 3–5, a progression which establishes first that the love is a "mystery" that cannot be understood in terms of the laws of this world, proceeds next to develop the contrast in ethical value between things material and things spiritual, and concludes finally that the lovers are therefore philosophically justified in renouncing the material realities of the world because the love affair has enabled them to apprehend the spiritual reality of "the whole world's soul." Looking back from this conclusion, one can see that stanzas 1 and 2 have formed the initial step in this logical progression by setting up the conceptual pattern on which the argument is based—the antithesis between the World (things material) and Love (things spiritual). These stanzas have dramatized the ethical opposition between the speaker's love and the material values which reside in health, youth, or money, and which are pursued by seeking a "place" in such fields of worldly enterprise as the Law, the Church, the Court, and commerce. The latent organizing concept beneath all the realistic details of the picture of life in "countries, towns, courts" in stanzas 1 and 2 has been that of the ethical category of Things of This World, in contrast to Things of the Spirit, and the opponent with whom the speaker is arguing at the opening stands as the spokesman for the World which is well lost. The vigorous debate which begins the poem, then, is merely a dramatization of the conceptual antithesis which is the basis for the dialectic of the poem's argument. The opening stanzas have therefore laid the logical foundation both for the metaphysical conclusions arrived at in the rest of the poem and for the central conceit of saintliness which gives imaginative form to the poem's statement.

Furthermore, the solid philosophic force which Donne gives to his religious metaphor by the rich metaphysical implications of the last stanza makes clear finally that, despite the witty ingenuity with which they have been developed, the sainthood conceit and the general identification of love with religious experience throughout the poem do have a firm conceptual basis and are intended to imply a serious philosophic statement. Donne commits himself, at least in part, to the logical implications of his central religious metaphor, and, in a sense, the analogy is actually meant as a conceptual proposition. The poem says, in effect, that, fantastic as this analogy may seem, it may contain elements of truth beneath its surface improbability. Viewed in the light of Donne's personal modification of the orthodox metaphysics of Platonic Love, some of the logical parallels which the poem draws between the experience of the lovers and the spiritual progress of the Christian saint do have both a psychological and metaphysical validity. The paradoxical wit of "The Canonization" is, therefore, essentially a serious wit, and the major paradoxes of the poem—the imaginative incongruity between the traditional concept of sainthood on the one hand, and on the other the far from saintly character of the speaker's antics in the first two stanzas and his emphasis on his sexual indulgence in stanza 3—merely accentuate the intellectual drama of a daring philosophic speculation.

This analysis defines what I think Donne was trying to do in "The Canonization." But I do not think he quite succeeded. My own feeling is that he never fully resolves the imaginative incongruities of the poem. For all its theatrical power and intellectual brilliance, "The Canonization" never achieves that effect of final logical and emotional integrity which makes poems like "The Good-Morrow" and "A Valediction: Forbidding Mourning" so impressive. If Donne was fully clear on the plan of writing a poem which would seem at first merely a lively and clever literary enterprise, and which would reveal itself finally as a serious philosophic poem about spiritualized love—and the concealed but careful logical planning of the opening stanzas certainly suggests that he had that purpose in mind from the start—then the trouble may be merely technical: Donne tried to accomplish too much in the concentrated final stanza. After four stanzas which have seemed predominantly witty and intellectually flamboyant, the single serious stanza with which he concludes does not seem enough to establish a base of philosophic seriousness for the whole poem and to resolve all its ambiguities of tone. And even in that final stanza there are still suggestions of slick cleverness in Donne's elaboration of the sainthood conceit, so that some loose ends of levity and of wit-for-wit's-sake are left dangling at the end of the poem. Too much of what Donne was trying to express in "The Canonization" may have remained in his own mind; it was either not said in the text or said so elliptically that one has to surround the poem with "The Ecstasy" and "The Good-Morrow" and even some of the personal facts of Donne's life to feel confident of the essential seriousness behind the play of wit in stanzas 3 and 5 and to be sure that the central analogy between love and religious experience is being presented with full emotional commitment.

The poem certainly invites a reader who knows anything about the facts of Donne's life to speculate about John Donne personally. Whether it is to be read as completely autobiographical, and whether the speaker in the poem is exactly and entirely John Donne, is something known only to the Mind of God; but it contains so many references to the generally known facts about Donne's personal circumstances in the years after his marriage that Donne himself must have expected his contemporary readers to see the speaker as John Donne *in propria persona* and to read the poem as a commentary on his personal life. And I think "The Canonization" certainly is that, however much the personal situation has been dramatized for literary purposes. When one reads the letters which Donne wrote in those years from his "hospital at Mitcham"—with their accounts of his sufferings from poverty and from recurrent attacks of sickness, of his depression over finding himself in middle age with all his prospects of advancement in the world ruined by his marriage, and of his remorse over having "transplanted" his gently bred wife "into a wretched fortune"— the details of palsy, gout, gray hairs, and ruined fortune in the opening lines of the poem, and the statement "We can die by it, if not live by love," take on a sharp actuality. And the problem of finding an answer to some worldly-wise friend's argument that his love had been an act of folly can hardly have been wholly imaginary. In this biographical context the dramatic tension of the poem, its tough-minded balancing of what has been lost against what has been gained, and its difficult progression to the philosophic conclusion that the world *has* been well lost for love take on a richer significance as an expression of a hard-won intellectual victory.

But in actuality that victory was anything but final, as even a glance at Donne's letters shows. The debate with himself over the rightness of what he had done went on. And perhaps the equivocality of tone in "The Canonization" derives partly from that fact. I think it is likely that Donne's failure to commit himself fully to seriousness in the poem, to throw the whole weight of artistic conviction behind the portentous philosophic statement which the last stanza presents, and to tune out, finally, the suggestions that the whole business is perhaps just a playful speculation, came from his own uncertainty of mind about these conclusions. The dramatic character of the opponent, that voice of worldly wisdom with whom Donne is debating in the poem, could have been drawn, no doubt, from a number of Donne's friends, but Donne could also have found the materials for this imagined figure closer to home. The realist who believes in getting ahead in the world, who enjoys the materialistic satisfactions of "countries, towns, courts," and who takes a cold view of the impracticalities of spiritual love and is thick to the subtle intellectual mysteries of spiritual phenomena, is the same dramatic character who speaks in "The Blossom" as the voice of John Donne, engaged in debate with his impractical soul. The personal reality behind the imaginary debate of "The Canonization" was certainly, in part at least, Donne's debate with himself. And the other-self who is reflected in the opponent of the poem was probably enough of an actuality in Donne's mind when he wrote "The Canonization" to cast a sly smirk over the whole poem, a realist's ironic suggestion that of course one's mind keeps cutting up in these fantastic ways, and it's a lot of fun, but that we certainly can't get really solemn about this argument that sexuality is a means to religious intuition and that it is sound philosophic sense to renounce the world for love.

In the last analysis, however, Donne *is* being solemn in this poem, and I think "The Canonization" reveals indirectly a good deal about his personal attitudes in the years just after his marriage. The poem's argument for putting his worldly other-self behind him, and its unflattering picture in the first two stanzas of the values of the whole society of his time, surely derive from personal conviction. The poem reflects a hardening in Donne's sense of philosophic alienation from the normal concerns of English life in the early seventeenth century, a strengthening of the feeling latent in his earlier verse that his own experience is separate and unique, something which other men in his time are unable to understand. In "The Canonization" the view of the world which his love has driven him to renounce is not fundamentally different from that suggested by the "sea-discoverers" passage in "The Good-Morrow," but here the picture of that world is more sharply critical. The "world" which appears in this poem is a society motivated entirely by a soulless, self-seeking materialism. This view of his age as a time concerned only with

"cost" and with getting ahead, and blind to spiritual values and
to the reality of religious experience, is essentially the attitude
which Donne had expressed in the early Satire 3: "Of Religion,"
the most clearly personal of his Satires; and it is the same attitude
which he carried to extreme, perhaps about the same time that he
wrote "The Canonization," in the baroque extravagance of the
comprehensive pessimism of "The First Anniversary," that grotesque poem in which Donne treats the entire world as progressively decaying from the loss of its Soul.

Moreover, Donne was scarcely the only man of his time to
believe seriously that his world was going to the dogs. The view
that English society in the late 1590's and early 1600's was a culture in which moral values were on the decline, and self-centered
egotism and cynical materialism on the increase, had a wide currency in belief in the first decades of the seventeenth century, and
certainly also some basis in fact. In the general disillusionment
which followed the fading of the Elizabethan Dream, many
thoughtful Englishmen in the days of James I came to look on
their own time as an Iron Age which had succeeded the Golden
Age of the sixteenth century,[24] and to give serious credence to the
ancient philosophic doctrine of the Decay of Nature. In the early
1600's Shakespeare and Ben Jonson, to name only the outstanding
figures, saw the life of their time in terms not very different from
those in which Donne presents it in "The Canonization." And
the very circumstantial testimony of Jonson's comedies, of Shakespeare's "bitter comedies" and tragedies, and of the plays of Webster and other Jacobean dramatists indicates that this general attitude had a more solid basis in fact than we are likely to realize
from our twentieth-century point of vantage; and it suggests that
when in early seventeenth-century England modern man first
began to feel his philosophic oats in his new role as absolute Lord
of Creation, the resultant excesses manifested a degree of moral
squalor which would have offended ethical sensibilities much less
fastidious than Donne's. It was certainly more than a subjectively
motivated state of depression which caused Shakespeare, in those
years, to speculate seriously on the likelihood that humanity would
come to prey on itself like monsters of the deep. In this intellectual
climate, then, it was not wholly fantastic for Donne to think of

an intensely idealized love which had led him to reject the worldly ambitions that motivated other men as in some ways like the other-worldly dedication of religious experience, and, in moments of defensive self-justification, to think of his marriage as in some ways like a saintly act of ascetic renunciation. The hard intellectual pride behind such an attitude was scarcely foreign to Donne's temperament, and this was certainly not the first time he had thanked God that he was not as other men.

I think that this much of what "The Canonization" says can be regarded as having had a personal basis in what Donne had actually thought as he brooded to himself over the rights and wrongs of his marriage to Anne More. And I suspect that it is the self-righteousness lurking in this attitude which the calculated extravagance of the poem, and its excess of wit and irony, are playing against. The intellectual tensions and emotional ambiguities of the poem certainly derive from conflicting attitudes in Donne's own mind, and if those tensions are never quite resolved to set the poem in final artistic balance, I think the cause probably lies in a certain residuary irresolution in Donne's mind at the time when he wrote it.[25]

There is, finally, one other fact about "The Canonization" which opens up an interesting possibility for speculation—the striking resemblances which it bears to "The Sun Rising." That poem, which is a more open and much less intricate piece of work, was probably written earlier than "The Canonization," and I see no reason to connect it with Donne's love for Anne More. But both poems are built on the same strategic plan: they begin with explosive brusqueness, as the lover tells an intruder on his love to get away and leave him alone, and they then modulate to an expression of sustained romantic passion. Both start, also, with a sharp realistic picture of what other people are doing—a semi-satiric survey of types of worldly ambition which is intended to suggest the normal concerns of life in the World, a world that the lovers have chosen to renounce—and they conclude with a picture of the lovers withdrawn from that world and completely absorbed in the contemplation of one another. Furthermore both develop an ingenious argument to prove that the world has been well lost for love because the two lovers have found the whole world in each

other. But, along with these similarities, the two poems show fundamental differences. There are no gray hairs in "The Sun Rising":
the lover in that poem is young, as one sees from his initial annoyance at the sun as an "old fool" and from his later patronizing
condescension toward the sun's old age ("thine age asks ease").
His love, moreover, seems a matter of mere physical rapture, uncomplicated by intellectual analysis and without any suggestion of
spirituality. And after the similarly theatrical opening stanzas,
"The Sun Rising" develops a tone which is very different from that
of "The Canonization." It is a poem of youthful exuberance and
unclouded high spirits, a dramatic expression of the exultant brag
of a young lover after a night of love.

I think Donne could hardly have failed to notice the similarities
in theme and literary method between the two poems, and I doubt
that the resemblance between them is accidental. It seems probable
that when Donne decided to write, in "The Canonization," a poem
justifying the loss of the world for love, he thought back to an
earlier poem which he had written on the same theme, a poem expressing a very different state of mind and dealing with what he
would see at this time as a very different kind of love, and that he
took that poem as his artistic model. Probably he had already re-
worked the genre of "The Sun Rising," as well as the theme of the
world well lost, in "The Good-Morrow," and I think he may have
decided to rework "The Sun Rising" again, this time more closely,
in "The Canonization." The writing of companion pieces of this
sort—poems like "L'Allegro" and "Il Penseroso" and the two
matched songs at the end of Love's Labour's Lost, which are similar in literary form but express contrasting points of view—was
a Renaissance literary fashion. These two poems of Donne's do
not have the close, point-to-point formal parallel which one normally finds in the Renaissance poems that were written together
as two halves of a single literary structure, but I suspect that, though
"The Canonization" follows an inner logic of its own and stands
as an independent poem, Donne thought of it as to some extent a
companion piece to "The Sun Rising."

But if he did see the two poems as a matched pair, was the impulse which led him to play them off against one another nothing
more than an interest in an abstract pattern of artistic contrast?
If I am right in my belief that Donne was moved to write "The

Canonization" by the pressure of his personal distress in the years following his marriage, and by a personal need to justify, not only to others but to himself, the loss of the world for his love, then it seems likely that Donne thought of "The Canonization" as "The Sun Rising" rewritten by an older, a sadder, and a wiser man.

HYMN TO GOD, MY GOD, IN MY SICKNESS

Since I am coming to that holy room,
 Where, with thy Choir of Saints for evermore,
I shall be made thy Music; as I come
  I tune the Instrument here at the door,
  And what I must do then, think here before.   5

Whilst my physicians by their love are grown
 Cosmographers, and I their map, who lie
Flat on this bed, that by them may be shown
  That this is my South-west discovery
  Per fretum febris, by these straits to die,   10

I joy, that in these straits, I see my West;
 For, though their currents yield return to none,
What shall my West hurt me? As West and East
  In all flat maps (and I am one) are one,
  So death doth touch the resurrection.   15

Is the Pacific Sea my home? Or are
 The Eastern riches? Is Jerusalem?
Anyan, and Magellan, and Gilbraltare,
  All straits, and none but straits, are ways to them,
  Whether where Japhet dwelt, or Cham, or Sem.   20

We think that Paradise and Calvary,
    Christ's cross, and Adam's tree, stood in one place;
Look Lord, and find both Adams met in me;
    As the first Adam's sweat surrounds my face,
    May the last Adam's blood my soul embrace. 25

So, in his purple wrapped receive me Lord,
    By these his thorns give me his other crown;
And as to others' souls I preached thy word,
    Be this my text, my sermon to mine own,
    Therefor that he may raise the Lord throws down. 30

Chapter 4

"Hymn to God, My God, in My Sickness"

THE "Hymn to God, My God, in My Sickness" has never been as popular with modern anthologists of Donne's work—and therefore with most modern readers—as the "Holy Sonnets" and the fine but much simpler "Hymn to God the Father," but I think it is by far Donne's most distinguished achievement in religious poetry. None of his other religious poems can match its symphonic richness of suggestion, and its balancing of intellectual subtlety with sustained emotion, of intricate precision in detail with a controlling sense of form.

The poem takes us to the last decade of Donne's life, past his entrance into holy orders and the death of his wife, to the time when he was Dean of St. Paul's. Walton would have us believe that it represents the very end of Donne's literary career, that it is his last poem, written eight days before his death in 1631. But Walton was a dramatic artist who often found poetic truth more significant than the truth of objective fact, and his date for the poem is probably wrong: it is more likely that this "Hymn" was written in 1623, during the serious illness which moved Donne to write the *Devotions*.[1] But the question of whether Donne was actually dying as he wrote the poem, or whether he just thought he was, is a worry for the biographer rather than for the critic. Donne conceived the "Hymn" as a deathbed poem, a personal meditation in these circumstances. Here he seems to have laid aside the conscious self-dramatization before an audience which we find in many of his love poems and even in some of the "Holy Sonnets," and to be writing more for himself than for any particular group of readers. He casts the poem in the form of a hortatory and analytical sermon addressed to his own soul, an argument with himself which he must finally resolve to set his house in order; and he has blocked it out as a step-by-step intellectual progression to a logical conclusion. In the first stanza Donne states the psychological problem which this argument must resolve: he is trying to establish his peace of mind before he dies by coming to accept intellectually the justness of God's ways toward him in order to be spiritually prepared for entering into the serene joy of heaven. The essence of the argument which the rest of the poem develops is that death and the physical sufferings of his illness must be accepted willingly: first, because it is only through suffering and death that man can reach heavenly bliss; second, because this experience is a requisite if God's dealings with man are to be just; and finally, because Donne himself is confident of salvation through Christ's Redemption.

In the first stanza Donne presents the problem itself in argumentative form: since heaven is harmony, the individual soul must be "tuned," or brought to internal harmony, before death in order to prepare it for eternal life in heaven, where its bliss will be that of entire accord with the Mind of God ("what I must do then"). The philosophic doctrine from which this proposition derives—the analogical identification of musical harmony with the peace and perfection of God and with the perfect order of His universe—was a commonplace of Christian Platonism. Milton's treatment of the same analogy in "At a Solemn Music" indicates the rich intellectual and emotional suggestions which this stanza had for Donne and for readers of the seventeenth century, suggestions of quiet, wholehearted joy in the feeling of peace with oneself and with God and of harmonious oneness with the meaningful order of all existence. According to the normal form of this body of ideas, a doctrine which Donne uses elsewhere, the individual soul is harmonious at birth, but it is made discordant by the experience of life in the flesh, and it must therefore be reharmonized before it enters heaven.[2] But the rest of this poem makes clear that the particular discord which Donne is concerned to tune out of his soul is his intellectual unwillingness to accept the bodily sufferings of his sickness and his coming death.

The basic meaning of "I tune the Instrument" is simply "I compose my mind," since "instrument," as one sees from Donne's restatement of line 4 in lines 28–9, is an image for Donne's soul. This image is derived from a subordinate concept which was a part of the same Platonic tradition, the doctrine that the soul is by nature a harmony, like a well-tuned lyre.[3] In line 4, Donne compares his soul to some stringed instrument which must be tuned so that it can harmonize in heaven with the serene and joyous song of the Church Triumphant, the "Choir of Saints." [4] But the word "instrument" has a further, specialized meaning in Donne's vocabulary. He often uses it in its theological sense to refer to the individual soul who acts as God's agent on earth to lead other souls to religious certainty: most specifically, it means "a minister of the Gospel." [5] The final stanza, which shows parallels with stanza 1 in both content and imagery, makes clear that Donne is speaking in this poem as a clergyman, God's instrument, who has preached God's Word "to others' souls." In line 4, then, Donne is playing with this ambiguity of the word "instrument," and the word carries also a personal reference to his present profession as a Christian minister. But there is, finally, a further suggestion of "I tune the Instrument here at the door," a suggestion which dominates the other two meanings of the phrase at this point in the poem. The phrase refers to the writing of the poem itself, to Donne's act of composing his mind, here at the door of death, so that the instrument of his soul may resonate harmoniously with a hymn to God about his humble acceptance of death and his joyous hope of resurrection into eternal life.

Donne dramatizes his statement in these opening lines by using the doctrinal analogies to music to generate a concrete central image for the first stanza. From the imaginative complex of the general Platonic musical analogy, of the specific analogy of the soul to a musical instrument, and of the picture of heaven in the book of Revelation, with its account of the saints and angels singing and playing their golden harps around the throne of the King of Kings, Donne evolves the concrete metaphor of himself on his deathbed as a court musician who is tuning up his instrument outside the door of the King's throne-room in preparation for entering the Presence Chamber, where he will take his place as part of the "King's Music" (the court orchestra). This metaphor is a further development, in a musical context, of another image which appears several times in Donne's work, the comparison of this world to an anteroom in which the soul must wait before being received into the King's Presence Chamber.[6] And in developing the image of the King's throne-room, Donne introduces also, I believe, a shadowy pun on the word "room," which he normally uses in the more general meaning of "place." I think he implies that meaning —with its suggestion that heaven is the place where his soul properly belongs—as well as the more specific sense of a room in a palace, by the phrase "holy room" in the opening line of the poem.[7]

But there is a technical theological discrepancy between the doctrine implied in stanza 1, according to which the soul is musical harmony itself and will become after death a part of what Sir Thomas Browne described as "that harmony which intellectually sounds in the ears of God," and the implications of the central image of the stanza, which presents Donne as the musician who will sound the harmony on the instrument of his soul. This inconsistency is paralleled by the ambiguity which the phrase "I shall be made thy Music" would have, in this context, for a Renaissance reader. That phrase could mean either "I shall be made into the music itself," or "I shall be made a member of the band of court musicians who play the music." I think Donne was both too scrupulously exact as a theologian about technicalities of doctrine, and too sharply alert as a writer to ambiguities in phrasing and to the logical implications of metaphor, to be unaware either of this doctrinal inconsistency or of the double meaning of this phrase, and I believe that the ambiguity on the word "Music" is deliberate. If so, the phrase "I shall be made thy Music" implies a specific mystical doctrine which, because of its paradoxical character, seems to have appealed particularly to Donne's speculative imagination. According to this doctrine the individual soul is absorbed after death into the joys of heaven, but at the same time it retains its identity and can contemplate those joys as a spectator. Donne refers to this concept a number of times, but the closest parallel to these lines of the "Hymn" is in "The First Anniversary," where he describes Elizabeth Drury in heaven as "now a part of both the Choir and Song."[8] I think, therefore, that "I shall be made thy Music" means: "When I join the Choir of Saints I shall become, in some

mysterious way, not only one of the musicians around the throne
who produce the harmonious music of heaven, but also a part of
the music itself."

Structurally this first stanza is an introduction, a statement of
the personal problem which the poem must settle and a suggestion
of the intellectual and emotional resolution toward which its argument must proceed. The argument proper begins with stanza 2.
Stanzas 2–4 form its first logical unit, and they have also an imaginative unity from the metaphor of geographical exploration, which
Donne introduces in stanza 2 and elaborates through stanzas 3
and 4. Here, as usual, Donne is reasoning by means of analogy,
and throughout the poem the separate structural blocks of thought
are involved with separate blocks of metaphor. Reduced to plain-
est English, stanza 2 says, "While my physicians diagnose my case
and see only that I am going to die . . ." Donne evolves his geographical conceit from this statement by referring to the transformation of his physicians into "cosmographers," a transformation
which is accomplish~ᵈ "by their love." Donne's medical references
are normally to the "New Physic" of Paracelsus, rather than to
Galenist medicine, and this line evidently alludes to one of the
pervasive doctrines in Paracelsus' medical writings—that to practice the medical art properly the physician must feel love for his
patient, a love which gives him not only the selfless dedication
which is necessary to his profession but also the higher intellectual
insight which the medical art requires.[9] In lines 6–7 Donne combines this piece of Christianized medical science with another concept from the stock of Christian Platonism, the belief in the transforming power of love.[10] His physicians, then, having experienced
the love for the patient which is their professional obligation, are
transformed by that experience into cosmographers (geographers).

The submerged concept which justifies this equation of the
physicians with cosmographers is the doctrine that man is a microcosm, or a little world, a concept which is central not only in
Donne's thought but also in Paracelsian medical theory. If Donne
himself is a little world, then the physicians who are studying that
world may be thought of as cosmographers. But Donne introduces
a refinement on the stock analogy between man and the world:
as he lies in his sickbed, he is not the world itself but rather a map
of it. To see the implication of this new twist in the analogy, one

must recognize a special connotation which maps often had for the Renaissance imagination and particularly for Donne: he regularly thinks of a map as a scanty and inadequate picture of the world which it represents.[11] The analogy between the physicians who are examining the microcosm and cosmographers who are examining a map carries a suggestion, therefore, that the microcosm is an imperfect and merely partial representation of metaphysical reality, as the map is an inadequate representation of the actual world. This special maneuver in handling the microcosm image serves, tactically, as a preparation for the later map conceit in lines 13–15, and it also gives Donne an opening for drawing a distinction, in stanzas 3 and 4, between his own full philosophic comprehension of his death and the limited insight which his physicians have.

Having made an imaginative progression from medical science, via love and the microcosm, to geography, Donne introduces at the end of the stanza the Latin phrase that was probably the germ from which he developed the complex geographical conceit in these stanzas. The physicians see that he will pass to his death *"per fretum febris"*—through the strait of fever. As Donne translates "fretum" in the rest of the line, he pluralizes the word to permit a play on two meanings of the English word "straits": first, the geographical meaning, "a narrow passage," and second, "physical hardship, danger." This pun serves to equate his sickness with mortal suffering in general and also with a passage through geographical straits, and it thus accomplishes the imaginative transition to the image of geographical exploration, which he introduces at the end of stanza 2 and elaborates in detail in stanzas 3 and 4.[12]

By studying the map outspread before them (Donne's body lying flat on his sickbed), the physician-geographers can see that he has arrived at his "South-west discovery," the straits through which he will pass to die. Donne uses "discovery" here in the special sense which the word carried, at least in his own usage, in the phrases "North-west discovery" and "South-west discovery": it refers to the discovery of the navigational passage which the merchant explorers had sought for generations, an ocean passage to the Orient.[13] The "South-west discovery," then, is the discovery of the Southwest Passage, the Straits of Magellan. And, Donne suggests, as he starts to develop the conceit in exact detail, precisely as Magellan passed through the stormy straits which he discovered to die in the West, in the Philippines, so he himself is about to pass through the straits (sufferings) of fever to his own death ("my West").

The third stanza opens new imaginative reaches in this metaphor of exploration, and it moves a step further toward a resolution of the problem which the poem deals with, as Donne expresses his sure courage in facing death and his joyous certainty of resurrection. The beginning of the stanza is emphatic, with strong accents on both "I" and "joy." Donne is contrasting his own reaction to the fact of his imminent death with that of his physicians. Like geographers, who know the experience of exploration solely through maps and who therefore, as they look at the map, think only of the sad fact that Magellan's passage through his "Southwest discovery" had led him to his death, the physicians can see merely that Donne will die from his fever, and—"by their love"—they feel only distress. But Donne himself, who is in immediate contact with the reality of the experience, feels only the joy and excitement of the actual explorer who has at last found the long-sought westward passage to the Orient. He does not regret that the currents will allow him no return from his passage,[14] and he is not afraid to face the hardship and danger which he may expect as he goes farther into the West that now opens before him—"What shall my West hurt me?" He thinks of the West (death) simply as the region that he must pass through to arrive at the East (resurrection and the joy of eternal life in heaven), the goal which all men have dreamed of and which truly adventurous men have actually sought. He knows the whole actuality of death, as the "door" opening into the splendors of the "holy room" of eternity, not as the mere "map" which is all that his physicians can see.[15]

This use of the East as a symbol for the resurrection and for heaven was traditional in Christian literature, and conceits, derived from this symbol, which exploited the antithesis between East and West made a particular appeal to Donne's imagination during his later years. He used the conceit for a point of wit at the end of his own epitaph, and Walton records that when Donne posed for the portrait of himself in death which he commissioned as he was dying, he "stood with . . . his lean, pale, and death-like face . . . purposely turned toward the East, from whence he expected the second coming of his and our Savior, Jesus." [16] In this passage in the "Hymn," "East" has a richly evocative symbolic suggestion. The word carries not only the sensory and emotional connotations of sunrise which surround the suggestion of resurrection into the eternal day of heaven, where "there shall be no night," and the further powerful emotional suggestiveness which the Orient had for the Renaissance imagination: the word had also, in Donne's own mind, a particular association with Christ. Here, as in his epitaph, Donne is thinking of the Vulgate's translation of Zechariah vi. 12: *Ecce vir, Oriens nomen eius.* This particular connotation of the symbol of "East" serves, therefore, as a first hint of the motif of Christ as Redeemer which is developed later in stanzas 5 and 6.

Donne finally sums up the argumentative point of stanzas 2 and 3 in the map conceit of lines 13–15. Its intellectual implications might be stated as follows: "In looking at my dying body one might think (as my physicians do) that death is far removed from eternal life, just as in looking at a flat map one might think that West and East were opposite extremes; but my dying body, like the map, is an inadequate representation of the reality, in which death and resurrection, like West and East, merge into one another and are merely successive phases of a continuous progression." [17] And the last line of the stanza—"So death doth touch the resurrection"—falls with the sure finality of a conclusion to which Donne has built through two stanzas. It is the first of the poem's logical resolutions.

Logically, stanza 4 completes the phase of the argument which was begun in stanza 2 and continued in stanza 3. The third stanza has established the conclusion that sickness and death can be accepted with equanimity because they provide a way of reaching the joys of heaven. Stanza 4 pushes this conclusion further: the passage through the "straits" of suffering and death is the *only* way by which man can reach heavenly bliss. But the major force of this stanza is tonal: it provides the emotional climax of the poem. Here Donne releases the full emotional voltage of his exploration metaphor to raise the mood of joy and hope which has been established by the preceding stanza to a peak of intensity. Drawing on all the passionate romanticism with which the Renaissance imagination had responded to the discovery of the New World, and on the further evocative power of the picture of the Heavenly City in the book of Revelation, he presents heaven as a gorgeous and exotic new world which he is about to discover, the "new earth" of Revelation; and his emotions, as he contemplates in imagination its unknown riches, are those of wonder, excitement, and eager anticipation.

The basic metaphor in these lines—the parallel between a man's emotions as he contemplates life after death and the puzzlement or excitement with which men contemplated the new geographical discoveries—was no novelty, in itself, to the Renaissance reader.[18] The brilliant effectiveness of the image in this stanza of the "Hymn" comes from Donne's originality in developing a fairly conventional analogy, from the sharp concreteness and the rich suggestiveness which he gives to the conceit, and the elaborate formal pattern which he imposes on it. To particularize the general analogy between exploration and the soul's progress to heaven, Donne turns to one of the problems which had engaged the speculations of medieval geographers—the problem of the location of the Earthly Paradise, which was thought of as an analogue, or "type," of heaven;[19] and he develops from this problem the basic imaginative equation of this stanza: a comparison between heaven and the riches of the entire earth. But this general metaphor is not stated explicitly: it flashes on the reader as a final organizing pattern only after he has responded to the suggestions of all the particular details of the stanza. In analyzing the conceit, I must work backward from the end of the stanza, but its effect on the reader is precisely the opposite: he progresses through apparently random specific details to a climactic effect in the final line which throws all of these details into place as part of a single imaginative order. In the last line of the stanza Donne says that the new lands to which he is going are like those "where Japhet dwelt, or Cham, or Sem." He refers here to a doctrine from medieval geography— that each of the three continents was settled by the descendants of one of the three sons of Noah: Europe by the sons of Japhet, Africa by the sons of Ham, and Asia by the sons of Shem.[20] In late classical and medieval geography these three continents comprised the entire habitable world; they made up the hemisphere of land, and the remainder of the earth was the hemisphere of water. Even though Donne was keenly interested, as this poem shows, in new geographical discoveries, his imagination worked most characteristically in terms of the old geography, as it did in terms of the old astronomy.[21] He sometimes refers to the three continents—the Old "World," in contrast to the New "World" of America—simply as "the world," and he implies that reference here.[22] Line 20, then ("Whether where Japhet dwelt, or Cham, or Sem"), means essentially "the whole world," or, in the symbolic significance which the line takes on from the rest of the stanza, "all of the satisfactions which man has known in the sum of his entire experience on earth."

Having set up, by this reference to the three continents, a three-part division in his allusion to the treasures of the entire earth, Donne uses this division to schematize the other geographical references in stanza 4. This triplicate pattern can be indicated as follows:

Anyan (Bering Strait)—Sem (Asia)
—"the Eastern riches"

Straits of Magellan—Cham (Africa)
—"the Pacific Sea"

Straits of Gibraltar—Japhet (Europe)
—"Jerusalem"

$$= \text{the riches of the whole earth} = \text{the comprehensive bliss of heaven}$$

In developing his basic image to imply that all earthly riches can be reached only through straits, Donne parallels a particular strait with each of the three continents, and he then particularizes the reference to each continent by a more specific geographical allusion which has both the general suggestion of one of the possible localities of the Earthly Paradise and also particular connotations that define the qualities of heavenly bliss.[23] The overtones of "Pacific" suggest the peace of heaven. "Sea" calls up suggestions of "the sea of glass" in Revelation, and of the rich significance which that metaphor had taken on as it was elaborated throughout the literature of Christian mysticism in the symbol of God as the infinite Ocean of Being, the great calm flood into which every soul might sink and be surely borne through eternity. And "Jerusalem" evokes the vivid picture in the book of Revelation of the New Jerusalem, the Heavenly City shining with gold and precious stones.[24] The allusion to the Indies in "Eastern riches" is allied in connotation to the reference to Jerusalem, and Donne's imagination also associates the Indies particularly with the Earthly Paradise.[25] The general effect of the imagery of this stanza, therefore, is to set up a series of powerfully vivid suggestions of the specific satisfactions of immortal life which builds to a cumulative suggestion of the entirety of heavenly bliss. In effect, the stanza implies that what Donne referred to in Elegy 19 as the "whole joys" of heaven, in contrast to the partial joys of mortal life, will be like every satisfaction which man has known or sought on earth, and more.[26]

After the ecstatic climax of stanza 4 Donne makes a sharp structural break in the poem; there is a shift in thought and a dramatic modulation to a different key. Stanza 5 begins the second logical unit in the argument, but it is linked to the final stanza by the transition passage of lines 26–7, so that the two concluding stanzas form a single structural unit with an internal division at the stanza break. Stanzas 2–4 have developed a single line of argument, have elaborated a single conceit, and have built a crescendo on a single tonal effect—the joyous assurance and excited anticipation which come to full expression in stanza 4. The concluding stanzas show a shift in argument, in imagery, and in tonality. The opening of stanza 5 breaks suddenly to quiet: it is meditative rather than assertive, and from here to the end the poem develops as a humble and fervent prayer. The last stanzas introduce also a new step in the argument. Stanzas 2–4 have presented the argument that Donne, and mankind in general, can reach heaven only by passing through mortal suffering and physical death. The two final stanzas present the theological justification for this necessity. They argue, in effect, that the ways of God, which have been shown in the preceding stanzas, are just, since suffering and death are the proper punishment for Original Sin, and that Donne himself may expect salvation, after he has duly suffered for Adam's sin, because he has accepted the Grace offered through Christ's Atonement. Donne caps the argument with a text from the Bible, which he quotes as a clincher in the final line of the poem.

As the argument turns theological, Donne looks to the Bible for allusion and for imagery. This imagery follows a traditional literary pattern: it is a series of conceits which analogize Adam's Fall to Christ's Redemption, and also—as Donne ties these traditional conceits into the structure of this poem—to Donne's own sickness and imminent death. These conceits, moreover, are bound logically to the argument of stanzas 2–4: they provide a series of analogies which join death with resurrection, and they thus develop further the conclusion reached in line 15, that "death doth touch the resurrection." This conclusion now emerges clearly as the basic form of the poem's central theme.

Lines 21–2 show, first, that according to Christian legend death and resurrection are conjoined geographically, topographically, and, so to speak, arboreally. Working with a traditional myth that the Cross was erected on the original site of the Garden of Eden,[27] Donne develops an antithetic parallel between two hills (Eden and Calvary) and two trees (the apple tree in Eden, and the Cross, which was traditionally referred to as a tree).[28] Paradise and Adam's tree, then, which brought death into the world, are related analogically to Calvary and the Cross, which brought resurrection and eternal life.[29] Death and resurrection, the Fall and the Redemption, are next shown to be conjoined in man and in the generic name of Adam. Donne implies this analogy by his allusion in line 23 to the fifteenth chapter of 1 Corinthians: to the passage "Since by man came death, by man came also the resurrection of the dead," and to St. Paul's description of Christ as "the last Adam." Donne himself partakes, from a theological standpoint, of the natures of both Adam and Christ ("find both Adams met in me"), and he is thus introduced as a third category in the system of parallels between Adam and Christ. As the argumentative conclusion to this series of analogies, therefore, death and resurrection are shown to be conjoined in Donne himself. Donne develops this conclusion further in the last two lines of the stanza. He prays that the two Adams (death and resurrection) will be met in him symbolically as he experiences successively physical death and immortal life. By equating the fever sweat of his sickness with the sweat which symbolizes the suffering and death that were the consequence of Adam's sin,[30] Donne implies that his present sickness and his coming death are a just punishment for his own share in Original Sin and that, because he has suffered this punishment, and has accepted Christ as Redeemer, he may expect to share in the promise of resurrection through Christ's summary Atonement.

Donne gives these concluding lines of his argument an effect of artistic finality by casting them into one of the formal patterns of Renaissance rhetoric, a sustained, term-by-term antithesis between two Adams, two enveloping liquids, the mortal body and the immortal soul, and—by implication—death and resurrection. The first Adam's sweat (death) which "surrounds" [31] Donne's face (his mortal body) is paralleled to the last Adam's blood (resurrection) which will "embrace" Donne's immortal soul.

I have allowed myself an irreverent smile at the fantastic analogical ingenuities of these lines. But no thoughtful man of the Middle Ages, and very few of the early seventeenth century, would have found anything to smile at in Donne's ingenious exercise in paradox-spinning at this point in the poem. Like many of the serious paradoxes in Donne's other poems, these conceits derive from a traditional imaginative vocabulary which is profoundly alien to the modern mind. But this vocabulary seemed not only valid but also deeply significant to the mind of an age which saw the world of concrete reality encompassed by the clear actuality of a strange other world of "things invisible," and which was philosophically beset on every side by logically proved intellectual "mysteries" which often contradicted every rational deduction from the daily evidence of one's senses. Donne presents his analogies between Eden and Calvary with a skeptical reservation: "we think." Perhaps, he suggests, they are not factually true. But it is not factual, scientific truth which a man contemplates as he stands on the shores of Time and Space and looks out into the opening mysteries of the vast Ocean which is God. These analogies are at least symbolically true, and that truth is now of greater moment: they are traditional imaginative patterns which men have contemplated throughout the ages as they have let their imaginations play, with wonder and delight, over the intricate system of "correspondence" in which was made manifest the great fact of Design in the Nature of Things. And their paradoxical character served merely to dramatize, to a medievalized imagination, the incomprehensible mystery of the Wisdom at the heart of things and of the Word which was made flesh, the mystery of a fixed order behind the ceaseless flux of phenomena, of eternity in change, corruption which could put on incorruption, and mortal things which could put on immortality.[32]

It is this grave significance which the brilliant cleverness of stanza 5 dramatizes, and Donne continues to elaborate this pattern of profound paradox as he moves into the solemnities of his closing stanza. Once again, his virtuosities of wit are simply the poetic vehicle for intense emotion.

Having attained, by the argument of stanzas 2–5, both to personal peace of mind and to a theologically solid bargaining position, Donne is able to present his prayer for salvation in the final stanza with the assurance of a man who has arrived at a logical conclusion ("So . . .") and who is entering a plea for favorable judgment which is legally sound. The first lines of this plea echo the content, imagery, and structural pattern of the last two lines of stanza 5. In this way they effect a logical and artistic transition from the final section of the argument to the conclusion of the poem. Into these two opening lines of the final stanza Donne has compacted several layers of meaning: they are the most complex passage in the poem, a climactic moment of impassioned private intrication before the poem opens out into the simple candor of the three closing lines. On one level of meaning lines 26–7 repeat, with the rhetorical trick of a reversal of syntactical order, the sweat-blood antithesis of lines 24–5. On this level, line 26 is a rephrasing of line 25: Donne asks that his soul ("me") [33] be received by God because it will be wrapped in the "purple" (= red) of Christ's redeeming blood. And "by these his thorns" in line 27 repeats, through one of its connotations, the significance of line 24: "because I have undergone, in the pangs of my mortal illness, the suffering and physical death which are the punishment for Original Sin." [34]

But this backward glance at the reference to the two Adams in the conclusion of stanza 5, which seems at first the principal implication of line 26, becomes an undertone in line 27 as the imagery of the red robe and the crown emerges as the dominant metaphor of these lines. The "thorns" referred to in line 27 are, primarily, Christ's crown of thorns, and the chief function of the image is to equate Donne's sickness with Christ's mortal suffering. In this context, the phrase "in his purple wrapped" becomes an allusion to the robe that Christ wore when he was crowned with thorns, which functions as a further image for Donne's suffering in his own mortal illness.[35] On the primary level of meaning, then, the imagery of the two lines discards the parallel between Donne and the first Adam and shifts the emphasis to the parallel between

Donne's own experience and the passion and death of Christ, who, as "very man," had embodied in his earthly life the perfect type of the experience of every mortal. Through this analogy between himself and Christ, lines 24–5 express Donne's hope that, since he participates by faith in Christ's Atonement, he may pass, like Christ, through death to resurrection and to a triumphant reception into heaven. They thus restate, in the conclusion of the poem, the final certainty which has been the logical premise for the entire argument: Donne's expectation of a victory over death through Christ's Redemption.

But the phrase "in his purple wrapped" carries still another implication. Since it occurs in the context of a reference to Christ's Triumph, and since it is logically and syntactically parallel to the analogy in the following line between the crown of thorns and the heavenly crown, it is meant to suggest not only the red robe which Christ wore when he was crowned with thorns but also the royal robe of his subsequent Triumph in heaven. The pattern of analogies between death and resurrection which began in line 21 carries over, therefore, into a final analogy between the robe and the crown which symbolize death, and the robe and the crown which symbolize resurrection and immortal life.

The imagery of lines 26–7 has, however, one other function in the imaginative structure of the poem. On a further level of implication it compares God's reception of Donne's soul into heaven to a King's reception of a suitor into royal favor. In this way the image of the entrance into the King's Presence Chamber from stanza 1 appears again, as an overtone, for a structural da capo effect in the conclusion of the poem. And this image generates a shadowy pun on the word "receive" in line 26: it is used, first, in the technical theological sense, to refer to God's act of taking a soul to Himself, and, second, with the ambiguity of "formally receive at Court."

The last three lines of stanza 6 also refer back to stanza 1—to the personal problem presented in that stanza, to the phrase "I tune the Instrument," and to the ambiguity of "a Christian minister" in the word "instrument." They define the character of the entire poem, in summary, by describing it as a private sermon which Donne has addressed to himself for the purpose of confirming his religious faith,[36] and they bring the sermon to a formal close by citing, as a final and unimpeachable argument-from-authority for its conclusions, a biblical text ("my text") which summarizes the statement of the whole poem: "Therefor [37] that he may raise the Lord throws down." The text is evidently based on the eighth verse of Psalm 146.[38] Donne has modified it slightly, probably in order to make it more nearly parallel with the central argument of the poem and to give his final line the punch effect of paradox. The text serves, then, as a paradoxical restatement of the theme of the poem, which was first stated, in its simplest form, in line 15 and then expanded into a theodicy in the two final stanzas: that death ("throws down") touches on the resurrection ("raise"), and that God must require man to experience death in order that ("therefor that") He may justly grant man immortality. And the phrase "throws down" carries not only a reference to Donne's lying in the grave in death but also, as an ambiguity, a final concrete reference to Donne's present situation as he lies in his sickbed.[39]

I have tried to suggest, as I have picked my way through this maze of detail, the architectural qualities of the "Hymn," which give order and shape to what would otherwise be chaos. Donne holds the entire poem together by the frame structure of stanzas 1 and 6. The opening stanza states the problem which the rest of the poem must settle, and the final stanza draws the poem into symmetry by the formal devices of its concluding "So," by its statement of the intellectual and emotional resolution which the intervening stanzas have arrived at, and by its backward reference, in both content and imagery, to stanza 1. Throughout the poem the development of the imagery is simply a function of the development of the thought. Within the two frame stanzas the argument divides into two logical units, those of stanzas 2–4 and of stanza 5, which are paralleled in the metaphoric structure of the poem by the contrast in imagery between these two sections. And within each section, as the argument evolves, Donne gives his structure of metaphor an effect of progressive shaping as he pushes it to final formulation in those rhetorical patterns which were so important a form of literary artifice to men of the Renaissance. The geographical image of stanzas 2–4 is elaborated with an effect of cumulative imaginative logic, and as Donne works out its full imaginative implications in stanza 4 he gives the metaphor an effect of ultimate formal definition by casting it into the triplicate

pattern of the conceit of the three continents. The antithetic patterning of the imagery in stanza 5 builds to a similar formal climax
in the sustained antithesis of the last two lines of the stanza. This
development of the imagery of each section into a sharp formal
pattern occurs at the points in the poem where each section reaches
its argumentative conclusion: it is a rhetorical device which provides, in the poem's evolution of metaphor, a climactic effect of
final imaginative definition which parallels the effect of logical
finality produced by the evolution of the poem's argument. Finally,
the first two lines of the last stanza serve the structural function
of providing a bridge passage from the argument proper to the conclusion. They focus the discussion of the two Adams into a consideration of the redeeming Christ, and they reshape the antithetic
imagery of the fifth stanza into the single image of the entrance
into the King's throne room. They thus provide a logical and
imaginative transition comparable in effect to a musical modulation to the key of the coda.

But another structural element which plays an important part
in the shaping of the poem is its music—the effect of the constant
plastic force of the disposition of metrical stress, of shifts in pace,
and of musical phrasing in ordering and communicating emotion.
I have commented incidentally, in examining other poems, on important effects of rhythm and verse movement, but I have not
studied the metrical evolution of any of those poems in detail because in most of them verse music seems to play a relatively small
part in the total effect of the poem. Normally Donne is not one of
the great musicians of English poetry. His verse is usually thin
in sensuous texture, and his musical effects at their best are not
those of lyrical lilt nor of rich, Miltonic orchestration but rather
those which one finds in "The Good-Morrow" and "The Canonization"—effects produced by subtle rhythmic inflections in a taut,
spare melodic line.[40] In most of his poetry the verse movement is
too nervous to generate sustained musical phrases; and sometimes
he throws aside phrasing almost entirely, so that one listens to the
jagged rhythms of excited talk in which the metrical beat is almost
wholly lost. There are times, in fact, when Donne seems to get so
excited over pursuing an urgent course of thought that he stops
his ear completely to the siren song of the rhythms of his verse: in
the second stanza of "The Good-Morrow," for instance, where,

after the fine effect of the firm, even movement through the first six lines, we suddenly find ourselves stumbling through the metrical gawkiness of "Let us possess one world, each hath one, and is one." At moments like this one would like to seek out Ben Jonson and shake his hand for the remark that for not keeping of accent Donne deserved hanging. But on occasion—in this "Hymn" especially, and also in "A Hymn to God the Father"—Donne can write with the ear of a master, sustaining long melodic lines and building them through a whole poem into a structure of severe and stately music.

A study of the verse movement, of the phrasing, and of the disposition of musical cadences in the "Hymn" will suggest how its music operates to mold the development of emotion to the development of thought, so that a logical resolution is felt also as a musical resolution. In general, the pace is slow throughout the poem, though there are many local variations, and the over-all tone is one of serenity and assurance. The poem does not actually present an emotional progression from uncertainty to confidence. It opens with the statement of an intellectual and emotional stability already arrived at ("I am coming . . . ," "what I must do then . . .") and then takes the reader through the process by which that assurance has been attained. The first stanza, like each of the other logical units of the poem, is shaped into a single musical phrase. The pace is slow and steady throughout the stanza, and the stress is firm and even, so that the verse moves with a grave insistency. This rhythmic effect is a musical equivalent to the suggestion of emotional serenity produced by the metaphors of musical harmony and to the implication of intellectual certainty in the stanza. The light caesura in the middle of line 5 produces a rhythmic suspension, so that the last half of the line has an effect of cadence:

And what I must do then, think here before.

Stanzas 2 and 3, which develop the first argumentative conclusion of the poem, form another continuous unit of musical phrase. The verse builds to a crescendo in an unbroken movement from the relatively light stresses and slack musical line of stanza 2 to the strong stresses and the taut line and firm verse movement which accompany the affirmation of the third stanza. The crescendo comes to climax on a strong suspension at the end of line 14, and then

the verse moves to a full cadence as the conclusion is stated in the
final line of the stanza:

> As West and East
> In all flat maps (and I am one) are one,   14
> So death doth touch the resurrection.[41]

Donne accentuates this suspension at the end of line 14 by a
rhetorical trick which he often uses, that of throwing emphasis
on a word by repeating it in the same line with a shift in meaning.[42] Thus one huddles through the parenthesis of "and I am
one" to pull up sharply with a heavy stress on "one" at the end of
the line, and the musical effect is like that of an unresolved fortis-
simo chord, followed by a rest, before the cadence.

Stanza 4, which advances the argument a step further, forms
another unit of musical phrase. In the first two lines the rhythm
is broken, with heavy accents, a hurrying of pace, and strong
caesuras, which underscore the effect of excitement in the eager
questions of these lines. But the verse steadies to a firm movement,
with strong, flung-out accents in line 18, builds a crescendo to the
heavy stress on the key word "none" in line 19, and then descends
to a slow cadence, checked by strong caesuras, which parallels the
effect of finality in the statement of the closing line:

> Ányan, and Mágellán, and Gíbraltáre,[43]
> All straits, and none but straits, are ways to them,
> Whether where Japhet dwelt, or Cham, or Sem.   20

As the tone changes from affirmation to humility in stanza 5, the
tension of the verse slackens, and the rhythmic units and light, flut-
tering stresses of the first two lines are the inflections of ordinary
speech. But the verse picks up tension and beat in the plea of line
23, and after a climactic stress on "both" in this line the stanza
settles to a cadence in the formal rhetorical balance of the two final
lines, with the phrasing inflected by mildly emphatic stresses on the
key words of the antithesis:

> Look Lord, and find both Adams met in me;   23
> As the first Adam's sweat surrounds my face,
> May the last Adam's blood my soul embrace.

The last stanza, which presents the statement of the final intellectual assurance of the poem, moves broadly and steadily, with a slow pace and heavy, even stresses, to the full cadence of the rhetorical close. In the last two lines the weight of stress increases, and the pace is slowed by caesuras in each line. There is a dramatic pause at the end of line 29, and then one drives through the last line to the full impact of the three weighty stresses which accentuate the grave finality of its statement:

> Be this my text, my sermon to mine own,   29
> Therefor that he may raise the Lord throws down.

This "Hymn" seems to me a magisterial performance, one of the few great religious poems in English. It is certainly Donne's richest and most finished work. And it has a quality which one rarely finds in Donne's verse: the quality of magniloquence, of that "impassioned majesty" which DeQuincey spoke of. DeQuincey found that effect throughout in Donne's work, but I think it is unusual in his poetry. The quality appears briefly in many passages, but Donne does not often sustain the effect for long; something lively breaks in, and he shies off from the settled gravity which attends the Sublime. But as one follows the solemn processional of this poem, the sure and stately deployment of its firm patterns of thought and feeling behind its grave arabesques of wit, one meets a fullness of utterance and a sustained poise of mind which seldom appear in Donne's other verse. He touched on this effect in "A Hymn to God the Father," but for all its ritualistic dignity, that poem manifests little of the scope, the organizing power, and the richness which are the qualities of the imagination that is at work in this "Hymn." This poem seems to reflect a wholeness of mind and an entire commitment of the personality to poetic utterance which Donne had not attained before.

It is dangerous, I know, to speculate too far into a man's mind as he faces death; and that prospect, as he contemplated it in his imagination, had given Donne the horrors so often that one hesitates to believe that he faced it in actuality with any settled equanimity. And the *Devotions*, which were probably written at the same time as this "Hymn," hardly show Donne with his face set boldly and calmly toward his West. Nevertheless, the wholeness

of mind which this poem expresses seems to reflect a conviction on
Donne's part that death is actually his way out, the passage which
he had sought for so long and has at last joyously discovered. I
think the effect of the achievement of final fullness of voice in this
deathbed poem can have come only from Donne's belief that he
would soon find in death emotional completion by experiencing an
ultimate release from all of those inner and outer tensions which
had beset his mind through life and had throttled the voice of his
verse.

Those tensions are slackening in his mind as he writes this poem,
but they are still there. The subject of the poem, its motivating
personal situation, is an inner argument. The "Hymn" is the last
in that long series of Debates between the Body and the Soul, between material and spiritual standards of value, which is the essential subject matter of Donne's poetry. In all the poems which
I have examined the intellectual structure of a debate, and sometimes the actual dramatic situation of a debate, has been the logical
form in which Donne has cast his literary materials. And I think
the personal reality behind the persistent recurrence of that mode
of literary formulation in Donne's verse can only have been the
psychological fact of the inner conflict between what Donne saw
as his two selves, the two personalities which he dramatized in the
debate of "The Blossom" in the conceptualized roles of his Body
and his Soul. Throughout these poems Donne has conceptualized
that opponent who stands at grips with his soul in "The Blossom"
in different ways—most often as the Body, but sometimes as the
World. And that general logical concept of Material Value, of the
concerns of the World and the Flesh, has appeared in these poems
in many different literary guises: as the speaker of "The Indifferent"; as Donne himself, though his assumption of this intellectual
role seems an unwilling one, in "Love's Alchemy"; as the Body
in "The Blossom," the sensualist lover in Elegy 19, the "sea-
discoverers" of "The Good-Morrow," and the worldly opponent
of "The Canonization." But all of these dramatic figures have been
embodiments of standards of value which are logically equivalent
to those of that other-self who is in debate with Donne's soul in
"The Blossom." And in all the poems these conceptualized dramatic figures have been balanced, as thesis or antithesis, in a dialec-.
tical pattern which has played them off against their logical op-

posites. Throughout these poems Donne, speaking to the reader through the persona of the speaker in his poem, has dramatized himself sometimes on one side of the debate and sometimes on the other. In "The Indifferent," Elegy 19, "Love's Alchemy," and "The Blossom" he has spoken through that self which he thinks of as the Body or as the World. But in most of his later poems, as in "The Good-Morrow" and "The Canonization," he tends to cast himself in the role of the other-self who is its opponent, of the Soul, who is arguing to fend off the demands of the Body and the World.

In the "Hymn to God, My God, in My Sickness" the inner argument is again essentially a debate between Donne's Body and his Soul, between the claims of the worldly desires of his suffering flesh and the other-worldly appetites of his mind. But here he enters securely into the conceptual role of the Soul, of his other-worldly intellect, and the anti-self of his worldly body is only dimly actualized in the poem. The debate, in fact, is virtually won before the poem starts. Moreover, in the logical terms in which Donne thinks of Christian death in this poem, that event would enforce a conclusive triumph for one of those two logical opposites by which he had defined the psychic tensions of his personality. I think the grave peace and quiet joy which inform the poem that Donne saw as his last argument with himself probably arise from the finality of his conviction that he will at last be quit of a World in which he had never felt fully at home, which he thought he had renounced on earlier occasions and which he had earlier tried to persuade himself—though never with full success—had been well lost. And he would be quit of the Body as well. It is significant, I believe, that the "resurrection" to which Donne looks in this poem does not include the resurrection of the body, though that mystery in Christian doctrine had particularly fascinated his mind and though he seems generally to have accepted it, both before and after he wrote this poem, as an article of belief. It is probable that the wholeness of spirit in this "Hymn" arises also from his hope that the long debate of his inner life is about to cease, and that its discords will soon be finally resolved in the release of his mind from that other-self of the body to discover unequivocal intellectual resolution in a harmony which it had long sought and had never long known.

Chapter 5

Some Conclusions

I

IN A famous critical pronouncement T. S. Eliot spoke of the "unification of sensibility" which Donne achieved in his poetry, and said that Donne, and other Metaphysical Poets of the seventeenth century, "possessed a mechanism of sensibility which could devour any kind of experience." [1] And Joan Bennett, enlarging, I believe, on this statement of Eliot's, has said that Donne "knew enough to portray and analyze a wider range of emotion than any other English poet except Shakespeare." [2] I don't think this evaluation of Donne is true, even if one allows for the rather special meaning which Eliot assigns to "sensibility": in fact, I think it makes very little sense. To place Donne's work beside that of Marlowe, Sidney, Spenser, and Shakespeare, or of Jonson, Browne, and Milton—those writers of the Elizabethan age and the seventeenth century who seem to me Donne's peers or his superiors—is certainly to see both the limitations of his sensibility and the limits to the kinds of experience which his poetry could master. If he achieved, however precariously, a unification of sensibility in his work, it was only by filtering out much of what comprises the sensibility of most men; and if he devoured all kinds of experience, many of those experiences were so badgered and mauled about in the process by which his mind assimilated them that they appear in his work in forms which bear little resemblance to the textural qualities which they normally have in the lives of others. It is true that Donne's mind could hold in one thought concrete physical fact and abstract metaphysical theory, and that his poetry, at its best, could achieve a unification of thought and feeling and of wit and seriousness. But these are only certain selected elements in experience which are often dissociated, and only selected poetic effects which are not always conjoined. They are, to be sure, some of the particular elements which Eliot and Ezra Pound were anxious to see combined in poetry at the time when they were trying to accomplish a poetic revolution and to create a New Poetry for the twentieth century in much the same way that Donne and Jonson had created a New Poetry for the seventeenth century; and it was for this reason that Eliot cried us off Milton and Tennyson and sent us all back to Donne. But to suggest in any way that Donne's poetry comprehends a great range of human experience seems to me gravely misleading.

We can see how misleading it is just by taking a short walk through the Gorgeous Gallery of Gallant Inventions which is English Renaissance literature, inspecting the slopes of England's Parnassus in that age and plucking a Handful of Pleasant Delights from the Hundred Sundry Flowers in its Forest of Fancy and its Arbor of Amorous Devices. It will be an agreeable experience; and to place these passages beside Donne's work will show us things about Donne. I am undertaking this little *florilegium* not because I want to belabor Eliot or Mrs. Bennett, both of whom have taught me useful things about Donne, but because Eliot's pronouncement has become so much a cliché in present-day thinking about Donne —often, I think, in senses which Eliot did not intend—that it is worth checking up on. And if we take a close look at some of the things that Donne's poetry is not, it will be easier for us to see what it is. To measure him against his contemporaries, moreover, will be more significant than what we would otherwise do: measure him against ourselves.

We might start with Donne's portrayal of the experience of love, or sex, since that is certainly one of his major fields of specialty. One of the motivating principles behind Donne's early love poetry was clearly the proposition which he stated in "Love's Growth," that

> Love's not so pure, and abstract, as they use
> To say, which have no mistress but their Muse . . .

And certainly he introduced into love poetry an exploratory curiosity in the treatment of love, and a clinical accuracy in defining

its varied physiological and psychological phenomena, which English literature had not known before. Beside Donne's love poetry
most of the love poems of the Elizabethan period look somewhat
literary, in the derogatory sense of that term, and do seem to owe
more to the Muse than to what the writer has known of love. The
naked, probing factuality of lines like these, from "Farewell to
Love," is the mark of the verse of Donne alone in the poetry of
the 1590's:

> But, from late fair
> His Highness sitting in a golden chair,[3]
> Is not less cared for after three days
> By children, than the thing which lovers so
> Blindly admire, and with such worship woo;
> Being had, enjoying it decays:
> And thence,
> What before pleased them all, takes but one sense,
> And that so lamely, as it leaves behind
> A kind of sorrowing dullness to the mind.
>
> Ah cannot we,
> As well as cocks and lions jocund be
> After such pleasures? . . .

Nor, for all his concern with arriving at a comprehensive philosophic theory which would account for love, was Donne ever
blinded by a theory about what love was, or should be, to the
diversity of what it could be in fact; nor to the remarkable difference, even, between what it could be on Thursday morning and
what it had been on Wednesday night. And he seems never to have
been inhibited by any such theory from an honest recording of the
data of love's infinite variety. A glance through "The Indifferent,"
Elegy 19, "Love's Alchemy," "The Blossom," "The Good-Morrow,"
and "The Canonization" suggests only a part of the wide range
in Donne's treatment of love. From the kaleidoscopic succession
of different attitudes toward love which one encounters in the
"Songs and Sonnets," one suspects, in fact, that an important intellectual purpose behind Donne's verse was to demonstrate how
rich and strange love could be.

But there was much of its richness and strangeness which he
seems never to have encountered, areas of the experience which

he was either not interested in exploring, or had never stumbled into, or was incapable of entering. The most considerable of Donne's blind spots in love was in the area which most modern men have tended to think of as the citadel of love's kingdom—that of romance. I think the kind of erotic experience which Spenser recorded in the "Epithalamion" is something which Donne never knew:

> Now cease ye damsels your delights forepast;
> Enough is it, that all the day was yours:
> Now day is done, and night is nighing fast:
> Now bring the bride into the bridal bowers.
> Now night is come, now soon her disarray,
> And in her bed her lay;
> Lay her in lilies and in violets,
> And silken curtains over her display,
> And odoured sheets, and arras coverlets.
> Behold how goodly my fair love does lie
> In proud humility;
> Like unto Maia, whenas Jove her took,
> In Tempe, lying on the flow'ry grass,
> 'Twixt sleep and wake, after she weary was,
> With bathing in the Acidalian brook.
> Now it is night, ye damsels may be gone,
> And leave my love alone,
> And leave likewise your former lay to sing:
> The woods no more shall answer, nor your echo ring.

It is not just the ecstatic romanticism with which Spenser idealizes physical passion in these lines which seems alien to anything that Donne ever wished to record about love: the whole complex of sensibility behind the passage is utterly foreign to Donne's temperament. Its rich sensuousness, for instance—the delight of sense in lilies and violets, silken curtains, and odored sheets; the Keatsian response to the luxury of the rich bridal bed, to the silk, the perfume, and the arras coverlets; and the pleasure in the blissful physical relaxation of sensuality—

> 'Twixt sleep and wake, after she weary was,
> With bathing in the Acidalian brook—

this is something which one never finds in Donne's poetry. Placed against this warm physicality Donne's celebration of purely physical passion in the nineteenth Elegy, where he deals with much the same situation which Spenser treats in this stanza, looks coldly ascetic and almost abstract in its intellectuality. For all its ideality, Spenser's treatment of love in this passage is far more sexually suggestive than any of Donne's concretely physiological presentations of sexual experience. And the sensuousness of Spenser's temperament comes through also in something else which one does not find in Donne's poetry—in the sensuous texture of Spenser's verse, in his feel for the lovely harmonies and sonorities of his language, and for the lyrical glide and fall of the cadences of his lines.

There are many other components of the sensibility behind Spenser's lines which Donne evidently knew little of. Investigating them will take us far from the subject of love, because the imaginative aura with which a great poet surrounds romantic love involves a rich complex of attitudes, but it will take us into the characteristic romanticism of the Elizabethan imagination, of which Spenser's poetry was so typical an expression. Spenser's work embodies, in fact, almost everything in the dominant tradition of Elizabethan verse which Donne was reacting against in his own poetry, and it thus reflects many aspects of the dominant sensibility of his age from which Donne was estranged. One of these attitudes is the happy response, in Spenser's lines, to the flowering beauties of the summer earth, to lilies and violets, to the evoked scene of the idyllic pastoral loveliness of the flowery grass by the clear brook in the secluded valley of Tempe, and to the echoing woods which rustle through the whole poem. Those impulses seem scarcely to have stirred in Donne. There are few gardens in his verse, and the gentle, Herrick-like pathos of his treatment of the flower metaphor in the first stanza of "The Blossom" is unique in his work— and quickly undercut, moreover, by wit and realism in the rest of the poem. On the rare occasions when Donne lays literary hands on a flower, what he does to it would usually make a nature lover wince. "The Ecstasy" starts promisingly enough in a setting of Spenserian pastoralism:

> Where, like a pillow on a bed,
>   A pregnant bank swelled up, to rest

> The violet's reclining head,
> Sat we two, one another's best.

But that is the last look we get at that fertile, flowery bank, and
we jump quickly off it into seventy-two lines of theoretical analysis
of the physiology and metaphysics of love. The violet does thrust
up its reclining head at one point, but Donne lops it with a theory:

> A single violet transplant,
> The strength, the colour, and the size,
> (All which before was poor, and scant,)
> Redoubles still, and multiplies.
> When love, with one another so
> Interinanimates two souls . . .

Floriculture, it seems, manifests certain abstract principles which
bear a striking and philosophically suggestive analogy to the psychological phenomena of spiritual love.

When one notes Donne's strong inclination to attitudes of re-
tired contemplation, his settled aversion to the literary mode of
the pastoral is surprising. That rich myth of the contemplative
life, in which the Elizabethan imagination found so commodious
a vehicle for the expression not only of the attitudes of romantic
love and of delight in the beauties of the natural world, but also
of the temper of religious contemplation and of thoughtful criticism of the materialism and venality of the way of the world, seems
to have made no appeal to Donne. He was evidently more essentially a man of the City than even Ben Jonson, and when he wished
to say that the world was well lost for a love more ideal than anything which worldlings could understand, his thoughts never
dallied with Arcady. The mechanically written piece entitled
"Eclogue," which introduces Donne's "Epithalamion" for the marriage of the Earl of Somerset, is bare of pastoral machinery and
void of the pastoral mood; and Marlowe's "Come live with me
and be my love" became in Donne's hands a witty love poem on
the circumstantial details of catching fish.

The rich meaning which Spenser's mind saw in the setting of
the flowering earth in the "Epithalamion" is something else which
I think Donne never felt. The woods which echo and answer to
the marriage in every stanza of the poem, and which frame Spenser's

whole imaginative picture of his love, are answering with the voice
of the fertile earth; they echo and answer to the love because that
love is a healthy and natural manifestation in human affairs of
the beautiful sensuous fruition of all earthly things. The woods
speak with the voice of Spenser's response to the Mediterranean
temper of classical paganism which glows through all the high
spirituality and Christian idealism of the poem. Surely, one thinks,
Donne would have felt this pagan identification of the warm flesh
with the fruition of the blowing earth and would have responded,
if only as a witty libertine, to the Renaissance song of springtime
and sexual love:

> When daisies pied and violets blue
>   And lady-smocks all silver-white
> And cuckoo-buds of yellow hue
>   Do paint the meadows with delight,
> The cuckoo then, on every tree
> Mocks married men; for thus sings he,
>   Cuckoo:
> Cuckoo, cuckoo: Oh word of fear,
> Unpleasing to a married ear!

Donne did essay this theme once, in "Love's Growth." But he was
out to angle it in his own way and to make of the relation between
spring and love something different from what it had been to
Shakespeare and the Elizabethan lyrists. The access of sexual desire with the coming of spring, it seems, reveals that his theory
about his love is wrong, and that his love is less pure than he had
thought during the winter. Since it is subject to change, it cannot
be wholly spiritual in essence but must have a physical component;
and it cannot, strictly speaking, be considered infinite, as he had
thought it was, because it has increased with the coming of spring.
Perhaps, he reflects, the increase of his physical desire at this season
derives from the fact that his flesh has been activated by the masculine sexual principle which the sun's rays infuse into the passive
matter of the earth to produce spring growth. In this fluctuation
between spirit and flesh, love seems to parallel the religious life,
which alternates Contemplation with Action. But the increase of
his love is not actually an increase: just as stars in the firmament
reflect sunlight—and so on. The fertility of spring becomes simply

a problem in natural philosophy, and the poem takes off into an increasingly tricky intellectual analysis of the physiology and psychology of his love.

But there is another important imaginative element in Spenser's stanza which one misses entirely in Donne's work—the romantic response to myth. Thinking of the lofty ideality of his passion for his wife, Spenser's mind turns naturally to the loves of Jove, and he works with the evocative power of "Maia" and "Tempe" and "the Acidalian brook" to call up suggestions of the serene, idealized world of the myth-making imagination of classical times. The association would have seemed natural to most Elizabethans, to Marlowe and to the young Shakespeare, and in the seventeenth century to Ben Jonson and to that belated Elizabethan, John Milton. It would not have occurred readily to Donne, and he would probably have rejected it for poetic purposes if it had. When Donne's seventeenth-century literary disciple, Thomas Carew, eulogized the poetic innovations of his master, he praised Donne for having "banished" from serious poetry the "train of gods and goddesses" and the "tales i' th' Metamorphoses." [4] Those decorative allusions to classical myth, which seemed so normal a poetic vocabulary to most of his contemporaries in the 1590's, are almost completely absent from Donne's poetry outside of the "Elegies"; and even when he uses them there, rather mechanically, he sometimes gets them wrong, as he did with the allusion to Atalanta in the nineteenth Elegy. His factual and logically analytical cast of mind seems to have cut him off from any serious imaginative response to myth, and he was thus cut off from one of the fundamental traits of the Renaissance mind, from a pattern of thought and association which was one of the normal activities of the Renaissance imagination well into the seventeenth century.

But Spenser and his contemporaries did not regard the mythological allusions scattered through their verse as mere pretty ornament; and Spenser's use of classical myth in the "Epithalamion" reflects a further aspect of his sensibility, and of the sensibility of his age, from which Donne seems generally to have been cut off. Both the mythological decoration of Spenser's poem and his response to the paganism of the literary tradition of the classical epithalamion are symptoms of Spenser's excitement over the Renaissance rediscovery of classical civilization and of his sense of community with that culture. The classical machinery in his verse carried for Spenser and for most of his contemporaries powerfully evocative suggestions of the continuity of their culture and of their place in the great tradition of Western civilization. Through their ready response to the classical myths, and to the literary traditions of classical literature, they looked across the centuries to Greece and Rome and found there men much like themselves; and they found also a great civilization which opened to them rich new possibilities for the life of man and which gave them a proud responsibility for upholding its heritage. One searches in vain in Donne's work for evidence of this sense of enthusiasm over the renaissance of classical civilization. He ransacked the philosophic thought of classical times for usable ideas, and he found, in the Ovid of the *Amores* and in Martial and the Latin satirists, poetic temperaments which were somewhat congenial, but the fact of the classical origin of this material seems to have had little emotional significance to Donne's mind. Of that sense of easy affinity and proud community with the whole life of classical antiquity which is so strong in Spenser and Sidney, Marlowe and Shakespeare, and Jonson and Milton, Donne's work shows very little.

Spenser's response to the great tradition of the past is related, however, to another important attitude of the imagination which is at work in his marriage song. The processional of the damsels to the bridal bower; the "delights forepast" in the gay pageantry of the Masque of Hymen and in the solemn and lovely ritual of the sacrament of marriage; and the stately, traditional structure of the poem itself, the elegant, formal marriage hymn, with each of its elaborately patterned stanzas coming to rest on the formalistic gesture of the long-breathed refrain of the echoing woods—all of these things manifest Spenser's pleasure in pageantry, ritual, and ceremony, in that quality in life and art which the Renaissance would have summed up admiringly in the word "solemn." This feeling that life reaches its highest fruition when it is cast into the stately patterns of traditional forms, and that these forms in art are celebratory of life's dignity and highest joy, was an attitude which Spenser shared not only with Milton but also with most of his contemporaries, who crowded to public pageants and royal progresses and, thinking it passing brave to be a king and ride in triumph through Persepolis, flocked to hear actors in royal robes speak the proud rhythms of Marlovian blank verse in the tragedies and histories of the public stage. Solemnity came naturally to the Elizabethans, with their taste for tradition and their strong sense of the dignity of man. It did not come naturally to Donne, as one can see from the pervasive irreverence, levity, and lively and disjunctive energy of his verse. Even that pride in man's dignity, which no man of the Renaissance could escape feeling, is less marked in Donne's work than in that of most of his contemporaries, and there is little evidence that he had any essential personal taste for ritual, or ceremony, or tradition.

But it may seem unfair to measure Donne's treatment of love against something which he did not want his poetry to be. Perhaps if we look away from Spenser's romanticism to the contemporary love poetry in the Ovidian tradition, that tradition of the witty and sophisticated treatment of physical passion in which Donne felt somewhat at home, we will find Donne more open to the characteristic sensibility of his age. "Hero and Leander" has affinities with the kind of love poetry which Donne was experimenting with in the nineteenth Elegy. We must strip away, of course, its rich embroidery of classical myth, by which Marlowe creates so powerfully evocative a picture of the warm paganism which he saw in the Mediterranean world of antiquity; but let us turn to the passage in which Marlowe is directly concerned with Leander's sexual advances, the same subject which Donne treated in his Elegy:

> Albeit Leander, rude in love and raw,
> Long dallying with Hero, nothing saw
> That might delight him more, yet he suspected
> Some amorous rites or other were neglected.
> Therefore unto his body hers he clung;
> She, fearing on the rushes to be flung,
> Strived with redoubled strength; the more she strived,
> The more a gentle pleasing heat revived,
> Which taught him all that elder lovers know;
> And now the same gan so to scorch and glow,
> As in plain terms, yet cunningly, he craved it.

"A gentle pleasing heat." Again one is struck by the ascetic character of Donne's handling of the same experience. Marlowe wants to record the precise feel of sexual desire to the body, while Donne's imagination has abstracted from that complex of emotion and physical sensation only those elements which he can build into a structure of wit and intellectual passion. Donne devotes twenty-seven lines to the mistress' undressing and to the lover's passion as his hands explore her body, but we never see or feel her body in any sensory terms. Marlowe's imagination sees Leander's naked-ness, "his breast, his thighs, and every limb," his "ivory skin," and the "white limbs" of Hero as they "sparkle" through the "lawn" of the sheets, and feels the sensation of Leander as his cold skin touches the "lukewarm place" where Hero's body has lain in the bed. And when Marlowe wants to suggest the ecstasy of consum-mation he turns for a poetic symbol to the vivid actuality of classical myth:

> Leander now, like Theban Hercules,
> Entered the orchard of th'Hesperides,
> Whose fruit none rightly can describe but he
> That pulls or shakes it from the golden tree.

Donne's mind, at this point, is off on a passionate exercise in ab-stract theological speculation.

But perhaps one can find in the wit and the man-of-the-world cynicism of some of the anti-Petrarchan passages in Elizabethan literature the same quality which one gets in some of Donne's brash and cynical treatments of love in his early verse. Sidney's charm-ing, urbane ridicule of Petrarchism, as I have pointed out, is not Donne's mode, but here is Rosalind in *As You Like It,* doing a rough and rowdy job on the Petrarchan stereotype of love woe after Orlando has announced that he will die "in mine own person" from frustrated love; playing with the legal conceits which Donne was fond of; and debunking the standard literary types of ro-mantic lovers:

> No, faith, die by attorney. The poor world is almost six thou-sand years old, and in all this time there was not any man died in his own person, videlicet, in a love cause. Troilus had his brains dashed out with a Grecian club, yet he did what he could to die before, and he is one of the patterns of love. Leander, he would have lived many a fair year though Hero

had turned nun, if it had not been for a hot midsummer night; for (good youth) he went but forth to wash him in the Hellespont, and being taken with the cramp, was drowned; and the foolish chroniclers of that age found it was "Hero of Sestos." But these are all lies. Men have died from time to time, and worms have eaten them, but not for love.

"These are all lies"—that sounds like Donne's accent. But the tone of the comedy here is not at all Donne's: this is humor, warm, relaxed, and humane. The zany touches of sympathy in "the poor world" and in the parenthetical "good youth," and the antic casualness of "from time to time" in the last sentence are things which would never have occurred to Donne. They derive from a capacity for irrational let-go, from an unconstrained gaiety, and from a richness and subtlety of social perception which Donne barely touched on, and only occasionally, as in that uncharacteristic poem "The Blossom." There is little here of the calculated logical planning, the hard shock of wit, and the disruptive energy of Donne's comedy in "The Indifferent." And there is the further important difference that what Rosalind is actually ridiculing are the emotions which she herself deeply and delightedly feels.

Metaphysical poetry, however, is in essence intellectualized poetry. Ideas are its imaginative core, and it may be unreasonable to expect from Donne's verse the sensory and emotional qualities which one finds in those kinds of Renaissance poetry that are less conceptualized in nature. Perhaps his work should properly be measured against that of other poets of the Metaphysical school. Here, for instance, is Marvell, in "The Garden," elaborating clever conceits and developing a fanciful ethical and metaphysical argument about Platonic Love:

> Meanwhile the mind from pleasure less
> Withdraws into its happiness;
> The mind, that ocean where each kind
> Does straight its own resemblance find;
> Yet it creates, transcending these,
> Far other worlds and other seas,
> Annihilating all that's made
> To a green thought in a green shade.

Here at the fountain's sliding foot,
Or at some fruit-tree's mossy root,
Casting the body's vest aside,
My soul into the boughs does glide:
There, like a bird, it sits and sings,
Then whets, then combs its silver wings;
And till prepared for longer flight,
Waves in its plumes the various light.

But here the subtlety is not just intellectual: Marvell has a perception of emotional subtleties, of nuances of feeling and sensation,
to which Donne's poetic imagination was either blind or insensi-
tive. And Marvell's cool propriety of mind, which shows in the
sure artistic tact that tells him just how much of what will be
enough for the unified effect of this kind of poem, is also something which Donne rarely attained. By comparison, Donne often
seems to be operating on Blake's principle that "you never know
what is enough unless you know what is more than enough." His
headlong impetuosity of intellect makes his thought more original
and exciting than Marvell's, but it can wreck poems, as a glance
through the whole body of Donne's verse abundantly demonstrates.

Here is another Metaphysical poet, Henry Vaughan, who was
indirectly one of Donne's literary legatees. In the opening stanza
of "The Waterfall" Vaughan is laying the logical groundwork
for the development of a religious conceit; but at the same time he
is responding to the natural world with an acuity of sensation, a
feeling for mood, and a command of the subtleties of verse music
which any Spenserian might envy:

With what deep murmurs through time's silent stealth
Doth thy transparent, cool, and wat'ry wealth
          Here flowing fall,
          And chide, and call,
As if his liquid, loose retinue stayed
Ling'ring, and were of this steep place afraid,
          The common pass
          Where, clear as glass,
          All must descend—
          Not to an end,

But quickened by this deep and rocky grave,
Rise to a longer course more bright and brave.

We might look also to Sir Thomas Browne, who writes prose in the manner of a Metaphysical poet. In the following passage Browne is developing a sustained philosophic conceit (an analogy between the Holy Ghost and the sun) with as firm a logical plan, as elaborate an intellectual ingenuity, and as precise a workmanship in detail as one finds in any of Donne's metaphysical conceits. He observes as careful a philosophic rigor, and he plays just as cleverly with paradox and with ambiguities and puns. But Browne works also with the emotional suggestions of the sound and rhythms of his language, and with subtleties of sensation and feeling like those in Marvell's poem. And one sees also in this passage something which one finds in Marvell's lines but which one never encounters in any of Donne's many treatments of religious "mysteries"—an evocation of the sense of mystery, of the emotional quality of losing oneself in an *"O altitudo!"* to feel wonder and awe at the contemplation of infinitude:

> I am sure there is a common spirit that plays within us, yet makes no part of us; and that is, the spirit of God, the fire and scintillation of that noble and mighty essence, which is the life and radical heat of spirits, and those essences that know not the virtue of the sun; a fire quite contrary to the fire of hell. This is that gentle heat that brooded on the waters, and in six days hatched the world; this is that irradiation that dispels the mists of hell, the clouds of horror, fear, sorrow, despair; and preserves the region of the mind in serenity. Whosoever feels not the warm gale and gentle ventilation of this spirit, though I feel his pulse, I dare not say he lives; for truly, without this, to me there is no heat under the tropic; nor any light, though I dwelt in the body of the sun.[5]

The passages from Vaughan and Browne remind me, however, that love palls, and religion offers. It was as a poet of religious experience that Donne had his widest literary influence. Perhaps his religious work will show a unification of sensibility more comprehensive than we see in his love poetry and a greater openness to the many kinds of religious experience known to men in his age.

I have said that the "Hymn to God, My God, in My Sickness" is
more richly suggestive and more stately than any of Donne's other
religious poems, but let us place it for a moment beside the Renaissance religious poem to which I have compared it, Milton's "At a
Solemn Music." Here is a part of Milton's attempt to communicate
his experience of contemplating the serene bliss of heaven, a close
parallel in both thought and imagery to the first stanza of Donne's
"Hymn":

> . . . And to our high-raised fantasy present
> That undisturbed song of pure concent
> Aye sung before the sapphire-coloured throne
> To him that sits thereon,
> With saintly shout, and solemn jubilee;
> Where the bright Seraphim in burning row
> Their loud uplifted angel-trumpets blow,
> And the Cherubic host in thousand choirs
> Touch their immortal harps of golden wires,
> With those just spirits that wear victorious palms,
> Hymns devout and holy psalms
> Singing everlastingly:
> That we on earth with undiscording voice,
> May rightly answer that melodious noise; [6]
> As once we did, till disproportioned sin
> Jarred against nature's chime, and with harsh din
> Broke the fair music that all creatures made
> To their great Lord, whose love their motion swayed
> In perfect diapason, whilst they stood
> In first obedience, and their state of good.

One feels immediately the magnificence of the verse music, beside
which Donne's is thin indeed. One sees also Milton's full and easy
imaginative response to the myth of the Heavenly City in Revelation, whereas Donne, in the first stanza of his poem, has abstracted
from that myth only those details which bear an intellectual relation to the structure of his thought or his conceits. What occupies
Milton's imagination for eleven lines served Donne, in his first
stanza, for only a line and a half:

> Where, with thy Choir of Saints for evermore,
> I shall be made thy Music . . .

"Thy Music" and "thy Choir of Saints" are the only details which Donne found of use in the great baroque canvas of St. John's vision; and they are useful to him chiefly because they establish the doctrinal analogy between God and music, because they provide a logical foundation for his central conceit and permit a play on the word "instrument," because they suggest, through an ambiguity on "Music," a paradoxical doctrine of religious mysticism —and possibly also, since Donne speaks in the poem as a Christian minister, because "Choir of Saints" suggests the parallel between the Church Militant and the Church Triumphant. Donne's imagination has responded to the myth conceptually and analytically, and the myth stimulates him to intellectual analogies. Though he must have felt some response to the sensory and emotive suggestions of the scene which he is presenting, he did not concern himself to call them up in his poem. The harmony to which he is "tuning" his soul is an intellectual accord with the Mind of God, and it is arrived at in the poem by a process of logical argument. But in Milton's lines one is hardly made aware of the intellectual implications of the scene, apart from the incidental detail of the pun on "concent," until more than halfway through the poem, when Milton turns to pointing the philosophic meaning of his picture, and we first encounter conceptual language like "sin" and "obedience." The harmony of soul which Milton contemplates is primarily an emotional harmony, and his major concern in the poem is to suggest the emotional texture of a sense of accord with the Mind of God. And in communicating this feeling of serenity and joy, his imagination re-creates the myth of heaven in full pictorial and auditory terms, terms in which Donne's imagination does not operate. Milton's mind sees the visual splendor of the "burning row" of the "bright Seraphim," the gold of the harps, and the sapphire color of God's throne, and hears the timbres and resonances of the harps and trumpets and the choral harmonies. Milton's imagination is excited also, as Spenser's would have been, by the "solemn" character of the scene, by its effects of stately ritual and ceremony. As his title suggests, it is this quality in the actual circumstance from which the poem derives—perhaps a court performance of choral music—which had stimulated his "high-raised fantasy" to religious meditation on the similar joyous solemnity which inheres in God's plan for the life of man.

If one wished to illustrate the "unification of sensibility" in Renaissance poetry, to find an example of a poetic sensibility which has not been "dissociated" into separate components of thought and feeling, I think no poem by Donne, or by any of the other Metaphysical Poets, would provide so good an illustration as this poem of Milton's, a poem in which observed fact blends with the constructs of the imagination, and in which thought gradually evolves out of physical sensation and emotion to function together with them in a unified and fully organic pattern of consciousness.

There is little of this deeply resonant harmony of soul in the kind of peace and gravity of mind which Donne's "Hymn" expresses. I think that Donne, in his religious experience, probably knew moments of intensity, an intensity of both joy and despair, beyond anything which Milton's more balanced temperament ever encountered, but those moments were never articulated in his verse with anything like the rich emotional and sensory texture of Milton's religious contemplation in this poem.

But the most striking quality of the greater part of Donne's religious poetry is not its intensity but its emotional poverty. When one gets away from the three "Hymns," parts of "The Litany," and the "Holy Sonnets" into the rest of his religious poetry, one finds, for the most part, verse as coldly intellectualized and as dully ingenious as Donne's commendatory epistles to Noble Ladies. In these meditative poems Donne's meditation tends to take the form of an intellectual fussing around with theological concepts, doctrinal paradoxes, and ambiguities on words. They seem forced or pointless twitchings of the analytical mind in a state of "holy discontent," [7] and only rarely do they spring to life in passages of intellectual intensity or organized imaginative power. I find the same spiritlessness behind the lengthy logical ingenuities of most of Donne's sermons: they suggest an intellect doggedly—and at times, I think, compulsively—analyzing and analyzing, but the analysis is rarely exciting even as thought, and the sermons come alive artistically only in occasional great passages of drama and rhetoric. The life of those great passages, moreover, is often of a peculiarly strained and melodramatic kind.

Donne suggests his own judgment on these excesses or sterilities in his religious work, and in his personal religious experience, in some passages in "The Litany," that revealing poem in which he

analyzes, for once with balance and sanity, the psychological evasions, abnormalities, or morbidities of the religious life:

> Those heavenly poets which did see
> Thy will, and it express
> In rhythmic feet, in common pray for me,
> That I by them excuse not my excess
> In seeking secrets, or Poeticness.

.   .   .   .   .

> When we are moved to seem religious
> Only to vent wit, Lord deliver us.

"Poeticness" of Donne's special kind—the venting of empty wit
—and the "excess" of playing around intellectually with the secrets
of theological mysteries are the curse of the more feeble of Donne's
"Divine Poems." And later in "The Litany" he prays

> That we may change to evenness
> This intermitting aguish piety;
> That snatching cramps of wickedness
> And apoplexies of fast sin, may die . . .[8]

"Intermitting aguish piety," "snatching cramps of wickedness,"
and "apoplexies of fast sin"—this is the pervasive character of the
religious experience which Donne's "Divine Poems" express, and
the metaphors of disease suggest his own sound judgment on what is
often its quality.

But there is no emotional poverty in some of the apoplectic
literary seizures in the sermons and the "Holy Sonnets," and here
one is sometimes literally embarrassed with riches. There are times
when a cramp over sin or damnation can produce poetry of superb
dramatic power, bursting on the reader with those coups de théâtre
which Donne often used in the openings of his love poems:

> What if this present were the world's last night?

> Spit in my face, you Jews, and pierce my side . . .

> At the round earth's imagined corners, blow
> Your trumpets, angels, and arise, arise
> From death, you numberless infinities
> Of souls, and to your scattered bodies go . . .

But this dramatic bent can also lead Donne to the forced sensationalism of melodrama, especially when he gets his hands on an erotic conceit:

> Batter my heart, three personed God; for, you
> As yet but knock, breathe, shine, and seek to mend;
> That I may rise, and stand, o'erthrow me,'and bend
> Your force, to break, blow, burn and make me new.
>
> .   .   .   .   .
>
> Divorce me,'untie, or break that knot again,
> Take me to you, imprison me, for I
> Except you'enthrall me, never shall be free,
> Nor ever chaste, except you ravish me.

And this tendency to slip over into sensationalism can carry him, in some of the sonnets of penitential tears, to distressing extravagances of self-display. Even a sonnet which opens as promisingly as "I am a little world" can lead us into these personal indecencies:

> I am a little world made cunningly
> Of elements, and an angelic sprite,
> But black sin hath betrayed to endless night
> My world's both parts, and (oh) both parts must die.
> You which beyond that heaven which was most high
> Have found new spheres, and of new lands can write,
> Pour new seas in mine eyes, that so I might
> Drown my world with my weeping earnestly,
> Or wash it, if it must be drowned no more:
> But oh it must be burnt! alas the fire
> Of lust and envy have burnt it heretofore,
> And made it fouler; let their flames retire,
> And burn me O Lord, with a fiery zeal
> Of thee and thy house, which doth in eating heal.

I think Christian humility came hard to Donne. The haughty egotist of the earlier poems, with his calculated reticences and his disposition to hold the reader at arm's length and to push him around, often seems in his religious poetry and prose to be trying to atone for this past poetic superbity by a blathering anxiety to Tell All. The result, in many of the "Holy Sonnets," is poetry which can be agreeable only to those who are edified—or titillated—by the pathology of religious self-abasement.

There is no evidence, in all of the logical and psychological analyses of Donne's fluctuating states of soul in his religious poems, that he ever attained that gentle and happy religious assurance which Walton would have us believe Donne often felt in his last years. The quality of the religious experience behind Herbert's "Virtue," which is so like Walton's, was something which Donne seems never to have known:

> Sweet day, so cool, so calm, so bright,
>   The bridal of the earth and sky;
> The dew shall weep thy fall tonight,
>   For thou must die.
>
>   .   .   .   .   .
>
> Only a sweet and virtuous soul,
>   Like seasoned timber, never gives;
> But though the whole world turn to coal,
>   Then chiefly lives.

Nor, for all that one sees in Donne's poems and sermons of his desire to be "burnt" and "ravished" by God and to "know" utterly by seeing Him face to face, does Donne seem ever to have experienced anything like the Mystic Rapture or the Mystic Ecstasy. Donne was fascinated all his life by the Mystic Experience and, like other tense and divided religious temperaments who have felt racked by the conflicts of the body and the soul, he seems to have wanted on many occasions to feel an ecstatic release in the sense of the annihilation of his troublesome individuality by the "death" of the Beatific Vision. "The Ecstasy" is Donne's attempt to record a moment when he felt he had touched on something approximating the Mystic Ecstasy, a serene and logically incomprehensible experience in which he was suddenly "unperplexed." But there is little effect of ecstasy in the tricky enterprise in logical analysis by which he tried to articulate the experience, and I think that that blissful sense of the sudden collapse of the analytical reason which mystics have felt at the Mystic Moment was an experience Donne could never have had. The sensations of religious mysticism remained for Donne something to be ought

after, and something to be analyzed intellectually, but all the religious "mysteries" which his work deals with are intellectual puzzles that he presents by trying to define them in logical terms, not
hovering moments of wonder and of awe. There is no indication
that he ever experienced the kind of religious vision which seems
to have come, faintly and at rare moments, to Henry Vaughan,
clearing the mists with which his arguing intellect had clouded
his mortal glass to let him see with naïve clarity:

> I saw eternity the other night
> Like a great ring of pure and endless light,
> All calm as it was bright . . .

There is, however, one important aspect of Donne's religious
experience in which he seems, at first glance, very much at one
with the characteristic sensibility of his age: his obsession with
mortality and with the physical phenomena of death. But it seems
to me that the great theme of the Lament for Mutability, of the
appalling presence of the inescapable facts of Time and Death in
the midst of all earthly joy, the theme which sounds like a ground
bass through all the literature of the Renaissance and which gives
that distinctive quality of poignancy to its sweetest songs, takes on
a different character in Donne's hands from the quality which it
has in the work of most of his contemporaries. Here is the characteristic Renaissance note, in Nashe, Peele, Herrick, and Shakespeare:

> Beauty is but a flower
> Which wrinkles will devour:
> Brightness falls from the air,
> Queens have died young and fair,
> Dust hath closed Helen's eye,
> I am sick, I must die.
>   Lord, have mercy on us!

> His golden locks time hath to silver turned;
>   Oh, time too swift, oh, swiftness never ceasing!
> His youth 'gainst time and age hath ever spurned,
>   But spurned in vain; youth waneth by increasing.
> Beauty, strength, youth, are flowers but fading seen;
>   Duty, faith, love, are roots, and ever green.

Fair daffodils, we weep to see
  You haste away so soon;
As yet the early rising sun
  Has not attained his noon.
      Stay, stay,
  Until the hasting day
      Has run
  But to the even-song;
And, having prayed together, we
  Will go with you along.

We have short time to stay, as you;
  We have as short a spring,
As quick a growth to meet decay,
  As you, or anything.
      We die,
  As your hours do, and dry
      Away
  Like to the summer's rain,
Or as the pearls of morning's dew,
  Ne'er to be found again.

Time doth transfix the flourish set on youth
And delves the parallels in beauty's brow,
Feeds on the rarities of nature's truth,
And nothing stands but for his scythe to mow.

Fear no more the heat o' the sun,
  Nor the furious winter's rages;
Thou thy worldly task hast done,
  Home art gone, and ta'en thy wages:
Golden lads and girls all must,
  As chimney-sweepers, come to dust.

The common quality in all of these passages from Elizabethan and
seventeenth-century poetry is the quality of poignant lament, either
gently pathetic or sternly tragic; and that poignancy derives from
the juxtaposition of the dusty fact of death with the physical and
emotional delights of love and of the beauties of the natural world
—the brightness of the air, young and fair queens, golden locks,

daffodils and sunrise and the pearls of morning's dew, and the
flourish set on golden lads and girls. It is this particular unification
of sensibility—the conjunction of the medieval *contemptus mundi*
with the new, pagan delight in the flesh and the earth—which
produced the distinctive vividness and pathos which the literature
of the Renaissance gave to the medieval theme of the Lament for
Mutability. And beneath that pathos lies another attitude: a sense
of tender, humble, and sympathetic community with the lot of
all mankind and of all earthly things.

One finds little of this precise intellectual and emotional quality
in Donne's treatments of mutability and death. The motif of death
appears often in his love poetry, and sometimes with startling concreteness, as in the "bracelet of bright hair about the bone" in
"The Relic." But in that poem the conjunction of the facts of
death and of love is of a different kind, and it generates not pathos
but shock, and also the grim comedy of a conceit about Judgment
Day. Death often enters Donne's love poems either in the form of
the Petrarchan conventions of the murdering mistress or of the
"death" of lovers' parting, where it leads to witty conceits or to
cynical realism; or it may enter in the form of a logical concept,
as in the nineteenth Elegy, where it generates effects of excited
philosophic speculation. And occasionally it appears, as in this
passage in "The Relic" and also in "The Funeral," as an ugly
physical fact, an irruption of a grim thought which jars rudely
against the generally cheerful tone of a poem of social wit and
sophistication. The predominantly intellectualized quality of
Donne's handling of the theme of mutability in his love poems
shows also the recurrent images which he uses to suggest the impermanence of the flesh and all worldly things; they are thin in
sensuous or emotional suggestion, drawn mostly from prosaic
things or from concepts—clothes, a book, straight lines, a dream,
play-acting, the sphere of the earth, the four elements.

Moreover, one looks in vain through all the appeals to coy
mistresses in Donne's love poetry for the characteristic Renaissance
effect of the *carpe diem* theme, the effect of Campion's adaptation
of Catullus:

> My sweetest Lesbia, let us live and love,
> And though the sager sort our deeds reprove,

> Let us not weigh them. Heav'n's great lamps do dive
> Into their west, and straight again revive,
> But soon as once set is our little light,
> Then must we sleep one ever-during night.

It is only rarely that Donne contemplates in this way the poignant emotional significance of death when he treats of the pleasures of love. "The Anniversary" has something of the serenity and pathos of Campion's poem, as Donne thinks of the aging of the two lovers and reflects that they

> Must leave at last in death, these eyes, and ears,
> Oft fed with true oaths, and with sweet salt tears . . .

But this poem is distinctly less this-worldly in its emotional orientation than the other Renaissance treatments of mutability which I have quoted, and the calm of mind which it expresses has a a logical basis quite different from Campion's pagan acceptance of the final obliteration of the sensuous and emotional joys of man's life in "one ever-during night." To Donne, the love which the poem celebrates is not essentially a physical union but a relation of the lovers' souls, and therefore the impermanence of the flesh offers only a slight ground for regret. And the lovers will not actually be parted by death; rather, they can look forward with assurance to a union in heaven, where their souls and their bodies, which will have been spiritualized through the resurrection, can join and at last be "thoroughly blest" in a love which is "increased" to ultimate spirituality and finally freed from the fleshly limitations of earthly love.

In "The Canonization," where Donne also juxtaposes the happiness of love and the limitary fact of death, there is even less of the delight in the pleasures of the flesh, and of the sure identification of oneself with the common mortal lot, which we see in Campion's poem and in the other passages that I have cited. In his acceptance of love as man's answer to death, Campion's speaker enjoys a sense of community with "all lovers," who will come, "rich in triumph," to grace his "happy tomb"; it is only "the sager sort"— the "crabbed old men" of Catullus' poem—who will not approve his act. Donne's speaker, however, feels proudly separate from other men and from other lovers: their sensual love is merely "rage," and

it is only a small élite, a saving remnant, who will be able to understand the exceptional experience in love which sets him apart
from the rest of the World. Nor does death stand in Donne's poem,
as it does in Campion's, as something apart from, and in tragic
antithesis to, the joys of fleshly love. In "The Canonization" the
ugly fact of death is seen as inherent in those very joys; it is vividly
present in each act of sexual indulgence, an indulgence by which
the lovers are certainly destroying themselves physically. But their
willingness so to mortify the flesh, Donne suggests, stands as evidence of their essential contempt for all material things. The attitude of tense asceticism which underlies this imaginative conjunction of love and death in "The Canonization" seems much closer,
in fact, to that reflected in a striking passage in Donne's sixth Elegy
than it does to the motif of carpe diem. This Elegy starts as a witty
and sardonic poem on the frustrations of love, but near the end
we come suddenly on two powerful lines which seem to be written
in Black Letter:

> Then with new eyes I shall survey thee,'and spy
> Death in thy cheeks, and darkness in thine eye.

This is not the gentle acceptance of the sad fact of mortality which
we find in "My sweetest Lesbia": it is the sudden shudder at the
ugliness of the corrupt flesh, the medieval note of the Dance of
Death, and the quality of a Dürer engraving. Nor does the awareness of death stand here, as it does in Campion's poem, against a
sense of the rich satisfactions of fleshly love, as the "crown" of life,
the experience which is man's "triumph" over death, enabling him
to face it with equanimity because he has known to the full life's
joys. It stands, instead, against a treatment of the folly of sexual
passion and an expression of an ascetic desire to renounce the stings
of the flesh and to learn to "hate" love.

The asceticism of temper which excluded Donne from the full
pagan delight in the flesh and the earth excluded from his work a
major ingredient in the normal Renaissance lament for the tran-
siency of mortal beauty and joy. T. S. Eliot has written perceptively
of Donne's awareness of the skeleton beneath every "contact possible to flesh," and has compared him to Webster, who

> was much possessed by death
> And saw the skull beneath the skin;

And breastless creatures under ground
Leaned backward with a lipless grin.

Daffodil bulbs instead of balls
Stared from the sockets of the eyes!
He knew that thought clings round dead limbs
Tightening its lusts and luxuries.[9]

But if Donne saw the skull beneath the skin, he did not at the same time see the skin, as Webster did, and the daffodils. And it was in that fleshly natural context that the skull normally appeared to the Renaissance imagination.

Donne's religious poems and his prose, however, show him possessed by death as few men of the Renaissance were, by the "sickly inclination" of mind to which he confessed in the Preface to *Biathanatos*, that odd treatise in defense of suicide for which Donne seems always to have had a lingering fondness. And in the theatrical power of the great passages on death in his sermons his contemporaries found some of the most arresting expressions of the "metaphysical shudder" at mortality which their age had seen. Whatever these passages are not, they are certainly exciting. With his dramatic sense and his talent for actualizing ideas by exploiting the philosophic significance of concrete, familiar things, Donne could electrify a congregation by pointing around the dirty and drafty church, with tombs and graves along the walls and beneath the floors, and crying:

> Every puff of wind within these walls may blow the father into the son's eyes or the wife's into her husband's or his into hers or both into their children's or their children's into both. Every grain of dust that flies here is a piece of a Christian; you need not distinguish your pews by figures; you need not say, I sit within so many of such a neighbor, but I sit within so many inches of my husband's or wife's or child's or son's grave.[10]

This is potent stuff. But the brilliance which flashes off these passages is often the hard, reflected brilliance of the limelight; and Donne's burrowing into the putrescence of corpses frequently verges on the queer. Even when I make every allowance for the great difference between what Donne's age and my own have regarded as a healthy attitude toward death—for that medievalism of temper which led the thoughtful man of the Renaissance to keep a skull on his study table and to regard the circumstantial contemplation of mortuary particularities as provocative of philosophic health—there is still enough difference between these passages on death in Donne's prose and the similar passages in the work of his contemporaries to make the circumstantiality of Donne's fixation on death seem morbid. Here, for instance, is Browne in a *momento mori* frame of mind:

> I thank God I have not those strait ligaments, or narrow obligations to the world, as to dote on life, or be convulsed and tremble at the name of death. Not that I am insensible of the dread and horror thereof; or by raking into the bowels of the deceased, continual sight of anatomies, skeletons, or cadaverous relics, like vespilloes, or grave-makers, I am become stupid, or have forgot the apprehension of mortality; but that, marshalling all the horrors, and contemplating the extremities thereof, I find not anything therein able to daunt the courage of a man, much less of a well-resolved Christian. . . .
>
> . . . I am not so much afraid of death, as ashamed thereof. 'Tis the very disgrace and ignominy of our natures, that in a moment can so disfigure us that our nearest friends, wife, and children, stand afraid and start at us. The birds and beasts of the field, that before in a natural fear obeyed us, forgetting all allegiance, begin to prey upon us. . . . Not that I am ashamed of the anatomy of my parts, or can accuse nature for playing the bungler in any part of me, or my own vicious life for contracting any shameful disease upon me, whereby I might not call myself as wholesome a morsel for the worms as any.[11]

And here is Donne pulling out the stops on the same theme:

> When of the whole body there is neither eye nor ear nor any member left, where is the body? And what should an eye do there where there is nothing to be seen but loathsomeness? or a nose where there is nothing to be smelt but putrefaction? or an ear where in the grave they do not praise God? . . . Painters have presented us with some horror the skeleton,

the frame of the bones of a man's body; but the state of the body in the dissolution of the grave no pencil can present to us. Between that excremental jelly that thy body is made of at first and that jelly which thy body dissolves to at last there is not so noisome, so putrid a thing in nature.[12]

Alongside this, Hamlet's fondling of the bones seems hearty and vigorously sane:

Alas, poor Yorick! I knew him, Horatio. A fellow of infinite jest, of most excellent fancy. He hath borne me on his back a thousand times. And now how abhorred in my imagination it is! My gorge rises at it. Here hung those lips that I have kissed I know not how oft. Where be your gibes now? your gambols? your songs? your flashes of merriment that were wont to set the table on a roar? Not one now, to mock your own grinning? Quite chapfallen? Now get you to my lady's chamber, and tell her, let her paint an inch thick, to this favour she must come. Make her laugh at that.

When one contrasts the wit or humor which give an effect of intellectual control to the other two passages—the wit which plays not only in Browne's expression of philosophic equanimity but also in Shakespeare's expression of philosophic bitterness—with the utter humorlessness of Donne's voluptuous abandonment to his necrophilous ardors, one wants to minister to a mind diseased, possessed of the Green Shudders and out to give them to everybody else. Moreover, that possession seems anything but reluctant. The brutal circumstantiality of Donne's passage is not just a technique for dramatizing the tough-minded integrity of a balanced Christian conviction that all flesh is grass and that we are but strangers and pilgrims on the earth, journeying to our own country which is heaven: it is the self-indulgent theatricality of a man who is enjoying himself in the striking pose of self-abnegating rejection of all the pleasures of the world, and who is hopping himself up to gag the flesh—the prurience and loose immodesty of the sawdust-path evangelist. And Donne himself, in his saner moments, knew this exhibitionist neuroticism for what it was. In the reasonable and self-effacing frame of mind in which he wrote "The Litany," he prayed to be delivered from these ascetic grossnesses:

From being anxious, or secure,
  Dead clods of sadness, or light squibs of mirth,
  From thinking, that great courts immure
All, or no happiness, or that this earth
      Is only for our prison framed,
      Or that thou art covetous
To them whom thou lovest, or that they are maimed
From reaching this world's sweet, who seek thee thus,
With all their might, Good Lord deliver us.[13]

I echo that last phrase feelingly as I read many of the passages on
mortality in Donne's religious work, and I think that, despite
Walton's approbation of these goings-on, and despite Donne's
great popular following as a preacher, many of Donne's intelligent
contemporaries must have felt the same way.

Moreover, in these passages where Donne contemplates the corruption of that body whose desires had both delighted and repelled
him for so long, one usually finds Donne square in the center of
the stage. It is John Donne who is about to die and who is shudder-
ing at that ugly obliteration of himself. Nor is he particularly inclined, at these moments, to that sympathetic outward projection
of himself by which he might feel, through this fact, a sense of
emotional community with the humanity which faces the same
fate. And it is this sense of the sad but rewarding community with
the lot of all things of the earth which gives the distinctive qualities
of satisfaction and philosophic peace to most of the Renaissance
laments for mutability. In his sermons Donne can abase himself
before his congregation and suggest that he is nothing, and just
as they, and that all are nothing in the grave; but the humanity in
which he participates imaginatively seems to remain essentially
an intellectual abstraction, or a set of particularized abstractions—
the merchant, the lawyer, the courtier, the magistrate, the king.
This was the "mankind" in which Donne saw himself involved in
that Meditation in the *Devotions* which Hemingway has popu-
larized:

No man is an island, entire of itself; every man is a piece of the
continent, a part of the main; if a clod be washed away by
the sea, Europe is the less, as well as if a promontory were, as
well as if a manor of thy friends or of thine own were; any

man's death diminishes me, because I am involved in mankind; and therefore never send to know for whom the bell
tolls; it tolls for thee.

"Mankind" here is a theological concept to Donne's mind—the
Mystic Body—as the earlier part of the Meditation shows:

> The Church is catholic, universal, so are all her actions; all
> that she does, belongs to all. When she baptizes a child, that
> action concerns me; for that child is thereby connected to that
> Head which is my Head too and engraffed into that body,
> whereof I am a member. And when she buries a man, that
> action concerns me.

Donne did not mean here what Hemingway has twisted his quotation to mean—a statement of every man's obligation, by the fact
of his common humanity, to feel a personal emotional involvement
with the struggles of other suffering human beings. Donne is involved in mankind, and concerned with the particular man whose
passing bell is tolling, theologically and conceptually, not by emotional attachment. There is no thought in the entire Meditation
about that man personally, nor any inclination to imagine sympa-
thetically what his life or death may have been—"never send to
know for whom the bell tolls." To watch Sir Thomas Browne pursuing the same train of thought provides a revealing contrast:

> I never hear the toll of a passing bell, though in my mirth,
> without my prayers and best wishes for the departing spirit;
> . . . I cannot see one say his prayers, but, instead of imitating
> him, I fall into a supplication for him, who perhaps is nothing
> more to me than a common nature: and if God hath vouch-
> safed an ear to my supplications, there are surely many happy
> that never saw me, and enjoy the blessing of mine unknown
> devotions.[14]

But Donne's emotions, at a similar moment, are involved only
with himself: "So this bell calls us all; but how much more me,
who am brought so near the door by this sickness!" The really important fact is that the bell tolls for John Donne: "any man's death
diminishes *me*." And it is the mortality of that "me," the precise
physiological and psychological phenomena and the metaphysical

implications of John Donne's own sickness unto death, which is the sole and inexhaustibly fascinating subject for Donne's meditation through all of the *longueurs* of the *Devotions*.

This inability to feel outside of himself and with the rest of mankind, which shows through in the general deficiency of Donne's work in the qualities of tenderness, pathos, and sympathy, is the limitation of mind which keeps all Donne's vivid treatments of the tragic fact of man's mortality from ever attaining to that typically Renaissance quality which one finds even in the work of John Webster, whose temperament was quite as proudly egocentric and as abstractly philosophical as Donne's and even more torn by inner conflicts and morbidities of mind—that broadly humane tragic sense of life which pervades all the literature of the Renaissance and which is its highest philosophic dignity.

I am not censuring Donne for not having written all the finest literature of his age, and I know that every poet has his limitations. But the limitations here are extraordinary. How much those which we see in Donne the writer were also limitations in the personality of Donne the man, we can never know with certainty. But in the personality or personalities which reached articulation in his literary work we find an ear relatively dull to the sonorities of language; a limited sensory response and an insensitivity to many subtleties of emotion; a lack of pleasure in the beauties of the natural world and an inability to invest its physical facts with the aura of the romantic imagination; an absence of any strong feeling for the cultural traditions of his own civilization, or of any strong sense of personal community with the rest of mankind; and a certain deficiency in human sympathy. Whatever the qualities of Donne's mind or sensibility were, it was certainly not a poetic sensibility which could devour or assimilate any kind of experience. Contemplating these severe inadequacies, one wonders. What was left to make poetry out of? Not very much, and certainly very little of what is normally thought of as promising poetic material: a hard eye for physical fact; a clean and brilliant analytical mind, and a lively but predominantly conceptual imagination; wide learning in fields of abstract thought; a theatrical sense; a personal concern with religious experience, psychological analysis, and getting ahead in the world; a strong animal sexuality and a strong egotism; and driving energy.

But it was enough. Donne's answer is in the seven poems which I have discussed in earlier chapters, and in a sizable number of other poems which, after more than three hundred years, are still worth reading and rereading for anyone seriously interested in literature. Donne's poetry triumphs by virtue of its limitations. Energies which might otherwise have been diffused over wide areas of consciousness have been channeled and caught into a tight constriction which makes them operate with brilliance and intensity. As I contemplate his work, I think of D. H. Lawrence's characterization of the fictionalized portrait of his mother in *Sons and Lovers* as a temperament in whom the "sensuous flame of life" was "baffled and gripped into incandescence by thought and spirit." A tense incandescence is the constant quality of the imagination which operates in Donne's best poetry: it is the incandescence of the tight grip of thought and spirit on all his consciousness. With a poetic sensibility as narrowly intellectualized as Auden's, and a poetic eccentricity as strong as Dylan Thomas', Donne had an energy and definiteness of mind which drove those limitations and eccentricities to produce some of the most impressive and boldly original poetry in English. His poetry is, in the literal sense of the phrase, a *tour de force*. I am reminded of an aesthetic pronouncement of Virgil Thomson's: "In art anything is all right as long as it's enough so."

2

That intellectuality of temper which set Donne always to the task of grappling his sensations and his emotions into thought is certainly one of the reasons why his mind has proved so congenial to the strongly intellectualized temper of our culture in the first half of the twentieth century, and it is one of the qualities which has made him so effective an interpreter to our times of the thought —if not of the whole sensibility—of his age. Of all the major writers of the 1590's and early 1600's, he is the one who most successfully articulates the philosophic ideas of his day in terms which make me realize the actuality of those beliefs to the men of that age; and I think that can only be because Donne's mental processes

conform more nearly to our own than do those of most of his
literary contemporaries. But the quality of those mental processes
awakened a sympathetic response also in many Englishmen of the
seventeenth century. I have gone to some lengths to show that
Donne was in many ways alien to the characteristic sensibility of
his time, especially of the Elizabethan period, but the quality of his
mind cannot have been so very different from that of other men
in his age if he established something like a new school in seventeenth-century poetry; and this school, unlike the school which
Ben Jonson created, seems to have been established inadvertently,
without Donne's making any personal crusading effort to reform
English poetry. Donne found literary imitators and enthusiastic
readers till near the end of the century; and even if one makes
some discount for the operation of Wordsworth's sound principle
that a major poet creates the taste by which he is judged, Donne's
break with the dominant traditions of English poetry in the 1590's
would not have caught on so widely in the following century unless his work had been in some essential ways an anticipation of a
new spirit which was beginning to appear in that century. It clearly
was, and I think Donne's reflection of that new temper of mind
has had much to do with the appeal of his poetry not only to the
seventeenth century but also to our own time; because that new
temper which modified the consciousness of the seventeenth century is one which has dominated the modern consciousness as well:
it was the scientific attitude. The men of the seventeenth century
responded to Donne because, living in a period of major intellectual transition and being analytically concerned with the old and
the new in the realm of ideas, they found in his mind something
like the conjunction of medieval doctrines with the developing
mental attitudes behind the new science which they found in their
own. And I think that is a major reason why he has also appealed
so strongly to many of us in the middle of the twentieth century,
living in a similar period in intellectual history, when science
is beginning to slacken its hold on our minds and when something like both the concepts and the habits of mind which science gradually tuned out of the Renaissance consciousness are
beginning to reassert themselves. In my analyses of particular
poems I have often pointed to the medievalism of Donne's mind,
and that is certainly the characteristic of his thought which first

strikes a reader of the twentieth century; but it is time now to qualify that suggestion by looking at those of Donne's intellectual biases and instinctive impulses of mind which are not medieval at all and which are very similar to those of the scientifically conditioned mentality of our own time.

Donne does not look, at first glance, much like a scientist, in that picture which he gives of himself in the first Satire, where he is seen turning away from the busy practicalities of the world to sit up nights over Aristotle and scholastic theology and to puzzle his mind over the logical mysteries of traditional metaphysics. But when he puzzled over the Mystic Experience and the other philosophic esoterica of theology, it was because they baffled him as "mysteries," as phenomena which did not accord with the normal laws of nature and which seemed rationally inexplicable. And, unlike most men of the Middle Ages and the mid-Renaissance, he was not content to leave them as mysteries, to feel wonder and pleasure—as that professional scientist Sir Thomas Browne did— over the fact that "the whole creation is a mystery," and to find in the contemplation of these things which one's mind could not understand a satisfying sense of the finitude of man's reason:

> As for those wingy mysteries in divinity, and airy subtleties in religion, which have unhinged the brains of better heads, they never stretched the *pia mater* of mine. Methinks there be not impossibilities enough in religion for an active faith . . . I love to lose myself in a mystery, to pursue my reason to an *O altitudo!* 'Tis my solitary recreation to pose my apprehension with those involved enigmas and riddles of the Trinity, with incarnation, and resurrection. I can answer all the objections of Satan and my rebellious reason with that odd resolution I learned of Tertullian, *Certum est, quia impossibile est.*[15]

Donne did not "love" a mystery in this way, much less the sense of losing himself in it. He came to believe much that was impossible, in Browne's sense of the word; but, with that tendency to "excess in seeking secrets" which he spoke of in "The Litany," he was always trying to figure out just how the impossible was possible. He was busy, for instance, to collect all the data that he could about the Mystic Experience, to define it exactly in intellectual

terms and analogize that logical definition to the conceptual defini-
tions of other phenomena which he had observed, and, if possible,
finally to experience it himself and see what it felt like. But to find
a parallel to the attitude behind his curious probing into the phenomena of religious experience I would turn, not to the parallel
which Donne himself might have drawn, to St. Augustine, that
great analyst of the states of the soul and sometime mystic, but
rather to a man like William James. There was much of the same
attitude of the research psychologist behind Donne's investigation
of the similarities between religious experience and eroticism, and
behind his probing into the physiological and psychological phenomena of love. It is this cast of mind which underlies his concern,
in a poem like "Love's Alchemy," to record the personally observed
data which make a previously held theory seem inadequate or untenable; or his concern in "The Ecstasy" to erect a theory which
will explain newly encountered data that do not fit into any previously held theories about love, and then to try to validate that new
theory by demonstrating its logical consistency with the generally
accepted theories about the natural phenomena of astronomical
motion, alchemy, flower breeding, the astrological influence of the
stars, and medical science. The scientific quality of Donne's analytic
conceptualization of love in "The Ecstasy" shows through also in
the startlingly modern usage of the word "sex" to refer to a general
biological and psychological concept, a usage which Donne seems
to have introduced into the English language.

> This ecstasy doth unperplex
>   (We said) and tell us what we love,
> We see by this, it was not sex,
>   We see, we saw not what did move . . .

The scientific attitude is, after all, not a matter of the content
of belief but rather of the mental processes by which one feels
belief should be attained, of particular habits and impulses of
mind and of the combination in the consciousness of certain faculties of intellection. Donne's mind combined all the faculties which
are the major ingredients of that attitude: a cold eye for concrete
fact, which is seen unromantically, in a bleak light, without any
pleasure in the emotional or physical texture of sensation; a conceptualized imagination eager to speculate on those facts and on

their logical relation to other facts, and anxious to dispose them into the patterns of abstract theory; a tendency to regard those theories as tentative and to keep checking them against the data of further observation; and a lively but skeptical intellectual curiosity about all available and well-established theories—that tendency which Donne saw in himself to "perplex security with doubt." [16] This is not a comprehensive list of all of Donne's characteristic mental attitudes and faculties of mind, but it comprises a great many of them, and it comprises all of the major psychological components of the scientific temper.

One can see all these components at work together in a passage like the third stanza of "The Good-Morrow." There is, first, the intellectual impulse behind the whole poem: the personal psychological experience with which the poem is concerned is something new which invalidates the ideas about love that Donne has held before; apart from its emotional satisfactions, the novelty of the experience has produced an intellectual awakening to further data about love which he had not encountered previously, and it must therefore be measured against more usual varieties of love in order to define that difference and to arrive at a theoretical explanation of these new phenomena. It is the conclusion of this analysis which Donne presents in the third stanza. The theory that he arrives at lies in the realm of the traditional metaphysics of his time, but Donne's intellectual progress to metaphysical generality begins with the sharp observation of physical particularity—with the concrete fact of the lovers' gaze. The scene of two lovers gazing with contented absorption into each other's eyes is a tempting opening for the romantic imagination in a poem about the joys of a passionate and idealized love affair. But Donne declines that opening. His imagination plucks those eyes out of the misty region of romance —and virtually out of their sockets—and lays them on a microscope slide. His bleak, minutely particular observation shows him the reflecting surface of the eyeball, the convex curve of that surface, the images which have impinged on it and are reflected there, and the hemispheric convexity which the curved surface gives to these images. And his mind then quickly whisks through the most reputable scientific account of the function of these images in initiating the psychobiological process by which visual sensation activates the soul to enter into the experience of love, notes the evidence of the "true plain hearts" manifested in the lovers' faces which indicates that this process has actually taken place—and there he is at his theoretical definition of a kind of love which has a physical component but which is essentially a relation of souls. But that theorizing process has begun with the careful observation of sense data, and those observed data of the images in the eyeballs, and of the true plain hearts in the faces, stand as evidence for the theory's validity.

Donne's mind moves, next, to check this theoretical definition of a novel variety of love against the laws governing the natural world. He notes the parallel between the principles operating behind the psychological phenomena of this love and the principles by which physics has defined the structure of all matter in the created universe; and he shows also that the psychological difference between this new love and more normal varieties of eroticism is precisely what one would expect from the different component elements of the two experiences: they manifest the same contrast in quality which physicists have found between the properties of the two different substances which comprise the world of nature, two kinds of substance which have also been found to comprise the two kinds of love. And, from this solid basis of the laws of physics, Donne is able, as any scientist must be if he is to win his professional spurs, to venture a prediction: this love, therefore, unlike more normal erotic phenomena, will be peaceful and enduring. The analogies on which Donne bases his scientific argument are, of course, analogies whose probatory validity no modern scientist would accept. But Donne was living in an age which was only proto-scientific, and this kind of analogical reasoning had been regarded as a sound method for arriving at scientific truth since the days of Aristotle, the first great natural scientist. To have rejected it, moreover, would have meant rejecting the whole structure of belief about the world, built upon this intellectual principle of the "correspondence" of all created things, which Western man had accepted for two thousand years. And the modern scientist, though he has learned to distrust reasoning by analogy and to scrutinize the corresponding terms of an analogy more carefully than men about 1600 had thought to do, certainly uses the suggestive value of analogies which are not very different from Donne's when he is starting to formulate new theory.

But before Donne is through expounding his analogy he has

manifested another trait of the scientific temper—caution in employing accepted theories which are not fully proved. In Donne's time there was more than one theory about the exact method by which lovers' souls were conjoined to produce the psychological phenomena of spiritual love, but other Renaissance love poets were usually content to settle for one generally accepted theory about the phenomenon and let it go at that—it was not the theory which they were most interested in anyhow. I know of no Renaissance poet before Donne who would have stopped in the climactic concluding lines of an impassioned love poem to investigate alternative hypotheses of exactly how this union had been produced. But Donne does just this at the end of "The Good-Morrow." The mechanics of the operations of the soul in love were, after all, still somewhat in the realm of speculation, and one couldn't be sure which of two widely accepted theories was factually true. And since factual truth was important if the argument of this poem was to be valid, one had better observe a little scientific caution and put both theories down as hypotheses. Fortunately, however, this uncertainty on an important point did not invalidate the poem's general conclusions about the love, because both hypotheses yielded identical logical predictions on the basis of the laws of physics.

I have dramatized these processes of mind somewhat, and simplified them by abstracting certain thought processes from a psychological and philosophic context which is more complex, and which contains other ingredients that are historically alien to the scientific attitude; but I do not think this account fundamentally distorts some of the operations which Donne's mind goes through as he evolves his argument in this stanza. And those processes of mind are much more closely analogous to scientific methods of reasoning than the processes which I can see behind the poetry of any of his contemporaries about 1600. One sees, from this evidence of Donne's affinity with the scientific temper, why he was the first literary man of his age to grasp the full philosophic significance of the new astronomy, and to realize with a shock, long before most of his contemporaries did, that "the new Philosophy calls all in doubt."

And I cannot resist a parenthesis on something else which I think one can see from this analysis: that the ancient quarrel between science and the arts is at bottom just as absurd—and absurd for just the same reasons—as that "ancient quarrel between poetry and philosophy" which Plato spoke of. In "The Good-Morrow" a contemplative imagination, working by processes very like the characteristic mental processes of a scientist, has been occupied to create an object of great aesthetic attractiveness. But I think that that impulse is in no way alien to the major impulse which motivates the research of most theoretical scientists. Wordsworth recognized this fact long ago in his Preface to the *Lyrical Ballads,* but we may turn also to the testimony of the scientists themselves. As one of them, a mathematician and writer on modern physics, has said, "the most important consideration of all to scientific men" in the personal value which they find in scientific thought—though it is usually the least of the values which most laymen see in science— is that "it provides the contemplative imagination with objects of great aesthetic charm." [17]

One of Donne's closest affinities with the scientific biases of the modern mentality is in that materialist, empirical cast of mind which was always applying the brakes to his impulses toward abstract speculation about metaphysical theory. His long philosophic struggle to pull his consciousness free from the suction of matter, and from the practical claims of the world of Things Material, lies behind Elegy 19 and "Love's Alchemy," as well as behind the explicit materialist-idealist dialectic of his mature love poems. But he never succeeded. The hard facts remained, and theories had to be checked against them. One of the ways in which Donne's mind seems least medieval and most like that of a modern scientist is in his tendency to think of any theological or philosophic doctrine which he accepts as though it were literal, factual truth, and to try to visualize it in terms of concrete fact and the practicalities of the physical world. It was that tendency of mind which I was suggesting, in my comments on "The Good-Morrow," when I referred to Donne's investigation of the "mechanics" of the union of the lovers' souls; because, unlike many other Renaissance poets who employed the doctrine, Donne seems to imagine this union in terms of something like the dynamics of an actual physical process.[18] Most of Donne's contemporaries seem to have thought of the union of lovers' souls more as Browne did, as simply a "most mystical union" [19] and therefore something which might be speculated on but was not to be visualized in concrete terms.

But Donne's imagination was always trying to materialize most

mystical doctrines in this way. The theological mystery of the resurrection of the body, for instance, fascinated Donne endlessly, and
he worried the problem from some of his early poems to some of
his last sermons. What kept puzzling him about that doctrine was
exactly what would puzzle a modern biologist or physicist: the apparently insuperable mechanical difficulties of the process by which
the decomposed body would have to be recomposed if resurrection
in the flesh was actually to take place on the Day of Judgment.
After all, as he kept pointing out in his sermons, within a few centuries the component atoms of that body would have been scattered by the winds and the waters over the whole world, and some
of them would have entered into plants and thence into living
beings in the form of food. But the soul, on the Last Day, would
have to locate, and recognize, and collect every single atom of its
original body, and then recompact it to stand at the Bar of Judgment. How in the name of heaven the soul was going to do this
Donne could never see. And the soul would be working against
time, too—Judgment *Day,* twenty-four hours. Of course the "day"
which the Bible referred to might not be a day in the normal sense
of the word—but then it might be; and the time-factor would surely
be an additional practical complication: it seemed hardly enough
time for so big a job. The soul was certainly going to have its hands
full. Donne speculated in "The Relic," this time in a comic mood,
on that problem of the time-factor, and, visualizing something of
the traffic difficulties which would arise on the Day of Judgment,
he referred to the occasion, with a snicker, as "the last busy day."
He was sure, of course, that the soul would pull it off somehow,
because the doctrine of resurrection in the flesh was established
on highly reputable authority, because almost all sharp-minded
intellects had accepted it for centuries, and because it was logically
consistent with other Christian doctrines and had a necessary place
in the logical structure of Christian theology. Donne was sure it
must be true. But for the life of him he still couldn't see how the
thing was going to work. Because if something was true it was
literally, factually true, and if we really believed that this business
was actually going to happen, right here in the physical world, we
had to try to understand it, didn't we, in terms of that world, as
a practical, scientific problem involving concrete things?
This utterly nonmedieval feeling that logically established theo-

logical dogma must regularly be referred to the observed facts of physical phenomena as something of a yardstick—a materialist yardstick—for philosophic truth, underlies all of Donne's puzzlings over theological mysteries. And that inclination of mind lies at the core of the scientific attitude. It is the assumption implicit in the sentence of William James which Whitehead cites as a statement-in-a-nutshell of the revolutionary intellectual principle which seventeenth-century science introduced into the modern consciousness: "I have to forge every sentence in the teeth of irreducible and stubborn facts." [20] But this principle was stated more dramatically, long before James, by Donne's contemporary, Sir Francis Bacon. Propagandizing for the scientific attitude and speaking of his great instauration in thought which will eventually make all existing knowledge obsolete, Bacon explains the new method of thinking that he has hit on which will "establish for ever a true and lawful marriage between the empirical and the rational faculty" and thus open to man this challenging intellectual adventure. In a statement with far more heretical implications for a good Renaissance Christian than I think even Bacon realized, he explains that he has attained this new way to truth by the intellectual process of "submitting my mind to things." [21]

Donne was always inclined to submit his mind to things in this way, even at moments when the content of his thought was most medieval. He was doing this in the "Hymn to God, My God, in My Sickness" when he threw in the skeptical, factual qualification, "we think," just before he let himself go on elaborating those traditional symbolic analogies between Eden and Calvary by which the medieval mind had dramatized its sense of the factual improbability of the mysterious ways in which God moved to perform His wonders for mankind. And this lurking inclination to run a quick laboratory check before he would cut his mind loose on a traditional religious concept flashes out most dramatically in Donne's vivid presentation of the actuality of Judgment Day in the opening of the seventh Holy Sonnet:

> At the round earth's imagined corners, blow
> Your trumpets, angels, and arise, arise
> From death, you numberless infinities
> Of souls, and to your scattered bodies go . . .

"*Imagined* corners?" And at a moment like this, when one is contemplating, with feelings of awe and terror, the dreadful reality of the Day of Doom as manifested to us in the book of Revelation, and when one is working poetically for effects of headlong rush and powerful excitement? But, as Donne must stop to point out, that account in Revelation is a little off on its facts. Four angels cannot possibly stand at the four corners of the earth and blow trumpets when, as any schoolboy knows, it is a "round earth." And one must remind the reader that the business about the earth's four corners isn't factually true, but just a liberty of the poetic imagination, if one is to present the reality of Judgment Day in fully convincing terms. That great myth, which had overwhelmed man's imagination for centuries, must still be haled by Donne before the bar of scientific judgment and made to answer to the stern philosophic tribunal of the "irreducible and stubborn facts" of the physical world.

It would never have occurred to most Renaissance poets to throw this skeptical, empirical qualification into a poetic picture of the Day of Judgment. They knew that the earth was round, but they would not have bothered to make a fuss over the fact at a poetic moment like this, not only because their more fundamentally medievalized minds would have been less inclined than Donne's to check religious doctrine against scientific fact, but also because their imaginations were more at home with myth. Donne's mind seems nowhere more scientific in its biases, and more psychologically unlike the imaginations of many of his literary contemporaries, than in this estrangement from the myth-making faculty of mind, to which the scientific attitude has been, from its inception, an inveterate foe. John Milton was in many ways more modern-minded than Donne, and he lived later in the seventeenth century, knew more of the new science, and had a serious intellectual interest in its doctrines; but he never troubled himself to run this kind of scientific check on the myth of Judgment Day, or on most of the other Christian myths which he treats in *Paradise Lost*. Like Donne, he believed that those myths were essentially true, but he was not worried by their factual inaccuracies of detail because he understood that they were also myths; and myth was a mode of imaginative expression to which his mind was habituated. Milton thought that great poetic pictures like those in Revela-

tion contained important elements of fact, because they were revelations by which the Holy Ghost had inspired the mind of St.
John the Divine with supernatural truths beyond man's normal
reach to know; but he also knew that St. John was a poet, and that
myth was a form of poetic symbolism whose essential validity lay
in its articulation of truths apprehended by those areas of consciousness that were beyond the reach of logic and the scientific intellect.[22]

Milton's imagination, moreover, shuttles easily between the intellectual realms of myth and scientific fact without finding any
incongruity between them. There are passages in his treatment of
the myths of Eden and Heaven and Hell in *Paradise Lost* which
strike us as incongruously materialistic and which seem to show
Milton's imagination at work to visualize his myths poetically in
concrete, scientific terms—passages like those on the digestive processes of angels or on what happens when a cannon ball goes
through angelic substance. But, as C. S. Lewis has shown, the thinking behind these passages does not reflect the conditioning of Milton's poetic imagination by the materialist bias of the new science,
but rather Milton's literal belief in the doctrines of the new Platonic Theology of the Renaissance, which maintained the corpo-
reality of angelic substance. Milton was at equal intellectual ease
in the realms of religious myth and of scientific doctrine, not just
because he regarded myth as a form of truth, but also because he
regarded scientific truth as a form of myth and not as an absolutely
accurate philosophic description of reality. At the end of Book II
of *Paradise Lost* he can glide smoothly from the scientifically accurate picture of the violent physical turbulence of the embryon
atoms in Chaos, and from the picture of the created universe as
Satan first sees it in his approach from outer space—a picture which
would accord with a Renaissance astronomer's visualization of the
cosmos—to the picture of the golden chain by which the earth is
suspended from the Empyreal Heaven. The golden chain is myth,
and the embryon atoms and the spherical cosmos are science, but
this does not worry Milton, as it would have worried Donne. He
knows that the golden chain is not actually there—he got it, in fact,
out of Plato and Homer—and that this part of his picture is not true
to the physical facts of how the universe is constructed. But it is
symbolically true, a mythical poetic symbol for the undeniable

facts of the Chain of Being and of the tie of God's love which binds earth to heaven and which binds all the discords of sublunary things into order. Moreover, at a time when laboratory method was still only a novel and embryonic scheme of investigation whose usefulness had not been proved, and when the telescope was only a recent invention, how could one know for sure what the actual physical facts of the structure of the universe were? Perhaps the warring atoms in Chaos were no more physically there than the golden chain was. They might be merely a myth of the scientific imagination, and there need therefore be no imaginative incongruity in injecting into this scientific picture the mythical allegorical figures of Chaos and Old Night. But that scientific myth also symbolized an important fact—the fact of the action of God's love in reducing Chaos to order and thus creating the beautiful form and the reasonable design of the cosmos. And it was those facts of the perfect order and reasonableness of God's world—and also the facts of man's central importance in God's design, and of the scheme of an upward progression from the imperfection of earth to the perfection of heaven—which the spherical perfection of the Ptolemaic cosmos symbolized. Perhaps that astronomical picture was also merely an inspired myth of the scientific imagination, as Milton suggests in Book VIII when he balances the Ptolemaic against the Copernican astronomy and concludes, quite properly for a thoughtful man of the mid-seventeenth century, that it is impossible for man to know certainly which of these accounts is a factually accurate description of the physical appearance of the cosmos. The Ptolemaic picture was, however, a more satisfactory poetic symbol, because it carried a rich reference to the essential philosophic facts about God's world, and the Copernican picture did not adapt itself so readily to these poetic purposes.

Milton was eager, of course, to know what the concrete physical facts about the universe were, and he was at pains to record in his poem the data about what Galileo had seen through his telescope; but he also knew that nobody had yet assembled much reliable information on those facts, and that to stop at every point to submit his mind to things was not required. The traditional method of articulating the basic philosophic truths about the world by means of symbol and myth was perfectly respectable intellectually; it came naturally to his mind, and it was also poetically more rewarding. When he presented the mythical picture of the Limbo of Vanity, located on

> the firm opacous globe
> Of this round world, whose first convex divides
> The luminous inferior orbs, enclos'd
> From Chaos and th' inroad of Darkness old,

he was no more concerned over whether the Limbo had an actual physical existence, or whether it was located at that particular astronomical spot, than Dante was concerned over whether the Mount of Purgatory was actually a mountain, really terraced into seven stages and geographically located at the antipodes of Jerusalem, or whether the individual souls which he assigned to his Limbo, or to the particular spheres in Paradise, were actually there. The concrete facts about matters like this were things which man's mind could not know—and the most important facts about the world were not concrete anyhow. For all Milton's curiosity about the new science, and all his aggressive individualist rationalism, his temper was medieval enough to enable him to subscribe equally to Raphael's advice to Adam, when Adam was trying to learn the actual facts about the two astronomies: "Solicit not thy thoughts with matters hid."

That medieval, anti-scientific intellectual principle of Forbidden Knowledge was something to which Donne could never accustom his mind: for all his efforts to do so, the "excess in seeking secrets" remained as a driving force in his temperament. And his habitual disposition to try to give supernaturalist doctrine concreteness by imagining it in terms of the irreducible and stubborn facts of the natural world cut him off from any real comprehension of the traditional process of mythical thinking which seemed so natural to others of his time. Moreover, this intellectual inclination does not seem to have derived from any conviction on Donne's part that his age had accumulated any substantial body of evidence to show that those facts of the natural world might now be better known than they had been to men of medieval times and might therefore be more worthy of intellectual scrutiny. It seems probable that Donne would have known of Bacon's hortatory scientific works, but there is no indication that they interested him particularly. This empirical inclination seems rather to have been an inherent and fundamental bias of Donne's mind. And in the conjunction of that empirical philosophic bias with a ruthless inquisitiveness of intellect lies Donne's most profound estrangement from the temper of the Middle Ages and his most essential bond with the new intellectual temper which was evolving in the Renaissance—with that spirit of unfettered intellectual adventurousness in Tudor humanism which led Sidney to define the impulse behind learning and the arts as the impulse "to know, and by knowledge to lift up the mind from the dungeon of the body to the enjoying of his own divine essence"; and with the later modification of that spirit, by the new science of the seventeenth century, into an empirical and individualist bias of mind which held that truths were not really known as truths until one had proved them by the evidence of one's own senses.

There is, finally, one other way in which Donne's mind shows a kind of instinctive intellectual affinity with the mental dispositions of the scientific temper—in the logical precision and logical consistency of his poetic vocabulary. No Renaissance poet was so little prone to that scientific vice which was soon to trouble Hobbes and the members of the Royal Society and which Bacon stigmatized as the pursuit of the Idols of the Market Place: the use of words loosely, or poetically and symbolically, without regard to their exact conceptual meaning or to their referential validity. Living in an age in which writers were pushing the English language around as they have never done since, luxuriating in the adventurous exploration of a "New World of Words," tipping old words off their logical bases to cant them on their connotative edges, and inflating the English vocabulary with countless new metaphoric usages, Donne wrote a language as chemically pure and as logically and referentially precise as the terminology of Newtonian physics. To his mind a word was a hard, objective fact. Its sound, or its emotional connotations, did not much concern him. He was concerned with what it really meant, or should mean, with its precise conceptual or denotative content and with its ambiguities of logical reference, which were to be carefully defined and exploited whenever possible. And to Donne that conceptual meaning was usually the meaning which the word had originally carried in the logical framework of the body of thought from which it had been torn by the rude hands which were rubbing it to a counter in common usage. That original, and proper, logical content must be restored to it and must be observed with absolute consistency. And it was against that irreducible and stubborn fact of what the word really meant that Donne played the ambiguities of its contemporary neologistic meanings. When I watch Donne scrutinizing his words in this way to find out exactly what they should mean, I think of Yeats's remark about "our common English . . . that needs such sifting that he who would write it vigorously must write it like a learned language." [23] Donne's poetic vocabulary is full of words which are given an effect of fresh vitality because he treats them in this way, with a sense of their precise, technical meaning in their native intellectual habitat. "Refine," for instance, always carries a reference to alchemic distillation: Donne never uses it, as it was coming to be used in his time, to refer to purification of some general sort. "Contemplate" always implies religious contemplation; "mysterious" never refers just to mystery in general; "form" regularly denotes metaphysical essence; "reveal" never means just "show"; "ecstasy" is not used metaphorically to refer simply to a sense of bliss; and so on, through a list of dozens of words which, in the usage of Donne's time, were rapidly losing their original limited reference and taking on their looser or different modern meanings. The result of this egregious logical responsibility toward language on Donne's part is a poetic vividness of a most unusual kind—the effect of constant, pinpoint jabs to the mind from the hardest, cleanest, most conceptually acute poetic vocabulary in English.

3

But if Donne had many affinities with the new attitudes of mind which gradually came to dominate English culture as the seventeenth century progressed, he certainly had much less in common with the dominant temper of the Elizabethan period, particularly of that great decade of the 1590's in which he began his artistic and his worldly careers, or with those characteristically Elizabethan attitudes which hung on in English culture until well after his death in 1631. The examination earlier in this chapter of the many ways in which Donne was alienated from the typical tastes and imaginative inclinations of his literary contemporaries in the 1590's and early 1600's certainly indicates some of the reasons why Donne felt at odds with the society of his time, and why even his earliest poetry reflects an attitude of something like hostility toward his reader, a desire to shock and startle him and to devise poetic stratagems which seem designed as an assault on his normal literary expectations. It was this hard intellectual pride, this individualistic sense of personal separateness from the concerns of "every Jack and Jill" which Yeats was responding to when he wrote:

> There is not a fool can call me friend,
> And I may dine at journey's end
> With Landor and with Donne.[24]

I have touched in earlier chapters on some of the reasons why Donne was inclined to feel that he was not as other men, and to take pride in that fact, but I think this attitude needs exploring further, though I do not believe I can account for it fully. The lordliness toward his reader which one sees in Donne's mature love poems reflects an individualism of an exceptionally haughty and condescending kind. One can see its distinctive quality by contrasting it with the individualism and the hostility toward the conventional, mindless mass which one finds in a poet like Cummings. Cummings is just as aggressively at odds with the man on the street as Donne was; as scornful of the materialism and self-seeking which he sees as the dominant concerns of his society; and as ready to clown his seriousness for effects of theatrical surprise, and to dramatize his proud selfhood by writing poems which, he confesses, are calculated to shock the reader and to hit him like a brick, directed at him with "that precision which creates movement." But Cummings nevertheless feels a generous and even sentimental sense of community with those who will read his poems, and says to his reader, with warmth and cuddly intimacy: "The poems to come are for you and for me and are not for mostpeople." [25] The aloof individualism and egocentricity behind Donne's later love poetry does not have this custard beneath its crust. It is rather a hard intellectual aristocracy which often seems to be saying to the reader: "The poems are for me, and make of them what you can."

Certainly one of the grounds for Donne's feeling of estrangement from the life of his time at the start of his career was an attitude which was more significant in his day than it may seem, at first glance, to a modern reader: his distaste for Queen Elizabeth. There is not much direct expression of that distaste in his work, but in the 1590's to write out plain one's scorn for the Queen would have brought the Privy Council down about one's ears, and the loss of those ears was one of the lesser of the penalties that might be expected under the government of the last of the Tudors. But the almost complete absence of reference to Elizabeth in Donne's work is significant: there is no trace in his poetry of that extravagant adulation of the Virgin Queen to which most Elizabethan poets turned their hand, if only their left hand, at some time or other in their literary careers. And Donne's feelings about Elizabeth show clear, for once, in his unfinished satire "The Progress of the Soul." There, giving his own sarcastic twist to the myth of Cynthia, he speaks with heavy irony of

> the great soul, which here amongst us now
> Doth dwell, and moves that hand, and tongue, and brow,
> Which, as the Moon the sea, moves us; to hear
> Whose story, with long patience you will long;
> (For 'tis the crown, and last strain of my song)
> This soul to whom Luther, and Mahomet were
> Prisons of flesh; this soul which oft did tear,
> And mend the wracks of th'Empire, and late Rome,
> And liv'd when every great change did come,
>   Had first in paradise, a low, but fatal room.[26]

There is conflicting evidence on how Donne planned to finish the poem. Jonson told Drummond that

> the conceit of Donne's Transformation or *Metempsychosis* was that he sought the soul of that apple which Eva pulled, and thereafter made it the soul of a bitch, then of a she-wolf, and so of a woman. His general purpose was to have brought in all the bodies of the heretics from the soul of Cain, and at last left it in the body of Calvin. Of this he never wrote but one sheet, and now, since he was made Doctor, repenteth highly and seeketh to destroy all his poems.[27]

But it is clear from this stanza near the start of the poem, and from the preceding stanza, that Donne's original plan in the satire was to trace the soul through this unedifying historical progress to its final resting place in Queen Elizabeth, and, as the "crown, and last strain" of his song, to reveal the Queen as the shining contemporary avatar of the spirit of that forbidden tree which brought death into the world and all our woe. Donne wrote the poem about 1601, when the mortal Moon was sadly on the wane, and it probably derived from his bitterness over Elizabeth's treatment of Essex, that courageous but headstrong idealist who stood, to many of the intellectuals of that day, as a symbol for the good old English moral virtues which were going by default in the increasing sycophancy and degeneracy of the court of the old Queen. Donne may have felt, at this time, that the spread of popular antipathy to Elizabeth made it a little safer to vent a long-standing bitterness. Nevertheless, to write so vicious an attack on the Queen and her courtiers, even if its circulation was to be restricted, as it seems to have been, only to Donne's close friends, was an act of danger and some daring in those authoritarian times.[28]

This hatred for Queen Elizabeth sets Donne apart, on a matter of major intellectual and emotional consequence, from all the important writers of the late 1580's and 1590's. The extent of Marlowe's Elizabethan patriotism is a question, but he seems at least to have worked as an undercover agent for Elizabeth's government. Sidney had his difficulties with the Queen, and felt, on occasion, the sting of her autocratic hand, but he apparently remained to the end her loyal and chivalrous servant. Spenser and Shakespeare grew sadly disillusioned with Elizabeth and her ministers in the late 1590's, as did Sir Walter Ralegh, but they had all known her once as Cynthia, as the "fair vestal throned by the West," as the Faerie Queene who had called up in her countrymen the slumbering spirit of old Arthur of Britain and who fired her subjects with the impulse to Magnificence. And they had seen her also as the symbol for an England which—as one could believe with some soberness of mind for a few enchanted years around 1590—might actually become Fairyland, an Earthly Paradise more happy than fruitfullest Virginia and more sumptuous than the Indian Peru. It was this dream which possessed Shakespeare when he wrote:

> This royal throne of kings, this sceptered isle,
> This earth of majesty, this seat of Mars,

This other Eden, demi-paradise,
This fortress built by Nature for herself
Against infection and the hand of war,
This happy breed of men, this little world,
This precious stone set in the silver sea,
Which serves it in the office of a wall,
Or as a moat defensive to a house,
Against the envy of less happier lands;
This blessed plot, this earth, this realm, this England,
This nurse, this teeming womb of royal kings,
Feared by their breed and famous by their birth,
Renowned for their deeds as far from home,
For Christian service and true chivalry,
As is the sepulchre in stubborn Jewry
Of the world's ransom, blessed Mary's son . . .

Ben Jonson came later to the scene, and when he began to
write it was harder to see Elizabeth as the goddess-symbol for
God's Chosen Nation; and he was temperamentally more like
Donne and disinclined to myth-making idolatry—as his observation to Drummond on the reasons for the Queen's much-admired
virginity so strikingly demonstrates. But even Jonson undertook
a patriotic epic poem on "the worthies of this country, roused by
fame"; and he could still feel enough of the fading Elizabethan
Dream to write "Queen and huntress, chaste and fair":

Earth, let not thy envious shade
Dare itself to interpose;
Cynthia's shining orb was made
Heaven to clear, when day did close:
Bless us then with wished sight,
Goddess excellently bright.

Donne seems to have felt none of this. And to be cut off from
any regard for the Queen in the early 1590's was to be cut off
from any sense of real community with the nation of which she
was the mythicized symbol in the days of that nation's greatest
glory, from what Shakespeare saw as "this land of such dear souls,
this dear dear land." It would have removed Donne from any
feeling of enthusiastic involvement in the life and the flowering

culture of an age which the cool and judicious mind of Samuel Daniel could sum up, in 1599, in these terms:

> For now great nature hath laid down at last
>   That mighty birth wherewith so long she went,
>   And overwent the times of ages past,
>   Here to lie in, upon our soft content,
>   Where, fruitful, she hath multiplied so fast
>   That all she hath on these times seemed t' have spent.
> All that which might have many ages graced
>   Is born in one, to make one cloyed with all,
>   Where plenty hath impressed a deep distaste
>   Of best and worst, and all in general,
>   That goodness seems goodness to have defaced,
>   And virtue hath to virtue given the fall.[29]

And Donne did feel thus cut off from this sense of being a proud part of England which most of his contemporaries felt in those days. This attitude must have contributed to his lack of any real enthusiasm for what had particularly excited Daniel in this poem, for the New Poetry inaugurated by Spenser and Sidney and Marlowe and brought to fruition in the last decade of the century. And I think Donne's setting of his face against Elizabethan nationalism must have been a contributory cause behind his unwillingness to participate in the general patriotic endeavor of the Elizabethan poets to produce, by writing deliberately within the poetic traditions of foreign literatures, a native English literature which insisted on comparison with the national literatures of the European Renaissance and of Greece and Rome. Other Elizabethan poets had their fun with the artificialities of Petrarchan sonneteering, but no other good poet of the time seems to have looked on the vogue of Petrarchism, as Donne regularly did, as just an empty social fad.[30] "Englishing" the numbers which Petrarch had flowed in meant more to the Elizabethan poets than that: it meant an English literature.

It is easy to see one major cause for Donne's antipathy to the Queen and to the ideology of Elizabethan patriotism, and for the chilly view which he seems to have taken of everything in English culture in the early 1590's which gave grounds for the optimism and idealism endemic among other writers of the time—the fact that he was born and brought up as a Roman Catholic. For to be a Catholic in Elizabethan England put one in a position not very different from that of a Marxist in America in the 1950's. It exposed one to the same popular opprobrium, the same official injustice, and the same cruelties from recurrent surges of witch-hunting hysteria, when Englishmen began to smell out all Catholics as potential underground agents for that atheistical monster, Philip of Spain and to see them as ready at any moment to lend a hand in one of his plots to murder the Queen and destroy the English bastion of Christianity. Donne's own brother evidently died in prison as a result of this attitude: his crime had been that of giving shelter to a Jesuit uncle who had secretly visited England. Moreover, from what we know of Donne's family background—a home environment which had family ties with the circle of Sir Thomas More and which must have surrounded him in youth with people of exceptional moral courage, intellectual integrity, and personal cultivation—it is clear that his early life would have dramatized sharply for him the thick intolerance of a popular attitude which cast people like himself beyond the pale, not only socially and intellectually, but also in their legal rights as English citizens. With this background it was not hard to feel alienated from the normal course of English life, and also to feel proud that one was not as other men and to find one's imagination recurring to self-congratulatory religious metaphors which stigmatized the mass of one's contemporaries as "the laity." I think, in fact, that this background helps to explain—though certainly only in part—why Donne's literary imagination could never get far from matters of religion, and why imagery from scholastic theology kept crowding into even his flashily cynical early love poems.

Donne's concern over the oppression of Catholics, and his intellectual development toward renouncing his own Catholicism, show indirectly through all of his Satires. He treats that personal problem explicitly in Satire 3: "Of Religion," where he expresses himself guardedly but bitterly on the subject of sovereigns as enforcers of conscience. Donne handles this problem of the abuse of temporal power with gingerly generality and comes no nearer to Queen Elizabeth than a reference to Henry VIII—a reference, however, which parallels him, with a show of impartiality which may be deceptive, to Philip of Spain:

        men do not stand
In so ill case here, that God hath with his hand
Signed Kings blank-charters to kill whom they hate,
Nor are they Vicars, but hangmen to Fate.[31]
Fool and wretch, wilt thou let thy soul be tied
To man's laws, by which she shall not be tried
At the last day? Oh, will it then boot thee
To say a Philip, or a Gregory,
A Harry, or a Martin taught thee this?

Exactly when Donne finally abandoned his Catholicism is not certain—it was probably in his middle twenties—but the break evidently cost him something and left him with lingering feelings of guilt and apostasy. He was at pains to retrace the road from Rome with the greatest intellectual scrupulousness, and he explained publicly in the Preface to *Pseudo-Martyr*, in a passage which sounds rather touchily defensive, that those "who have descended so low, as to take knowledge of me, and to admit me into their consideration" could testify that he had entered on this undertaking with

> no inordinate haste, nor precipitation in binding my conscience to any local religion . . . And although I apprehended well enough, that this irresolution not only retarded my fortune, but also bred some scandal, and endangered my spiritual reputation, by laying me open to many mis-interpretations; yet all these respects did not transport me to any violent and sudden determination, till I had, to the measure of my poor wit and judgment, surveyed and digested the whole body of divinity, controverted between ours and the Roman Church.

But, with all concession to the undoubted truth of this account, expedient considerations cannot have been negligible for a young man who found himself caught in the position of a Catholic in Elizabethan England, especially for a young man as promising and as ambitious as Donne was in his early years, and as sharp to the ways of the world. There is often something a little forced about Donne's jibes at the papists in his later verse and prose, and I think that this excess is not merely the attitude of public overassertiveness which one sees in our times in the reformed Marxist. Elements of that public defensiveness against those who might still suspect him of Catholic sympathies are certainly present in Donne's work, but I think the attitude had deeper roots in Donne's defensiveness against himself, against a lurking sense that he had sold short his conscience at the counter of the World.

Donne never said this in so many words, but it is striking to see how readily his imagination snaps back into specifically Catholic patterns of thought in poems which were almost certainly written after he had abandoned Catholicism, and particularly in poems of a satiric cast in which he voices his distaste for worldly values and his sense of separateness from the normal concerns of English life. At moments like this, he seems to think of himself almost instinctively as an oppressed Catholic, suffering at the hands of the World. In the third Satire Donne dissociates himself sarcastically from the type figure of Mirreus, who naïvely and superstitiously loves the rags of Rome, but in the passage which I have cited from that Satire, and in other passages in the poem, his bitterness over the oppression of religious nonconformists shows clearly; and in the fourth Satire, probably written several years later and certainly after 1597,[32] his Catholic bias is still in evidence. It is strong also in "The Progress of the Soul," as Donne originally planned the poem, and that poem was certainly written after he had publicly stripped off the Romish rags. It shows in the fact, as reported by Jonson, that Luther and probably Calvin were to appear in the poem as incarnations of the soul of evil which had finally entered into Queen Elizabeth, and also in Donne's sarcastic reference to Elizabeth, in the stanza I have quoted, as one of the great souls who have torn and mended "the wracks of th'Empire, and *late* Rome." In-a poem like this, which could never have been intended to pass beyond the inner circle of his friends, Donne evidently was willing to show himself clear as still a Catholic, and proudly so, in his emotional attachments, and bitter toward the royal symbol of the England which looked on that honorable intellectual estate as moral degradation and treason of mind.

But the most revealing glimpse of Donne's latent attachment to the Catholicism of his birth, and of the tendency toward haughtily defensive poses with which this early experience had marked his mind, is in "The Canonization." That self-defensive poem about John Donne's renunciation of worldly values, which, as I have argued, must have derived from his inclination to feel a certain private righteousness as he brooded on the suffering which he had incurred by his marriage, is the most clearly Catholic in its imaginative pattern of all of his major love poems. The doctrine of the personal intercession of saints was an article of belief on which the Anglican church, and Protestantism in general, had divided sharply from Rome; and to Donne's mind, skilled in the technicalities of ecclesiastical controversy, the central conceit of sainthood in that poem would have had distinctively Catholic associations, as would the comparison of the lovers to ascetic anchorites, withdrawn into their "hermitage" from the world in which ordinary people got ahead by observing "his Honour, or his Grace" and worshipping "the King's real, or his stamped face." Watching Donne's imagination go suddenly Catholic as he defends himself against the World, I think of his statement in the Preface to *Biathanatos,* one of the few direct and candid statements which Donne ever made about the formative effect on his mind of his early environment. Confessing there to "a sickly inclination" which had often disposed him to think seriously of suicide, he suggests that this cast of mind may have derived in part from the fact that "I had my first breeding and conversation with men of a suppressed and afflicted religion, accustomed to the despite of death, and hungry of an imagined martyrdom."

I think it is precisely this attitude of mind which lies behind "The Canonization," and we might take another close look at that poem, examining it now not as a poem but simply as a psychological document. I have argued earlier that the sainthood conceit must be considered as an analogy whose logical implications are, to some extent at least, to be taken seriously, and that, in view not only of Donne's personal circumstances in the years after his marriage but also of the social and intellectual climate of early Jacobean England, it was not entirely fantastic for Donne to look on his marriage as actually similar to a saintly act of renunciation. I have suggested also that the poem's equivocality of tone may have derived from the ironic self-criticism which Donne directed against the ingredient of pompous solemnity in that dramatization of himself. But I think there was a further reason for some comic self-criticism in this poem, because there is another attitude lurking behind "The Canonization" which needed all the debunk-

ing that a lively and irreverent wit could give it. A poem whose
final stanza thrust itself on the reader with such urgency must be
taken as a poem which in some sense means what it says all the
way through; and if one does take Donne at his word in the poem
and reads the central religious metaphor as in any way actually
meant—at least, as a likely metaphysical speculation—one must
account for another logical implication in that metaphor: the suggestion of the *martyrdom* of these saintly lovers. If Donne had
been more successful in pulling "The Canonization" together as
a serious philosophic poem, what would we have had—a solemn
presentation of himself and his wife (or, if one prefers, of two very
similar lovers who are dramatic characters in the poem) as high-
minded saintly figures who have been martyred for their love by a
world too gross to appreciate the nobility and purity of their relationship? Perhaps the play of irresponsible wit and irony which
keeps "The Canonization" from achieving final artistic order as a
serious poem may have saved it from something worse; because
there is something a little ugly leaking through the cracks in the
poem: a hard self-righteousness on Donne's part, and a feeling that
the world has done him wrong. It is one thing to regard oneself, as
Donne certainly did, as set off from common men by a clear superi-
ority of intellect and moral sensibilities, and to feel that, in suffering for a devoted and idealistic love affair because one has violated
the codes of a somewhat materialistic and self-seeking society, one
is rather like the clergy, initiated into mysteries which "the laity"
will never understand. But to see oneself, on those grounds, as a
martyr, who can be properly appreciated only by after ages and
whose justifier will stand at the latter day upon the earth, is quite
another affair. And unless the thought had crossed Donne's mind,
he would not have written the last two stanzas of this poem—the
stanzas where effects of basic seriousness are most strongly in evidence. Perhaps it was just as well that Donne left some loose ends
of wit playing around those stanzas to suggest that maybe the whole
thing was merely a high-spirited antic of the imagination. But the
poem is not just that; and the inclination to present the speaker
in the poem, who is surely more than half John Donne, as in some
sense truly a martyr, is certainly there.

I think that the juxtaposition of the concept of martyrdom with
distinctively Catholic patterns of thought in "The Canonization"

provides a suggestive insight into one of the conditioning causes for that instability in Donne's mind which I have postulated as an explanation for the ambiguous tonality of the poem. The querulous letters which Donne wrote from his home at Mitcham in the early 1600's certainly suggest anything but a soul at peace with itself. Even when one makes the most sympathetic allowance for the obviously just cause for his personal distress and depression in those years, there remains something morbid about those letters, evidence of hypochondria and of intermittent neuroticism. It was out of this general state of mind that "The Canonization" was probably produced, and if the poem was conceived partly as a serious act of self-justification, its wit and irony are none the less busy to keep justification from going too far, from committing Donne fully to the morbid conclusion that he has been martyred by the world, and that his act should have an important moral significance to the degenerating materialistic society from which he has withdrawn. When I balance what Donne seems to be saying in the poem against its surface effects of cheerfulness and playful exuberance, I think of a statement of D. H. Lawrence's: "One sheds one's sicknesses in books."

The attitude of mind behind "The Canonization," then, seems very similar to that reflected in the passage which I have cited from Donne's Preface to *Biathanatos:* both reveal an ironic criticism playing against these defensive dramatizations of himself which Donne's imagination inclined to. But the disposition, in moments of depression, to imagine a martyrdom for himself, and to think of himself at those times as a Catholic at odds with the World— and perhaps also as a Catholic who has had to sell short his birthright to the World that he contemns—is certainly something which Donne felt more than once.

I am not offering Donne's Catholic background as a whole explanation for the complex phenomenon of his inclination to attitudes of ascetic renunciation, of his proud individualism and aloof sense of differentness from other men in his time; but it is certainly one fact lying open to view which would have shaped and powerfully enforced those tendencies of mind in anyone as gifted, as practical minded, and as ambitious as Donne. This early environmental pressure would certainly have laid a psychological base for other attitudes which are characteristic of Donne's maturity:

for the satisfaction which he found in the aristocracy and unworldliness of what Yeats has described as "that sweet extremity of pride
that's called platonic love"; [33] and for the separatist, egocentric cast
of mind which led him to look on his love as a "little room" in
which he had shut out the World, and to dramatize it, with a sense
of gratification, as an entire and exclusive private world on which
the outer world of other people could not encroach. And the extent of this proud egocentricity in Donne's mature love poems is
remarkable. It shows in the obscurity and privacy of his processes
of thought, which make parts of "The Good-Morrow" and "The
Canonization" so inward that they are accessible only to the most
careful reader. And it shows also in Donne's intense absorption
in analyzing, and defining, and justifying his own private and peculiar experience of love. In most of those poems, moreover, there
is very little which is tangible about the other party to that love,
and little suggestion, in all Donne's psychological analyses of the
precise quality of his love experience, of any real sense of the surrender of selfhood in this love. The love—in the "A Valediction:
Forbidding Mourning," "The Good-Morrow," and "The Canonization"—is, rather, something in which the contours of self can
be preserved, defined, and dramatized. The woman usually appears
in those poems as a shadowy "thou," or merely as "we," but the
"we who are this new soul," and who are made such by love, is
hard to distinguish from the "me" that was before. The utterly
compatible union of souls which Donne celebrates seems less a
mutual self-surrender than an entire conformity of her soul to his.
These poems are veritably—in a sense of the phrase which Donne
did not intend—"dialogues of one," and we hear little in most of
them but the voice of John Donne, talking about what is hap-
pening to him. Most of Donne's serious love poems set me thinking of the young Henry James's jibe at Walt Whitman: "For a
lover, you talk too much about yourself."

Donne's inclination to attitudes of withdrawn egocentricity
shows through also, I believe, in another symptom, one which
points below the conscious attitudes of his mind—in his strong
imaginative fixation on the concept of the microcosm. That notion
was a universal commonplace in Donne's time, and the statement
that man was a little world flowed easily from the pen of any
thoughtful writer of the Renaissance; but I know of no Renais-

sance writer, not even Browne, whose mind worried the doctrine as endlessly as Donne's. The concept has an important place in the thought of all the major poems which I have examined, and it is ubiquitous in the verse and prose of Donne's later career. Moreover, Donne's mind tended to exploit a particular implication of the microcosm analogy which it did not always have for the minds of others: its significance as a philosophic validation of withdrawal and introversion. This is the conclusion which Donne derives from the concept in "The Good-Morrow," "The Canonization," and "The Sun Rising," and it obviously lurks behind "A Valediction: Forbidding Mourning" as well: one is a world in oneself, and to oneself, and in that private world one can find all that other men desire; in fact—and here Donne wrests from the doctrine of the microcosm an implication which it did not normally carry—the private world of oneself is a *better* world than the world which ordinary people know. From the time of his marriage until near the end of his career, I think Donne would have echoed, with a cold intensity of commitment which that gentle and contemplative man never knew, Browne's statement that

> the world that I regard is myself; it is the microcosm of my own frame that I cast mine eye on; for the other, I use it but like my globe, and turn it round sometimes for my recreation.[34]

4

But when Yeats proudly proclaimed his own qualifications to dine at journey's end with Landor and with Donne, his sharp eye was seeing more than Donne's cold aristocracy of mind. Yeats saw also that the strong and definite public personality which we find in Donne's poems was only Donne's Mask, and that the private personality behind the mask was in many ways antithetic to that dramatic construct of the literary imagination. The rest of Yeats's poem, "To a Young Beauty," suggests that he was thinking particularly of the contrast between the ascetic intellectuality of Donne's literary personality and the intense sexuality of his private life; but the parallel with Landor makes Yeats's point fully clear, because Yeats regarded Landor as a man who compensated, in the cool, lapidary hardness of his literary persona, for the headlong passions, the strong sexuality, and the general emotional turbulence of his personal life.[35] Yeats saw this same compensatory psychological process at work behind his own poetry, and his comments on the contrast between his own poetic persona and his private personality will stand—by inference from "To a Young Beauty"—as one of the most penetrating insights into Donne's personality:

> As I look backward upon my own writing I take pleasure alone in those verses where it seems to me I have found something hard and cold, some articulation of the Image, which is the opposite of all that I am in my daily life, and all my country is. . . .
>
> It is perhaps because nature made me a gregarious man, going hither and thither looking for conversation, and ready to deny from fear or favour his dearest conviction, that I love proud and lonely things. When I was a child . . . I found one poem . . . that delighted me beyond all others: a fragment of some metrical translation from Aristophanes wherein the birds sing scorn upon mankind.[36]

With a private life similarly disordered by strong passions and by inner conflicts between a haughty impulse to solitary contemplation and counterimpulses to gregariousness and practical achievement in the world, Donne wrote poems in which feeling is disposed coolly into orderly patterns by the firm grasp of thought, and which often attain to Yeats's aesthetic ideal of poetry "as cold and passionate as the dawn."

I have attempted the job of getting behind Donne's mask to the privacies of John Donne's personal life in my reading of "The Canonization" and of some of the other poems, and I want to address myself to that job once again in conclusion, though I do not think the conclusion can be very conclusive. I have no final answers to the puzzles of Donne's personality, but they are certainly matters which one must speculate about if one is seriously interested in Donne's work.

To get at the workings of Donne's private mind is not easy, chiefly because for most of his life, at least until he broke the mask to become the public penitent and personal testifier that we see in some of the "Holy Sonnets" and the personal passages in the sermons, Donne himself seems to have been at pains to put barriers in the way. It was, I am sure, more than a passing whimsey which led him to write, in "The Undertaking,"

> I have done one braver thing
> Than all the Worthies did,
> And yet a braver thence doth spring,
> Which is, to keep that hid.

One of the major paradoxes of Donne's work is the contrast between a body of poetry which seems far more candidly personal and autobiographical than the verse of most of his contemporaries, and a considerable body of private letters—more than we have from any important literary man of his time—which reveals little of personal significance and which tells us very few of the things about Donne's private life that we would like to know. The man who seems to manifest himself in public so bluntly and openly in poems like "Love's Alchemy" seems oddly reticent and even evasive when writing privately to his friends.

It is true that men of the Renaissance did not have the modern view of the personal letter as a mode of expression in which one is supposed to take off one's clothes and let up the blinds. It was a literary genre which could be as artificial as the Petrarchan love sonnet, and any unlocking of the heart which it performed was likely to be accomplished only after elaborate genuflections of esteem and with endless rhetorical sarabands of style. Milton, for instance, apologizes at the start of one of his letters because he is writing

> among the distractions of the town, not, as usual, surrounded by books. So if anything in this letter fails to please you or to fulfill your expectations, it shall be made good in another, upon which more pains have been bestowed, as soon as I return to the haunts of the Muses.[37]

And Donne begins one of his letters to his friend Sir Henry Goodyere with a similar apology:

> I write not to you out of my poor library, where to cast mine eyes upon good authors kindles or refreshes meditations sometimes not unfit to communicate to near friends, nor from the highway, where I am contracted and inverted into myself; which are my two ordinary forges of letters to you.[38]

But the brusque and straightforward personality who hits hard in the opening lines of so many of Donne's love poems is not the man from whose letters we would expect much in the way of courtly conventionalities or conscious rhetorical artifice; and if we are to expect carefully formulated meditations based on his reading of authors suitable to provoke philosophic contemplation, we would expect also something of the timbre of Donne's personal voice at the times when he was contracted and inverted into himself. Moreover, these epistolary formalities were by no means constantly observed in the letters of Donne's contemporaries. Queen Elizabeth and Sir Philip Sidney could court it with the best in their letters, but they could also turn their private hands to letters which sizzled with personal irritation and struck as nakedly as a whiplash on a cheek.

There is hardly any of this quality of direct, wholehearted personal utterance in Donne's letters. Even when he is writing to men who were apparently close friends—to George Gerrard, for instance, and to Sir Henry Wotton—some impulse to reticence seems at work. We find little in the letters about Donne's literary career, almost no comments on other writers, and no reflection of what seems to have been a fairly close friendship, at least a professional friendship as men of letters, with Ben Jonson. Donne's few references to his own poems and prose works, even before he came to regret them as early indiscretions, seem guarded and oblique, and apologetic beyond the conventional deprecatory pose of the Renaissance gentleman toward his literary work.[39] And sometimes we find Donne expressing concern over the possibility that a letter might be opened in transit and fall into unauthorized hands, a concern that rarely seems justified by any indiscretions or personal confidences which the letters contain. The surface impression which one gets from the letters is that of a man strongly conventional; and when one looks beneath the surface, the pervasive lack of personal color and of personal information, even in the letters of complaint and depression which Donne wrote from Mitcham in the years after his marriage, suggests a man tensed up and holding himself in reserve, unwilling to manifest, even to such intimates as he had, much of what is in his private mind.

These letters show us, I think, how much the apparently frank personal revelations of Donne's love poems are calculated and selec-

tive, and they suggest the extent of the personal reticences which
those public literary disclosures conceal. But the explosive brusqueness and the open-throated forthrightness of speech in many of
those love poems suggest something else: that this vigorous, candid,
and clear-minded literary personality, who scorns the conventional
artifices of poetic expression and takes us roughly by the collar with
"For God's sake hold your tongue, and let me love," was not
only a dramatic creation which derived from only a part of what
Donne was personally; it was also a literary formulation which
served, for Donne himself, the psychological function of providing
a release for the inner tensions and conflicts of mind which choked
his utterance in his private letters.

The pattern of emotional logic which recurs in many of Donne's
love poems—in "The Sun Rising," for instance, "The Canonization," and "The Good-Morrow"—has just this suggestion of psychological release. Those poems burst on the reader with a spurt
like the opening of a safety valve, and it is only after they have
taken a stanza or two to blow themselves out that they settle to
emotional calm and intellectual harmony, and that the verse begins to move with evenness and stability. And other poetic effects
to which Donne inclines suggest that his verse had its origin in the
release of strong psychic tensions: his fondness for explosively
theatrical openings, for effects of intellectual shock and surprise,
and for verse movement which is rough and energetic. Like many
other critics of Donne's work, I have often had recourse to dynamic
metaphors in trying to describe the emotional suggestion of the
literary progress of Donne's poems, because those metaphors reflect the particular quality of my response to Donne's deployment
of his literary materials. Apart from the obvious suggestions of
energy and tension in the rhythmic surface of the verse, I find something fundamentally taut and dynamic at the core of Donne's
poems, in the psychological character of the experience that they
communicate, which eludes analysis and definition. I know of only
one other English poet, in fact, whose verse is as strongly dynamic
in its essential quality as Donne's—Gerard Manley Hopkins. And
in Hopkins' poetry this dynamism clearly derives from the dis-
charge of the psychic conflicts and repressions which clenched Hopkins' personal life.

I think, then, that the literary personality which we find in

Donne's poetry was a Mask in the full sense which Yeats gives to that special term: not only was it different from, and even antithetic to, much that Donne was in his personal life, but this vigorous and nonconformist persona also gave that private life completion by providing compensation and release for its inner conflicts, its reticences and evasions, and its many conventionalities. And the evidence that Donne saw his inner life as split and torn is very clear. I have spoken in the preceding chapter about the recurrence of the logical pattern of the Debate between the Body and the Soul as the basic subject matter behind a great deal of Donne's poetry. And that conceptual articulation of his personal experience as essentially an unstable conjunction of the disparate elements of Body and Soul is reflected also in Donne's thought—in his tendency to dispose all of his knowledge around the concept of the contrast between Matter and Spirit, to try to organize everything which he knew about the world into this logical pattern of conflict and antithesis. This concept of the conjunction in all nature of the disparate elements of "things visible" and "things invisible" was, of course, a fundamental logical pattern in all the thought of the Renaissance, and it was as much a universal commonplace as the doctrine of the microcosm. But what is unusual about Donne's employment of this philosophic commonplace is the avidity with which his mind seizes on it—to the virtual exclusion of other structural concepts by which Renaissance thought defined the principle of "correspondence" in the Nature of Things and the conformity of the macrocosm to the microcosm—and also the lengths to which he went in order to get all of his thought systematized into this dualistic logical scheme.

But I think Donne's best poems, in which this body-soul dualism is a recurrent structural concept, provide less significant evidence of the central place which it occupied in his thought than some of his worst ones. His generally feeble and listlessly written commendatory epistles to Noble Ladies labor this conceptual antithesis endlessly. It provides the recurrent subject matter and imaginative pattern for those poems in praise of the Countess of Bedford in which we see Donne just mechanically running through a routine of intellectual intrication, like a dutiful Boy Scout practicing the standard knots. The Countess was an important patron of poets, and though Donne never seems to have been able to work up much personal feeling for her, a patron was something that he needed, and she must get a poem from time to time in celebration of her exemplary virtues. What to write about?—oh, the way in which she shines above other ladies because her beauty is that of the soul and not just of the body, and how his love for her is Platonic, and all that: the rest can be filled out with plenty of analogies about the dualism of spirit and matter throughout the universe. Donne can do this with his left hand, turning his imagination out to grass and trusting it to follow, out of habit, the well-worn paths. As soon as we learn that the lady stands out above all other women, we can fill in the rest of the poem for ourselves if we know these deeply ingrained patterns of Donne's thought: she is to ordinary women as the soul is to the body, form to matter, the elixir to the mithridate, gold to dross, the king to the state, the clergy to the laity, the active principle of the sun to the passive principle of earthly matter, angels to mortals, the spheres to the earth, substance to accidents, and so on. When Donne's imagination is turning over on only a few cylinders, this is the way it works, because his more vigorous intellectual activity had been constantly occupied with fitting all of his ideas into this dualistic pattern.

One of the most revealing contrasts, however, between the workings of Donne's mind and those of the minds of many of his contemporaries as they explored the patterns of analogy which demonstrated the correspondence of all things in the Ordered Universe, is the narrowness of Donne's intellectual focus on this single principle of correspondence. Another structural principle, which was more interesting to the minds of Shakespeare and Milton and many other men of the Renaissance, seems to have had little imaginative appeal to Donne—the principle of organism, of the harmonious interaction of all the subordinate parts of the various subsystems in the cosmos, and the harmonious interrelation of all these subsystems in the great system of God's Design. Donne had little feel for those stock Renaissance analogies which paralleled the beehive, or the garden, or the harmony of the spheres, to the peace and happiness of the Body Politic when each citizen plays his assigned role in the state and is duly obedient to his natural superiors, or to the serenity in the "state of mind" of man when the emotions and the animal passions do not rebel against the sovereignty of reason and when the body answers happily and obediently to its natural lord, the soul. Donne employed these analogies on occasion, as any writer of the Renaissance would have, but they had nothing like the appeal to his imagination, nor the central place in his thought, of the analogies based on the principle of dichotomy. The philosophic imaginations of Shakespeare and Milton tended to see the natural state of both the great world and the little world of man as one of inner harmony and peace, but Donne's mind found it more congenial to regard the natural condition of the universe, and the natural state of man, as one of disunity and precarious balance between components which were inherently disharmonious. Even in "The Ecstasy," where Donne expressed his puzzlement at discovering that body and soul could be compatible and where he explored the evidence that this principle of the natural conjunction of matter and spirit was at work throughout the universe, he still saw man and the cosmos not as a richly organic harmony but rather as a resolution of the conflicting natures of two components. And the normal emphasis in Donne's macrocosmic analogies is on the fact of conflict and dichotomy. The world which he contemplated in himself was a world of two parts, split and at odds with itself:

> I am a little world made cunningly
> Of elements, and an angelic sprite . . .

And from that unstable microcosm his mind reached out to find that in this unhappy plight he was not alone, that this disharmony was also the condition of all created things.

Faced with this sense of a continual discord in himself, and concerned to analyze it rationally, it was certainly to Donne's advantage that the world with which he had to deal was, if not the "beautiful world" which Matthew Arnold thought an advantage to a poet, at least a logically ordered and reasonable world. It was fortunate that he could find in the traditional thought of his age, in the massive philosophic structure of the Christian world view, something which a similarly divided man like D. H. Lawrence could not find in the thought of the twentieth century: a metaphysical validation for his inner conflicts which provided psychological support for the burdens that experience had laid on his rationality, and which gave him the sense that, however different his life seemed from that of other men in his society, he nevertheless belonged to his universe. To watch Donne clutching at every instance of the dualism of matter and spirit throughout the universe is to see how much that soul which loved to be subtle to plague itself needed the psychological support of this metaphysical structure to give manageable intellectual form to the data of its personal experience.

For all of the skepticism and the irreverence with which Donne sometimes juggled the ideas of the Christian *Summa,* his mind never moved far outside the structural pattern of its basic concepts. The last section of the nineteenth Elegy, where Donne equates the body and the soul and parallels a woman's genitals with the Essence of God, is a piece of shocking heresy, but it is a heresy which operates within the logical frame of Christian theology and is developed in terms of its central concepts. Donne ventures his anti-Christian conclusions here by merely inverting the standards of value which Christian thought had assigned to matter and to spirit. His outrageous paradox in this passage actually reveals a far stronger dependence in his mind on the formulations of Christian metaphysics than we see in Marlowe's mind in the following relatively innocent-looking passage:

> Nature that framed us of four elements,
> Warring within our breasts for regiment,
> Doth teach us all to have aspiring minds.
> Our souls, whose faculties can comprehend
> The wondrous architecture of the world
> And measure every wandering planet's course,
> Still climbing after knowledge infinite,
> And always moving as the restless spheres,
> Wills us to wear ourselves and never rest
> Until we reach the ripest fruit of all,
> That perfect bliss and sole felicity,
> The sweet fruition of an earthly crown.

The speculations on Epicurean materialism, which Marlowe has here projected into the dramatic character of Tamburlaine, are much more fundamentally heretical than the materialistic implications of Donne's conceit in Elegy 19, because Marlowe has been able to pull his mind entirely free from the logical formulations of Christian theology. His speaker has blithely derived all the soul's thirst for philosophic knowledge, and all man's intellectual aspiration, simply from the physical principles of matter, and he entertains no philosophically idealist concepts whatsoever. And the intellectual shock of the word "earthly" in the final line, after the false imaginative leads provided by the Christian tags on the preceding lines have led us to expect "heavenly crown," makes the shock effects of the nineteenth Elegy seem merely naughty by comparison. Donne's imagination, at its most daringly speculative, never got this far from the philosophic structure of medieval thought, and I believe that Donne would have felt lost if it had.

The evidence that the strong speculative impulse which Donne himself described as a "voluptuousness, . . . an hydroptic, immoderate desire of humane learning and languages," derived from a psychological need much deeper and stronger than that which motivates the philosophic speculations of most men raises a fundamental interpretive question about all of Donne's poetry. To what extent are Donne's paradoxical conceits and philosophic analogies metaphors which are actually intended to establish a philosophic statement? Is Donne essentially a philosophic poet, throwing the whole weight of intellectual conviction behind these analogies between his subjective experience and the objective facts or theories about the heavenly spheres, alchemy, geography, and the mystery of resurrection, and using these analogies essentially as an imaginative mode for communicating metaphysical ideas? Or should we look on bursts of analogical philosophic ingenuity like the conceit of the earth and the spheres in "The Good-Morrow," or the Platonic Love conceit in Elegy 19, as primarily expressive vehicles for emotional states, literary formulations in which the statement of philosophic truth is not a major concern, and in which Donne has simply turned his imagination loose on ideas without bothering to observe a preliminary check of intellectual responsibility? [40]

I have leaned to the first answer—to the view that Donne's poetry is literally metaphysical in the common sense of that term —in my interpretation of some of the poems which I have examined. The other view, which has had some currency in modern criticism, is reflected in T. S. Eliot's statement that Donne "was more interested in *ideas* themselves as objects than in the *truth*

of ideas," that he derived some inner satisfaction merely from playing with philosophic doctrines, from "petting and teasing" these
"mental objects" as an activity which was an end in itself rather
than a means to truth.[41] Joan Bennett, in one of her essays on
Donne's poetry, expresses a similar view. She sees Donne as a
practitioner of Eliot's "objective correlative" theory of poetic creation, as a man who uses abstract ideas in his poetry because he is
searching for "the intellectual equivalents of emotion." Citing the
opening of the seventh Holy Sonnet and the passage on the "new
Philosophy" in "The First Anniversary," she argues that in these
passages Donne

> is not philosophizing, he is expressing a state of mind by re-
> ferring to a background of ideas. He is no more a philosophical
> poet because he makes use of ideas than Shelley is a descriptive
> poet because he makes use of things seen. . . . Donne is not
> discussing whether the world is round or flat, nor the validity
> of the "new philosophy"; he is using these exciting specula-
> tions to express and define his emotion.[42]

I think this view is largely wrong, though it has much to recom-
mend it. It is certainly true that Donne's virtuosities of metaphysical analogy are often poetic vehicles for states of emotional excitement; and when one sees him treating the doctrines of alchemy or
astrology seriously in the conceits of one poem and rejecting those
doctrines as imposture in the conceits of another, one is tempted to
conclude that he is using these metaphysical analogies simply because they are the mode by which his mind articulated states of
feeling and not because he is concerned to present statements of
sound truth about the objective world. But Mrs. Bennett's interpretation seems to me somewhat unhistorical, and I think it derives,
in part at least, from the fact that the modern mind has found it
much easier than the Renaissance mind did to draw a sharp division
between fact and fantasy in the realm of theoretical speculation
about the natural world. With its reliance on the test of experimental method, the modern mind can haul the theories of alchemy
and astrology into the research laboratory and settle, once and
for all, whether they work and therefore whether they are sound
doctrine; and it can be puzzled by Donne's failure to do the same
and to make up his mind about whether these ideas are true or

false. But to the man of Donne's age, living before the development of the experimental method, there was no such sure yardstick for measuring the factuality of theory, and many of the generally accepted metaphysical doctrines about the world of nature lay in an intellectual twilight zone between fact and fantasy into which the modern mind rarely ventures and in which it does not feel at ease. To men of Donne's age the skepticism suggested by the fact that alchemy did not always work in practice, and that alchemists were often charlatans, was of some importance; but it was also important that the alchemic theory of matter was, as they would have said, "reasonable," because it was logically consistent with the metaphysical principles of the Ordered Universe. These doctrines might therefore be true, whether any chemic had yet got the Elixir or not. The modern intellectual equivalent to this kind of Renaissance scientific speculation is not the body of empirically provable concepts found in the doctrines of Newtonian physics and of normal medical therapy, but rather the speculative adventures of Freudian psychoanalysis, or—for a closer parallel—the doctrines of atomic physics, in which the theorist finds himself in a fantasy world where little actually corresponds to the daily evidence of one's senses, and where matter and light seem sometimes particles and sometimes wave phenomena—and maybe both, or neither—but where abstract mathematical accounts of these phenomena do seem to demonstrate a logical consistency with pre-existing, and somewhat tentative, theories about the natural world. I think the thought of modern atomic physics offers a rough parallel to the kind of intellectual validity which Donne's critical mind found in many of the metaphysical analogies that he explored through the conceits of his poetry. And for this reason I think it is generally true that in his poems he is presenting those conceits fundamentally as philosophic statements which are, or may well be, factually true.

But that interpretation of the motive behind Donne's use of metaphysical concepts as poetic material, an interpretation which makes Donne fundamentally and consistently a philosophic poet, is too simple an answer; and it must yield about halfway to Eliot's view that Donne was not really interested in the truth of the ideas he deals with, and to Mrs. Bennett's contention that he used these ideas merely as "the intellectual equivalents of emotion."

Even when one grants that it was harder for the Renaissance mind than for the modern mind to decide finally on the objective truth of scientific or metaphysical theory, and that many such questions, like that of the choice between the Ptolemaic and the Copernican astronomies, offered an open philosophic option to men in Donne's time, it is still very clear that Donne's shifting emotional states could sometimes override the claims of intellectual consistency or factual probability in dictating his choice of metaphysical concepts for the imagery of his verse—so much so, at times, that one wonders whether Donne really cares very much about whether these concepts are objectively true. "The First Anniversary" and "A Valediction: Forbidding Mourning" were probably written within about a year of each other.[43] In the mood of personal depression and extravagant pessimism in which Donne wrote the "Anniversary," he turns, for the literary materials of his picture of the chaos of his world, to the doctrine of the Decay of Nature and to the theories of Copernican astronomy. But in the "Valediction," where his mood is one of intellectual assurance and emotional peace, the astronomical imagery is Ptolemaic, and we find Donne analogizing his personal experience to the sure, unchanging order of the pre-Copernican universe. Whatever degree of objective validity he may have assigned to the scientific doctrines which he used in the two poems, they are certainly, to an important degree, objective correlatives for the emotional temper of his own subjectivity. Moreover, for all his interest in the new astronomy and all the indications that, at the time he wrote "The First Anniversary," Donne had accepted its doctrines, his imagination kept reaching back to the logical pattern and system of the old world view. Most of the astronomical images in his later religious poems, and even some of the images in "The First Anniversary," are Ptolemaic. And in the "Hymn" written in his sickness, after manifesting his excitement over Magellan's voyage around the new continent of America, Donne turns to imagery based on the old three-continent world of medieval geography to express the emotional assurance of his belief in salvation. In this poem, the neat and logically symmetrical patterns of the medieval world view are obviously philosophic formulations which Donne's mind associates, perhaps subconsciously, with its emotional peace.

Moreover, if we try to regard all of the metaphysical analogies in Donne's verse as vehicles for intellectually valid philosophic statements, we can find him being oddly casual about the intellectual quality of the conceits which he combines in a single poem. In "A Valediction: Forbidding Mourning," for instance, the analogy between the two contrasting kinds of love and the contrast between the earth and the spheres would have seemed, to a thoughtful man of the Renaissance, a parallel of the highest philosophic respectability, at least as metaphysical speculation. But the analogy between the union of the souls of separated lovers and the ductility of gold would have seemed more dubious, though not entirely without significance, for purposes of sound argument. And the analogy between the lovers' souls and the legs of a compass has a validity of an entirely different kind, and very little philosophic significance. Similarly, in the "Hymn to God, My God, in My Sickness," the musical analogy of the first stanza derives from a thoroughly presentable philosophic doctrine, but the conceit from geographical exploration which follows has very little argumentative validity as a proof of the specific conclusion that "death doth touch the resurrection." And, after the qualifying skepticism of "we think," how much probatory value are we to assign to the Eden-Calvary paradoxes of the last two stanzas? A poet centrally concerned with devising an argumentative poetic presentation of objective truth would have given these conceits a more careful logical scrutiny before he bundled them together in a single poem. Donne's array of analogical arguments in these two poems would never have passed muster before a philosophic poet like Milton, who stands as though always on trial, ready to answer to any man for the degree of metaphysical validity which he assigns to any of the standard cosmological analogies which he uses in his verse, and for the soundness and logical consistency of his philosophic statements. In *Paradise Lost* Milton examines the two astronomies, shows why he thinks it impossible to choose surely between them and makes clear why he prefers the Ptolemaic theory; and when he introduces Copernican theories at some points in his narrative, he is careful to present them as alternative hypotheses for certain astronomical phenomena which are possibly true but less probable than the Ptolemaic accounts. Milton never treats the old astronomy as true in one poem and as false in another, as Donne does in the "Valediction" and "The First Anniversary," [44] nor combines in a single

poem the contradictory doctrines of the old and the new geography, as Donne does in the "Hymn." For all Donne's efforts to get
his ideas systematized around the logical antithesis between matter
and spirit, he never succeeded in being the kind of massively systematic thinker that Milton was; and I think it was partly for this
reason that Milton looked with scorn on Donne and his school as
lightweight and intellectually irresponsible poets, "fantastics" who
were taken with delight by "new-fangled toys, and trimming
slight." [45] In comparison with the scrupulous logical responsibility
of Milton's mind, the skittering of Donne's philosophic imagination often looks very irresponsible and seems directed by something
other than a thirst for philosophic truth.

I think it often was; and I believe that, though Donne probably
regarded his poetry as essentially philosophic, and though much
of it is, one must concede that his metaphysical conceits are at times
less devices for expressing what he has good reason to believe is—
or may be—philosophically true than they are modes for articulating subrational emotional states. It seems probable that a major
reason for Donne's addiction to exploring paradoxes in his verse,
and to elaborating philosophic analogies, in a *discordia concors*
pattern, around the concept of dualism of matter and spirit
throughout the universe, was that these logical formulations satisfied his psychological need to master the conflicts of his consciousness by giving them intellectual form. Certainly as we observe
Donne at work evolving the intricate conceit of geographical exploration in the "Hymn," excitedly working out the general analogy in terms which parallel his sickness point by point with the
exact history and even the precise navigational data of Magellan's
voyage, and then shaping the conceit up into the ingenious triplicate pattern of three straits, three continents, and three sons of
Noah, we are observing something which I can see only as the
pursuit of form as an end in itself. It is the effect of intellectual
form, rather than philosophic statement, which Donne is reaching
for here. I do not think he is concerned, at this point in that poem,
to reveal an order inherent in objective reality: I think he is concerned to impose an order on himself. The impulse behind his
development of that conceit arose from depths of the psyche which
Donne could articulate in no other way. And I think we must concede—unless we accept, as I cannot do, the scholastic explanation

for the pursuit of form in art—that our responses to the effects of
form in this passage derive from depths of our own consciousness
which we do not understand. The psychological need that drives
Donne in this passage is a need which all men feel in some degree,
but the passionate intensity with which he goes at the job here
shows that for him the imperative could sometimes be wholly
peremptory.

I think this need for the pressure of some external force of pattern on his consciousness shows through in Donne's work in another
way. I suspect that it was a major reason for his preference for
elaborate stanza forms in his poetry. Other critics, whose compe-
tence to speak with authority on these matters is beyond question,
have looked with admiration on Donne's virtuosity in exploiting
the metrical possibilities of those stanzas; and I can only register
my dissent. As I read the "Songs and Sonnets," I often find myself
almost entirely unaware of the stanza form as a device which enters
significantly into my experience of the poems. There are times when
Donne certainly makes his stanza pattern count, as he does in "Go,
and catch a falling star," in "Sweetest love, I do not go," and in the
first two stanzas of "The Blossom"; but there are also many times
when he does not. In "The Indifferent," for instance, is there any
sound artistic reason, in terms of the general or particular rhythmic
effects of the poem, for Donne to use so complicated a stanza pattern, with the number of stresses in a line varying 4–6–7–5–4–4–
5–5–5? I cannot see that this metrical variety produces in this poem
any significant effects which could not have been produced by a
series of pentameter lines, or at least by a combination of pentameter with tetrameter. I think it is only rarely that Donne exploits, as an important element in the literary effect of a poem, the
prosodic possibilities latent in these complex verse forms, possibilities for the effects of rhythm and sound which derive from variation
in the length of musical phrase and from the appearance of unexpected rime. I realize that in using these stanzas Donne was
working for the effect of the speaking voice, and not for the effect
of song which one gets from such stanzaic verse as the lyrics of
Jonson's masques. But Jonson, in poems like "A Pindaric Ode,"
could write verse as roughly muscular and as spoken as Donne's
and still exploit the rhythmic potentialities of a complex verse form
in a way that Donne rarely does. To my ear, many of the intricate

stanza forms in the "Songs and Sonnets" do not yield enough returns
to the reader to justify the trouble which Donne must have gone
to in order to use them, and I suspect that they were chosen with
an eye less to the satisfactions of the reader than to the needs of
the writer—because they served Donne's need for some patterning
force operating on his consciousness as he developed a poem. To
some extent, I suppose, this reason lies behind any poet's employment of set verse forms. In this matter, as in Donne's use of other
formal devices in his verse, the difference is not one of kind but
of degree: he inclines to extremely complex stanza patterns, and
to a great variety of them, and often makes very little purposeful
artistic use of them once he has set them up. To devise a stanza
form as complicated as that in "The Indifferent," only to ride so
roughshod over it that the reader is likely not to notice the stanza
pattern at all, seems rather peculiar.

This theory finds support in the contrast between the sharp
structural characteristics of most of the "Songs and Sonnets," where
Donne has before him the symmetrical blueprint of his stanza design as a device to enforce logical and imaginative organization,
and the relative formlessness of the logical and imaginative flow in
much of his verse in heroic couplets and in much of his prose.
Donne laid out the logical structure of his sermons with a ruler
and a compass, but within the major structural units, when his
mind is faced with nothing but a blank sheet of paper, he can break
loose and start spinning out analogies with as little controlling
design as we find in many sections of the *Devotions*. And some of
the "Elegies" and the verse letters in couplets just go on and on,
tumbling from conceit to conceit without any general artistic plan.
I suspect that it was Donne's awareness of how chaotically his
imagination could operate when it had nothing to check it but an
infinite series of couplet rimes which moved him to devise the
careful logical outline and intricate structural devices which he
used in "The First Anniversary." But despite the restraining force
of this elaborate mechanism of structure, that poem is more dis-
organized than most of the verse in the "Songs and Sonnets." I think
that Donne urgently needed the pre-existent structural blocks of
a stanza form to rein in his rampaging imagination and make it
operate at its best.

But when his imagination is operating at its best, the most

striking trait of Donne's verse is its sharp formal design. What-ever the disorders of Donne's private consciousness were, his literary persona could be a fanatic for order. There have been few poets in English whose imaginations were so strongly structural as the imagination which one sees at work in the poems that I have ana-lyzed. And sometimes—as in the Platonic Love conceit in Elegy 19 and the tricky imaginative patterns of the last two stanzas of the "Hymn to God, My God, in My Sickness"—one sees Donne push-ing devices of structure into minutiae of detail which might escape even the most careful reader. The closest parallel in English litera-ture to Donne's concern with intricacies of design in his verse, a concern which seems at times almost obsessive, is in the work of James Joyce. And that similarity points to other parallels between the work and the personalities of the two men. Joyce was a man whose inner life was clearly one of great disorder. Like Donne, he was much attracted by the concept of the conflict between the body and the soul: he employed that concept in *Ulysses* both as a central device of artistic structure and as a central thematic idea. And Joyce compensated for the chaos of his personal consciousness by a fanatical pursuit of artistic order in his work, a pursuit which extended into intricacies of pattern that few readers could be ex-pected to notice. He found in these imaginative patterns—in "the rhythm of beauty" which resulted from "the first formal esthetic relation of part to part in any esthetic whole"—an effect of emo-tional peace: in his view, these devices of form produced the "es-thetic stasis" which he sought in his work.[46] To Joyce's mind, the achievement of the artist in imposing an ideal imaginative fixity on the chaotic and disturbing flux of his consciousness, a conscious-ness which was as Protean as the shifting sands and the tides of the sea, was an act from which the artist, as well as his readers, derived the satisfaction of feeling that the disorder of life had been mastered by the mind and could therefore be contemplated with serenity. Joyce was, moreover, a writer who adopted an atti-tude of cold arrogance toward his readers, and this arrogance led him into privacies and obscurities of expression. He was a relapsed Catholic who was never at peace over that apostasy, who felt alienated from the society of his birth and persecuted by that society, and who tended to identify himself, for this reason, with the figure of St. Stephen the Martyr. And he was a writer whose work seems strongly personal and autobiographical but whose intellectualist and ascetic literary persona appears to have been very different from much that he was in his private life. Finally, one of Joyce's comments on the literary usefulness which he found in the philosophic structure of Vico's theory of history looks like something that Donne could have said about the usefulness which he found in the analogical intellectual patterns of the Christian world view: "I would not pay over-much attention to these theories, beyond using them for all they are worth, but they have gradually forced themselves on me through the circumstances of my own life." [47]

I think, however, that this statement of Joyce's is evasive and defensive, and that it is partially untrue. For Joyce, as for Donne, the analogical philosophic patterns which he used in his work unquestionably satisfied personal psychological needs, and they could, on occasion, be employed for that reason alone. But Joyce certainly thought of himself as fundamentally a seriously philosophic writer; and I think this is even more true of Donne, whose paradoxes and metaphysical analogies enjoyed a far wider intellectual acceptance among his contemporaries than Vico's cyclic theory has found in our own time, and could therefore be assigned a much higher logical probability, if not certainty, as vehicles for sound philosophic statement.

I do not know how far these analogies between the two men can be pushed—and the considerable difference between seventeenth-century England and twentieth-century Ireland certainly warns against pushing them too far—but they seem to me highly suggestive for anyone who wants to pry into the mysteries of Donne's personality.

I offer, finally, as a speculation, another personal analogy which may help us in looking behind Donne's literary mask—and it is an analogy which points, incidentally, to many of the temperamental affinities between Donne and T. S. Eliot. It should be of some significance, because it is a parallel which Donne himself tended to draw: the parallel with St. Paul. Many of Donne's sermons reveal, in an understandably oblique way, his inclination to identify himself with St. Paul in later life; and he spoke through the voice of St. Paul in the final stanza of his deathbed "Hymn." Isaak Walton, who was one of Donne's parishioners, was also inclined, probably in response to the hints of the sermons, to drama-

tize Doctor Donne as the St. Paul *de nos jours*. Donne identified
himself also with St. Augustine, on the same obvious grounds of
an early career of worldliness and fleshly sin which led to later
penitence, ascetic renouncement, and conversion to the preaching
of God's Word; but the figure of Paul seems to have occupied a
more prominent place in Donne's imagination in his later years.
The fact that in these years he was Dean of St. Paul's, and was
thus designated, by the accident of his position, as the recipient of
the mantle, was a fact whose significance did not escape Donne's
dramatic imagination, as one sees from his Paul's Day sermons;
and this apparent coincidence may well have led him to meditate,
in the manner of the Eden-Calvary analogies of his "Hymn," on
the mysterious suggestion of Design at work behind the apparently
casual process which had·brought John Donne, after long wander-
ings of soul, to speak in the place consecrated as the English pulpit
of Paul. Donne's explicit statements of his sense that he was in some
ways like the saint do not extend, naturally enough, beyond the
humbly penitent suggestion that his Jack Donne–Doctor Donne career had fallen, like Paul's, into the immemorial edifying pattern
of sin and reciprocal atonement. But I wonder whether Donne,
with his psychological curiosity and his skill at analyzing the subjective phenomena of religious experience, did not find other
points of analogy as he brooded over the personal similarities between himself and St. Paul. The parallel certainly extended to
Paul's great literary talent and power of mind, and to his sensational efficacy as a preacher of God's Word "to others' souls," an
efficacy which derived in large part from the fact that he was also
preaching to his own and was struggling to resolve his shakiness
of conviction and fears over his personal salvation. But I wonder
whether Donne saw the parallel as extending also to Paul's morbidities of mind—to his mercurial instability which led him to be all
things to all men and then to feel shame at that meretriciousness;
to his fascination with sex which struggled against his ascetic impulses of revulsion against the flesh; to his neurotic fear of death
and his concern with the corruption of the body in the grave; and
finally to his inclination to arrogant self-righteousness, and to
imaginings of personal martyrdom. As I read the embarrassing revelation in the last chapters of the second Epistle to the Corinthians
of a passionate ego in a state of very poor repair, of a man teetering

sadly in mental equilibrium as he tries to come out of his more comfortable pose of not suffering fools gladly and to put on humility, I find a record of private turbulences and vulgarities of soul which looks like something that the personal reticences of John Donne may well have concealed.

5

To say this is not to condemn but to define, and to account for the vicissitudes of Donne's reputation. There have been few writers of any consequence who were not, as Auden said of Yeats, "silly like us" in their personal lives. And against any suggestion of condescension in what I have said about Donne's personality stands the solid evidence of intellectual and artistic achievement in the poems which I have discussed in earlier chapters. In a sense, of course, Donne's morbidities of personality do not count in evaluating that artistic accomplishment, as the *locus classicus* of Richard Wagner serves to remind us. But Donne's poems partake, nevertheless, of his peculiarities of temperament: despite the deliberate dramatic projection through which those personal qualities find expression in his verse, they retain there an inescapably personal and autobiographic character. And to some extent those peculiarities do matter, as Wagner's do, in evaluating his work: they register in his poetry for virtue and for fault, though they appear in an altered form and stand judgment there before standards of value which are partially different from those by which one might reasonably judge a man's personal character. The fact that Donne's poetry has alternately been admired and scorned over the past three-and one-half centuries is largely a result of the difference in the value which different periods in our recent history have assigned to those temperamental peculiarities which his poetry reflects.

When Sir Edmund Gosse, some fifty years ago, made a careful and sympathetic effort to understand Donne's personality, the only conclusion which he could arrive at was that Donne was a riddle and very odd indeed, a conclusion which all the less sympathetic critics of Donne's work had been settling for since the middle of the seventeenth century. But I do not think that Gosse failed to solve the puzzles of Donne's personality just because he was an Edwardian. And Dryden and Dr. Johnson, to mention only two of those who have found Donne and his poetry peculiar or fantastic, were not men whose judgments one can just brush aside; nor do the tastes and values of their similar but somewhat different ages represent such aberrations from Dr. Johnson's narrow but not foolish standard of "that uniformity of sentiment" which characterizes "human nature," to justify one in dismissing those standards of judgment as negligible. Clearly Donne *was* odd personally, and, in a partly different sense, his poetry is. It is for this reason that he does not stand free, as Shakespeare does, and that he never will: his work will always have to abide the question of the dominant philosophic values of a particular era. And it is those values, whether they are consciously formulated or not, which, in the last analysis, determine literary taste.

But Donne's work could not have so strongly engaged the attention of serious-minded readers in two modern centuries if he had been just a brilliant freak, if his oddness had been a merely exotic and inconsequential aberration from the norm of human nature. If sober and thoughtful men in Donne's day and in our own have discovered much in his writings to occupy their minds, it must be that they have found him not merely silly like us but that they have seen in that apparent queerness substantial values which did not appear to most readers of the ages of Dryden and of Dr. Johnson. Donne certainly believed this himself, and to the end of his life, though with many vacillations, he stood to his conviction that he could not actually be as different as he seemed when measured against the conventional forms into which the more ordered lives of others had been cast, that the data of his personal peculiarities must be relevant to truth, and that these results of the experiment which was his life should be defined and recorded.

Obviously those data of the complexities and oddities of the human spirit and of the universe in which it found itself did not attract the men of the Enlightenment. In fact, I think the more thoughtful men of that time often found these facts rather frightening. Dr. Johnson, at least, seems to have had strong and practical reasons to be frightened at the circumstances of his own morbidities and oddnesses of mind and to cling tightly to the stabilizing values of Reason and Common Sense and conformity to the norm of Nature. But something of the same uneasiness, of a shudder and recoil before the strangeness of the abyss which the ruthless and disjunctive intellectual adventures of the late Renaissance had opened before man's mind, shows beneath much of the thought of the period of the Restoration in England, that period which first reacted strongly against Donne's kind of poetry. It was as much on this shaky irrationalist base as on the solid intellectual promise of the philosophic method of scientific rationalism that men built the great, impermanent structure of the Age of Reason. That disquiet over what might lurk behind the Veil of the Temple shows through in the eagerness of men of that time to call down the mind from impassioned private speculation about those problems of metaphysics and the mysteries of man's soul which it could not finally resolve, and turn it to the empirical enterprises of adapting oneself to the world of nature and of working out a modus vivendi with others in the world of society. And it shows in the general determination of Englishmen in the late 1600's to avoid rocking the boat by simply avoiding serious involvement with those philosophic questions of individual conscience and belief which had helped bring England to civil war in the middle of the century, and to confine the enterprise of thought, instead, to those matters on which all men could agree. It shows also in the avidity with which men of the late seventeenth century seized on the pragmatic intellectual biases of the new method of scientific research, a method of thought "so human for its use"—and also, as of course one must add, "for knowledge so divine"; [48] and it appears in the widespread popular satisfaction, in the early eighteenth century, over the fact that, after all which the seventeenth century had done to complicate the universe, Sir Isaac Newton had at last got it back into manageable form, into a simple and reasonable mechanism which the simple and reasonable mechanism of man's mind could understand. The same disquiet shows finally —and most importantly—in the general agreement that the time had come when rationality must learn to part society from the disorderly companions of its past, from the unruly emotions and from that faculty of mind which Dryden described, with a significant adjective, as the "lawless imagination." Something of this emotional uneasiness—and also of intellectual expediency—is mixed in with the spirit of serene, objective philosophic inquiry in that passage in the Preface to *An Essay Concerning Human Under-*

standing in which John Locke turns his back on the mentality of the Renaissance and begins his formulation of the philosophic biases which were to dominate the thought of the era that succeeded Donne's. The first problem of thought, Locke decided, was

> to take a survey of our own understandings, examine our own powers, and see to what things they were adapted. Till that was done I suspected we began at the wrong end, and in vain sought for satisfaction in a quiet and sure possession of truths that most concerned us, whilst we let loose our thoughts into the vast ocean of Being; as if all that boundless extent were the natural and undoubted possession of our understandings, wherein there was nothing exempt from its decisions, or that escaped its comprehension. Thus men, extending their inquiries beyond their capacities, and letting their thoughts wander into those depths where they can find no sure footing, it is no wonder that they raise questions and multiply disputes, which, never coming to any clear resolution, are proper only to continue and increase their doubts, and to confirm them at last in perfect scepticism. Whereas, were the capacities of our understandings well considered, the extent of our knowledge once discovered, and the horizon found which sets the bounds between the enlightened and the dark parts of things, between what is and what is not comprehensible by us, men would perhaps with less scruple acquiesce in the avowed ignorance of the one, and employ their thoughts and discourse with more advantage and satisfaction in the other.

Doubts, questions, and skepticism; finding one's mind astray in depths where there was no sure footing, and loose on the boundless extent of the vast ocean of Being with the horizon obscured—what secure satisfaction lay in this? Better, certainly, to acquiesce in ignorance, to set a firm bound between the enlightened and the dark parts of things, and within that narrow but safe circle, to seek to be "quiet and sure."

Despite the temporarily ineffective philosophic disturbance of the Romantic movement, these simplistic and pragmatic biases dominated most of the thought of the mid-nineteenth century, as they had dominated that of the eighteenth century, and it was in these periods that Donne's reputation came nearest to full eclipse.

But in the mentality of the twentieth century those biases have been progressively on the decline. Remarking breezily on some of the characteristic enterprises and achievements of modern thought, W. H. Auden has observed that

> Love like Matter is much
> Odder than we thought.

Our time has found it rewarding, as the Enlightenment and the Victorian period did not, to investigate this oddness, for all which that investigation has cost us. In fact, that intellectual bias is beginning to emerge, at mid-century, as a distinctive philosophic preoccupation of the twentieth-century mind, as it had been of the mind of the seventeenth century. Certainly a solid reason behind the fad for Donne's poetry in our own time is that his work dramatizes, with exciting vividness and conclusive particularity, the truth that not only love and matter but also abstract thought and art—in fact, to summarize what, for all practical philosophic purposes, this series adds up to, that we ourselves—are much odder than we thought.

CHAPTER 1: SOME MINOR POEMS

"The Indifferent"

1. The dates of all four of these poems are uncertain, since we have very little sure evidence for dating the greater part of Donne's poems and can set up only a conjectural chronology for most of them. Ben Jonson told Drummond that Donne had "written all his best pieces ere he was twenty-five years old," but Jonson probably meant this remark not as praise of Donne's precocity but rather as an expression of his distaste for the more complex and difficult poems of Donne's later career, which were being admired and imitated at the time when Jonson visited Drummond. At any rate, I am pretty sure that Jonson's "best" is not mine—he knew by heart, for instance, all one hundred and fourteen lines of the clever but trivial elegy, "Upon the Loss of His Mistress's Chain." But Jonson's remark does indicate that he recognized a general change in subject or in literary manner between the verse of Donne's early career and the verse of his maturity. And what we know about Donne's life in the years before and after the crucial event of his marriage in 1601 would lead us to expect a change to a greater seriousness and introversion, and to a more unworldly standard of values in the work of his later years. That he could have written poems like "The Indifferent" and Elegy 19 in the period after his marriage is certainly possible, since he remained till the end of his life a complex and various-minded man, and since he was the kind of poet who deliberately plays imaginary roles in his verse; but from the evidence of his state of mind afforded by his letters in these years, I think it is unlikely that he would often have found occasion to do so. It is very probable, then, that "The Indifferent," Elegy 19, and "Love's Alchemy" were written in the 1590's, before Donne's marriage to Anne More, and I think "Love's Alchemy" may be later than the other two. "The Blossom" is probably a later piece than any of these poems. Its sure technical control suggests mature workmanship, and the strong likelihood that it was written to Mrs. Herbert would place it after 1607, when Donne's friendship with Mrs. Herbert began.

2. Compare Donne's use of "know" in Elegy 3, line 6; Elegy 19, line 43; and Elegy 16, line 37 ("Will quickly know thee, and know thee, alas!" —the variant reading of the line which Grierson acknowledges embarrassedly as almost certainly what Donne originally wrote). "Rob

me" probably alludes to the Renaissance medical theory that each
indulgence in the sexual act shortened a man's life by one day. This
theory seems to have preyed on Donne's mind from time to time, and
he refers to it several times in his love poetry. (Cf. e.g., "A Farewell to
Love," 24–5, and stanza 3 of "The Canonization.") For the pun on
"travail," compare Elegy 20, line 43. In "The Indifferent" Donne's
play on this word involves not only the connotative suggestion of
"trouble" but also the meaning "travel," which makes an incidental
point of wit by the antithesis to "fixed" in the following line. In the
context of the sexual terms "know" and "travail," it seems likely that
Donne intended "do" in line 11 to carry a sexual ambiguity also. "Do"
is a common sexual pun in Elizabethan English, and Donne uses the
pun several times in other poems.

3. "An Essay of Valor," in Donne, *Complete Poetry and Selected Prose*,
ed. John Hayward (New York, 1932), p. 418.

4. *Lives of the English Poets* (World's Classics), *1*, 15.

5. "The Undertaking," 21–8.

6. "The First Anniversary," 216–18.

7. The passage in Jonson's memorial poem on Shakespeare in which
these phrases occur (lines 25–42) is a typical expression of the na-
tionalistic attitude to which I am referring.

8. Carew's "Elegy upon the Death of Doctor Donne" shows the reaction
of a contemporary to this aspect of Donne's work. In this poem Carew
eulogizes Donne as the master who has established for English poetry
the literary standard of boldly autobiographic individualism. Writing
in the more strongly individualistic atmosphere of the seventeenth
century, he has this to say of Donne's achievement:

> The Muses' garden, with pedantic weeds
> O'erspread, was purged by thee; the lazy seeds
> Of servile imitation thrown away,
> And fresh invention planted; thou didst pay
> The debts of our penurious bankrupt age;
> Licentious thefts, that make poetic rage
> A mimic fury, when our souls must be
> Possessed, or with Anacreon's ecstasy
> Or Pindar's, not their own . . .   (Lines 25–33.)

9. Donne was clearly attracted by the genre of the Ovidian love elegy,
because of the chances which it offered for plays of wit and for man-

of-the-world cynicism about sex, but his Elegies, as we will see later, have a way of getting out of hand and developing into poetry of a new kind. And Donne certainly made some attempt in the Satires to follow the conventions of the genre of formal verse satire—conventions which were fairly congenial to his temperament. But the blunt, crusty, chip-on-the-shoulder moralist who is snorting his indignation in the opening lines of Satire 3—the stock persona of Juvenalian verse satire —is not the same person as the troubled and carefully thoughtful man who is exploring a religious problem in the last section of the poem; and the second speaker looks very like John Donne in propria persona.

10. "The Bait," 1–4. The sardonic comedy in Donne's realistic debunking of the idyllic world of pastoral romance in the poem is also characteristic:

> Let others freeze with angling reeds,
> And cut their legs, with shells and weeds,
> Or treacherously poor fish beset,
> With strangling snare, or windowy net:
>
> Let coarse bold hands, from slimy nest
> The bedded fish in banks out-wrest . . .

11. See "Go, and catch a falling star," "Love's Deity," "Woman's Constancy," "The Damp," and Paradoxes 6 and 10. I will investigate later Donne's use of this reversal strategy in "The Blossom," and his use of the similar device of a false-lead opening in "The Good-Morrow" and "The Canonization."

Elegy 19

12. I am using terms like "school" and "opponents" purposely. Donne himself sometimes dramatized the contemporary analysis of love as a theological dispute between rival philosophic factions. In a letter to Sir Henry Wotton he wrote: "You (I think) and I am much of one sect in the philosophy of love; which, though it be directed upon the mind, doth inhere in the body, and find piety entertainment there." (*The Works of John Donne,* ed. Alford [London, 1839], 6, 352.)

13. The following words in the opening section either are sexual puns or carry sexual ambiguities: "powers" (1), "labour" (2), "standing," "fight" (4), "world" (6), "stand" (12), "tread" (17), "received" (20). Donne gets some minor shock effects by playing these suggestions against the theological ambiguities of certain words in these lines.

"Safely" in line 17 carries the ambiguity of "in a state of salvation,"
and "receive" (line 20) is a technical theological term for a mortal's
apprehension of supernatural influences or revelations. (Cf. Donne's
use of this word in "The First Anniversary," 416. For its sexual meaning, see Webster, *The White Devil*, III, ii, 102.)

14. Cf. Sidney, *Astrophel and Stella*, Sonnet 32; Spenser, *Amoretti*, Sonnet 15; and Romeo's speech in the balcony scene (II, ii, 82):

> wert thou as far
> As that vast shore wash'd with the farthest sea,
> I would adventure for such merchandise.

The image recurs throughout Donne's poetry, usually in the form of
the conventional antithesis between the two Indies—the "India of
Spice" (the East Indies) and the "India of Mine" (the West Indies).
The phrase "Mine of precious stones" in line 29 stands as a concrete,
factual detail of the general image of America, since Donne normally
thinks of the New World as the land which offers the voyager gold
and precious stones. Cf. Sermon 14: "This sets us upon the two
hemispheres of the world; the western hemisphere, the land of gold,
and treasure, and the eastern hemisphere, the land of spices and per-
fumes." (*Works*, ed. Alford, *1*, 281–2.)

15. The detail of the general conceit which equates the woman's body
with a "kingdom" also reflects the political cast of Donne's imagination in these lines. It derives from a conventional associative pattern in the Renaissance mind which was a part of the system of "cor-
respondences" in the Ordered Universe—the analogy between the
human body and the Body Politic, which the Renaissance mind usually thought of as naturally and properly a kingdom, an autocratic
monarchy.

16. For Donne's use of "seal" as a sexual pun see Elegy 7, line 29, and
"The Relic," 29. "License" (25) and "free" (31) both carry ambiguities
of licentiousness in Renaissance usage. (Cf. *As You Like It*, II, vii, 68,
where Shakespeare plays on the sexual suggestion of both of these
words.) And I think Donne intends also a sexual reference in the word
"mine" in line 29. (See the discussion below of the opening lines of
"Love's Alchemy.") In "A Rapture," which is based in part on this
Elegy, Carew makes a similar use of "mine" as a sexual metaphor
(lines 33–4). The pun on "discovering" (= undressing) is, of course,
the logical basis for the entire conceit, since it analogizes the situation
which the poem deals with to geographical exploration.

17. This metaphor evidently made a particular appeal to Donne's imagination. He uses it as the basic image for a love directed toward the
soul in his most explicitly Platonic love poem, "The Undertaking,"
13–20. See also the parallel use of the image in the verse letters "To
Mrs. M. H." ("Mad paper stay"), 29–32, and "To the Countess of
Bedford" ("Honour is so sublime perfection"), 26; and in "A Funeral
Elegy," 61. In "Obsequies to the Lord Harrington," 12–13, Donne
refers to an "ecstasy" as an "unapparelling" of the mind. The image
appears in a sexual context in the "Epithalamion" for the Earl of
Somerset, 208–11, and it recurs throughout his other poetry in connection with treatments of the doctrines of philosophic idealism.

18. Cf. Satire 1, lines 43–4:

> And till our souls be unapparelled
> Of bodies, they from bliss are banished.

19. Compare the different effect which Donne gets from the same analogy in stanza 6 of the "Epithalamion" for the marriage of the Princess
Elizabeth. His gingerly treatment of the comparison there makes it
a casual conceit, a piece of mere cleverness with little shock value.

20. These doctrines recur throughout Donne's work. (Cf., e.g., the distinction between mediate and immediate knowledge in "The Second
Anniversary," 290–314, and the contrast between the "accidental" joys
of earthly life and the "essential" joys of heaven in the conclusion to
that poem, lines 471 ff.) The casual, glancing reference which Milton makes to these ideas in a passage in *Areopagitica* suggests how
widely current they were in the Renaissance: "but he who thinks we
. . . have attained the utmost prospect of reformation that the mortal
glass wherein we contemplate can show us till we come to beatific
vision . . ." (*Works* [Columbia edition], *4, 337*).

21. Donne substitutes "gems" for "clothes" to permit the Atalanta conceit. He is thinking of the elaborately bejewelled dress of an Elizabethan lady.

22. The phrase "earthly soul" alludes to the scholastic doctrine of the
tripartite soul. According to this doctrine, man's soul was divided
into three parts: a soul of growth, which he shared with the plants;
a soul of sense, which he shared with the animals; and a soul of reason, which was man's distinctive possession and which was the only
part of his soul that was immortal. Or Donne may be thinking of a
variant of this doctrine in Renaissance Platonic literature which

divided man's soul into two parts, a soul of appetite and a soul of reason. (See the passage on Platonic Love in Castiglione's *Book of the Courtier* [Everyman edition], pp. 282–3.) The phrase "earthly soul" refers, then, to the soul of appetite, or the soul of sense. Compare "A Valediction: Forbidding Mourning," 13–20, where Donne draws a distinction between rational lovers, whose love is based on the soul, and common lovers, whose love is mere animal sensuality:

> Dull sublunary lovers' love
> (Whose soul is sense) . . .

23. The inaccuracy of Donne's reference to the Atalanta myth is interesting as an indication of the casualness of his interest in classical mythology. He evidently thinks that the golden apples were thrown by Atalanta herself to distract the lovers who were pursuing her. Donne's references to mythology are infrequent and occur mostly in the "Elegies"—probably because he had read Ovid before he wrote some of them, or because mythological allusions were part of the machinery of the genre of the love elegy.

24. Donne frequently uses this distinction between the genitive case and the other cases of personal pronouns to suggest the metaphysical difference between the body and the soul. This grammatical trick reflects the philosophic distinction between a man's "substance," his metaphysical identity (the soul—"he," "him") and the "accidents" of his substance (the body—"his"). Cf. Elegy 18, line 26; "The Ecstasy," 51; "The Cross," 36.

25. Donne is referring here to a traditional justification for religious iconography. Cf. Sermon 27: "They had wont to call pictures in the church, the layman's book, because in them, he that could not read at all might read much." (*Works, 1,* 542.) Donne cites Calvin as his source for this analogy in Sermon 122, where he presents an expanded discussion of the idea and distinguishes between the "right use" and the "abuse" of religious pictures. (*Works, 5,* 177.)

26. The contrast between the binding and the book as an image for the distinction between the body and the soul is a common metaphor in Elizabethan literature. Cf. *Romeo and Juliet*, III, ii, 83–4 ("Was ever book containing such vile matter / So fairly bound?"), and Lady Capulet's extended development of the conceit in I, iii, 81 ff.

27. For Donne's use of "self" to mean "soul" see Satire 3, line 37, and Sermon 38: "Remember that thy soul is thyself" (*Works, 2,* 80). This usage seems to have been common in the Renaissance. Cf. Sidney, *Astrophel and Stella,* Sonnet 52, line 13.

28. I am quoting here from Hoby's translation of Peter Bembo's speech in *The Book of the Courtier* (pp. 317–22). Bembo sums up this progression in his charge to true lovers: "Let us climb up the stairs which at the lowermost step have the shadow of sensual beauty, to the high mansion place where the heavenly, amiable, and right beauty dwelleth, which lieth hid in the innermost secrets of God, lest unhallowed eyes should come to the sight of it; and there shall we find a most happy end for our desires." (Pp. 320–1.) I am citing this passage not as Donne's direct source but rather as one of the chief sources for the doctrines of Platonic Love in Elizabethan England. As I have suggested, not only this section of the Elegy but also those of Donne's other poems in which he treats Platonic Love seriously indicate that Donne was influenced only in general by the literature of Renaissance Platonism: the details of his poetic treatments of Platonic Love are usually drawn from its collateral relative, Christian mysticism, and from scholastic theology. The theological reference of a number of the details in this passage of the Elegy (lines 39–40, 42, 43–5) suggests that Donne's primary sources here are sacred rather than secular. And it is worth noting that the use of sexual imagery in treating the Mystic Experience is frequent in Christian mystical literature. The central conceit in lines 33–45 of this poem derives from a simple inversion of this kind of imagery.

29. "Revelation" is one of the terms which Donne applies specifically to the Mystic Experience. Cf. "A Letter to the Lady Carey and Mrs. Essex Riche," 53–4: "This my Ecstasy and revelation of you both." Line 42 plays, of course, with an ambiguity on "revealed" = undressed.

30. See *N.E.D.*: "impute," 2; and Holy Sonnet 6, line 13: "impute me righteous."

31. Cf. Aquinas, *Summa Theologica*, Q. 12, Art. 4: "It follows, therefore, that to know self-subsistent being . . . is beyond the natural power of any created intellect. . . . Therefore a created intellect cannot see the essence of God unless God by His grace unites Himself to the created intellect." This line of the poem plays on the phrase "imputed grace" to suggest also a woman's gracious granting of sexual favors to a lover who is all unworthy—the conventional Petrarchan love situation.

32. The connotations of "mystic" (= pertaining to the direct communion of the soul with God) in line 41 help accomplish the imaginative transition from the subject of the spiritual love of woman to that of the Mystic Experience. But the primary function of "mystic

books" is to complete the layman image of lines 39–40. The phrase develops the implied contrast between the ordinary, sensual lover (the layman who must be attracted to sacred books by their bindings) and the enlightened lover (the clergyman who is permitted to read the book and who thus learns religious mysteries directly). But it is clear from *"see* revealed," and from the rest of lines 43 and 44, which certainly refer to the Beatific Vision, that Donne discards at this point the analogy to the clergyman's understanding of a sacred book. The "revelation" of a woman's body is analogized, not just to an understanding of the religious mysteries which are "revealed" to men in a "mystic book," but rather to a kind of revelation which is seen, to the Sight of God in the Beatific Vision. The woman's body is thus equated, at this point, with God's Essence as "known" directly by the soul of the mystic, and not merely with the kind of knowledge of God which the clergyman gains through a sacred book. The ultimate reference of the book analogy to the undressing situation which the poem deals with indicates also that Donne is punning on "mystic" in its Renaissance sense of "hidden" (= dressed).

33. Compare the prayer which concludes Bembo's exposition of Platonic Love in Book 4 of *The Book of the Courtier.*

34. "Self" is used here, as in line 41, to refer to soul, or metaphysical essence. The questions of whether all souls who experienced the Beatific Vision received an equally full comprehension of God, and whether God granted, through this experience, a partial or a complete manifestation of His Essence—and thus a partial or full knowledge of Himself—had been subjects of scholastic controversy. (See *Summa Theologica,* Q. 12, Arts. 6 and 8.) Cf. Sermon 21, where Donne describes the Beatific Vision and reviews some of the controversy:

> And then [in heaven] our way to see him is *patefactio sui,* God's laying himself open, his manifestation, his revelation, his evisceration, and embowelling of himself to us there. Doth God never afford this patefaction, this manifestation of himself in his essence, to any in this life? We cannot answer yea, nor no, without offending a great part in the School, so many affirm, so many deny that God hath been seen in his essence in this life. (*Works, 1,* 423.)

35. The source for Donne's phrasing in "since that I may know" is 1 Corinthians. xiii. 12: "For now we see through a glass darkly; but then face to face: now I know in part; but then shall I know even as also I am known." This biblical allusion operates to enforce the suggestion of the Beatific Vision in the other details of these lines.

The same text lies behind the image of the "mortal glass" in Milton's reference to the Beatific Vision in the passage cited above in n. 20. And compare Donne's Sermon 154:

> *Erimus sicut angeli,* says Christ, "There we shall be as angels." The knowledge which I have by nature shall have no clouds; here it hath. That which I have by grace shall have no reluctation, no resistance; here it hath. That which I have by revelation shall have no suspicion, no jealousy; here it hath. . . . There our curiosity shall have this noble satisfaction, we shall know how the angels know by knowing as they know. (*Works, 6,* 184.)

36. Donne makes the same pun in "An Epithalamion . . . on the Lady Elizabeth and Count Palatine," 96. Cf. *Hamlet,* IV, vii, 171: "That liberal shepherds give a grosser name."

37. Cf. *Hamlet,* III, ii, 155–9:

> Hamlet: Ay, or any show that you'll show him: be not you ashamed to show, he'll not shame to tell you what it means.
> Ophelia: You are naught, you are naught.

38. I think one can trace the steps of Donne's imagination here quite closely. He seems to visualize an essence, or "form," spatially, as something located in the center of a body. See his reference, in the passage cited in note 35, to God's manifestation of His Essence as "his evisceration, and embowelling of himself." Donne's use of the word "centric" to mean "essential" carries a spatial ambiguity in "Love's Alchemy," 2, and in Elegy 18, line 36. Both of these passages show a process of imaginative association similar to that in lines 41–5 of Elegy 19. The various ambiguities which they imply for "centric" set up the following analogical progression: spiritual essence = a woman's soul = a geometric center of a body = a woman's genitals.

39. I think this was the original form of the line. Bennett uses this version in his edition of Donne's poems, but Grierson and Hayward prefer the variant reading: "There is no penance due to innocence." Each version has the support of several manuscripts. Probably both are by Donne, and one is a later revision of his original text. The version I use seems to me almost certainly what Donne originally wrote. Its tough, man-of-the-world tone is perfectly consistent with the tone of the whole poem and with the kind of love affair which the poem deals with. Also, it gives the conclusion of this section a dramatic punch which is similar to the effect that Donne builds to

at the end of each of the preceding sections of the poem. The other reading of the line makes the poem go startlingly pure and sweet at this point, and for no intrinsic reason that I can see. Grierson agrees that the version which I give was probably the original form of the line and suggests a plausible explanation for Donne's having softened it up later: a marginal note in one of the manuscripts (which gives the sweeter version of the line) indicates that Donne may have revised the poem to use it as an epithalamion, possibly as his own. (*The Poems of John Donne* [Oxford, 1912], 2, 90.)

40. The marginal comment on a manuscript referred to in n. 39 suggests that a good deal of the poem went over the head of at least one of Donne's contemporary admirers. It reads: "Why may not a man write his own epithalamium if he can do it so modestly?" "Modestly" here may refer primarily to the poet's modesty about his sexual prowess, but even in this sense the word is hardly accurate for the sexual braggadocio of the speaker in the poem. And the word certainly carries connotations of a social attitude as well. When one makes every allowance for the wide difference between modern and seventeenth-century standards of sexual propriety—a difference which is suggested by the writer's feeling that this poem was perfectly proper for use as both a marriage gift to one's wife and a public document about the marriage—"modestly" is still pretty astonishing. I can conclude only that the unknown admirer who wrote this comment missed a good deal of what goes on in lines 33–45 of the poem.

41. The distinctive quality in Donne's handling of the materials of Ovidian love poetry can be seen if one compares this poem with Carew's "A Rapture." Carew's poem shows not only the general influence of the tradition of Ovidian verse but also the particular influence of Donne's work. The central theological conceit which the title suggests is a variation of the central conceit of "The Ecstasy," and the poem shows both general and specific debts to Donne's eighteenth and nineteenth Elegies. But the sustained lightness of tone and the effect of prettily decorated indecency in "A Rapture" place it in the main stream of the Ovidian tradition and give a tonal quality quite different from that of Elegy 19.

"Love's Alchemy"

42. Donne himself often uses the analogy without any suggestion of irony in poems which present an essentially Platonic conception of love. It appears, for instance, in "A Valediction: Forbidding Mourn-

ing," 13–29, as a metaphor for a love which is above sensuality and "inter-assured of the mind." There Donne describes this love as "refined" (using the word in its technical sense as a term for the process of alchemic distillation) and unlike the lustful love of common men, which is "elemented" of the flesh. The ambiguity on "elemented" refers to the four elements which composed all earthly matter and from which the alchemist "refined" by extraction the spiritual essence of the quintessence, or the "soul" of gold. In the "Valediction," then, alchemic theory is presented, at least within the imaginative logic of the poem, as sound doctrine, and not at all as the "imposture" which Donne seems to regard it in "Love's Alchemy." This ambivalence in handling images from alchemy appears throughout Donne's work, and it is characteristic also of his treatment of images from astrology. The reason for this logical inconsistency is that both of these bodies of theory had a somewhat ambiguous position in early seventeenth-century thought and lay on the borderline between scientific truth and quackery. For a Renaissance poet, therefore, imagery from alchemy and astrology could cut either way: it could imply either a swindle game or esoteric truth about the secrets of the natural world. In *Paradise Lost,* written long after Donne's poem, Milton treats both alchemy and astrology as essentially true, and at the end of the seventeenth century, scientists as reputable as Robert Boyle and Sir Isaac Newton were still engaging in alchemic research.

43. Lines 715–22. The completely stock character of the metaphor appears from Shakespeare's use of it in Sonnet 33:

> Full many a glorious morning have I seen
> Flatter the mountain-tops with sovereign eye,
> Kissing with golden face the meadows green,
> Gilding pale streams with heavenly alchemy . . .

Shakespeare does not expand the analogy here but uses the phrase "heavenly alchemy" simply as a piece of Platonic shorthand to support the parallel which the poem develops between the effect of the rising sun and the spiritualizing influence of a love which is not tainted with lust.

44. Donne uses "quintessence," "elixir," and "soul of gold" as interchangeable terms, though these terms were sometimes used in the writings of the alchemists to designate different substances.

45. See, e.g., Shakespeare's Sonnet 147: "My love is as a fever, longing still."

46. "Happy" in line 16 carries the same double implication.

47. Cf. the meaning of "mystery" in "The Ecstasy," 71; "The Funeral,"
4; "The Canonization," 27.

48. In Donne's vocabulary the word "mine" always carries the particular suggestion either of gold or of precious stones and is sometimes
merely a synonym for gold, as in the recurrent phrase "the India of
Mine." (Cf. n. 14, above.) For Donne's use of "mine" to mean "gold,"
see "The Sun Rising," 17, and the "Elegy on the Lady Marckham," 24.

49. This analogy was a commonplace in the doctrines of the alchemists.
Cf. Donne's sarcastic reference to it in Elegy 11, lines 43–6:

> Or were it such gold as that wherewithal
> Almighty Chemics from each mineral,
> Having by subtle fire a soul out-pulled;
> Are dirtily and desperately gulled . . .

But the Renaissance imagination readily analogized gold to the human soul on other grounds as well. In the analogical system of "correspondence" by which the universe could be understood, there were
similarities between parallel members of all of the hierarchies in
the subsystems which comprised the cosmos. For this reason gold,
which ranked at the top of the hierarchy of the minerals, occupied
a similar position—and therefore had similarities in nature—to the
top-ranking members of each of the other scales: to the sun, for
instance, in the astronomical world, to the eagle or the lion in the
worlds of the birds or the beasts, to the king in the world of human
society, and to the soul in the "little world of man."

50. Donne uses the same pun in his breezy ridicule of Platonism in
Elegy 18, line 36. There "centric" refers both to philosophic essence
and to the "centric part" of a woman's body. In that passage the
phrase "the earth we till and love" parallels the sexual pun on "dig"
in "Love's Alchemy." Cf. also Elegy 19, line 29.

51. "Told" in these lines evidently does not carry its modern meaning,
since the "kiss-and-tell" implication would make no real sense in the
poem, but rather its older meaning of "assess," probably with the
specific suggestion of counting up or accumulating data. The word
thus operates as part of the analogy between love and alchemic research.

52. For a more explicit treatment of this analogy between the limbec
and the womb see Elegy 8, lines 35–8, and also "The Progress of the

Soul," 494–5. The theoretical basis for the analogy was the alchemists' contention that the "soul," or elixir, was created in the "womb" of the limbec by the sexual union of the masculine, "active principle" of fire, with the feminine, "passive principle" of matter.

53. "Winter-seeming" derives from the stock Petrarchan metaphor of "colds" and "chills" to suggest the frustrations which the lover suffers from his mistress's unresponsiveness. The winter-summer paradox is a further formal device to give an epigrammatic finality to the last two lines of the stanza.

54. "Our day" in line 13 is evidently a reference to the medical theory that sexual indulgence shortened life. See above on "rob me" in line 16 of "The Indifferent" (n. 2).

55. Donne is using "angelic" here in a theologically precise sense, since angels were pure spirit without flesh and their loves were therefore sexless and purely intellectual. The analogy between spiritualized love and the love of angels is another commonplace in Platonic thought. Compare Donne's use of the analogy in his debunking of Platonism in Elegy 18, line 23 ("May barren angels love so"), and in the Platonic love poem, "The Relic":

> Difference of sex no more we knew,
> Than our Guardian Angels do . . .

56. Compare Sir Thomas Browne's use of this analogy in a Platonized passage in *Religio Medici* (Part 2, Section 9) which evolves from a discussion of "the silent note which Cupid strikes":

> For there is a music wherever there is a harmony, order, or proportion: and thus far we may maintain the music of the spheres; for those well-ordered motions, and regular paces, though they give no sound unto the ear, yet to the understanding they strike a note most full of harmony. . . . For even that vulgar and tavern-music, which makes one man merry, another mad, strikes in me a deep fit of devotion, and a profound contemplation of the first Composer. There is something in it of divinity more than the ear discovers: it is an hieroglyphical and shadowed lesson of the whole world, and creatures of God; such a melody to the ear, as the whole world, well understood, would afford the understanding. In brief, it is a sensible fit [= musical phrase] of that harmony which intellectually sounds in the ears of God.

57. The theory behind the Paracelsians' use of Mummy as a medicine was that dead bodies retained some of the Natural Balsam, the sub-

stance in the body which functioned during life to preserve the flesh from wounds and external infections.

58. I think the implication of the material nature of Mummy, in contrast to the spiritual nature of the Elixir, is certainly in Donne's mind. This implication fits precisely with the logical antithesis between the body and the soul which is the organizing concept for the thought of the poem, and it is characteristic of Donne to cast his conceits into the form of an antithetic pair of metaphors in which the two opposed terms are analogized to material reality and to spiritual reality. There are not many other references to Mummy in his poetry, but his imagery from Paracelsian medicine frequently is cast into the pattern of an antithesis between spiritual and material panaceas. The usual antithesis is between the spiritual Elixir, or quintessence, and the material *theriaca,* or mithridate. Compare "The Cross," 25–30, and the following passage from "Love's Growth," where the medical image applies, as in "Love's Alchemy," to the contrast between spiritual and physical love:

> But if this medicine, love, which cures all sorrow
> With more, not only be no quintessence,
> But mixed of all stuffs [= material things], paining soul, or sense,
> And of the sun his working vigour borrow,
> Love's not so pure, and abstract, as they use
> To say, which have no mistress but their Muse . . .

59. My punctuation of the two final lines differs from that of Grierson and other modern editors. Following some of the manuscripts, Grierson punctuates:

> at their best
> Sweetnesse and wit, they'are but *Mummy,* possest.

This punctuation is clearly wrong. It does not make very good sense; it blurs an obvious logical antithesis; and it is curiously slack in syntax for the ending of so tense a poem. It is hardly Donne's practice to let a poem go limp in the conclusion. My punctuation derives from that of the 1633 edition, which shows Donne's careful pointing of the reading pauses which he wanted in order to produce the punch effect of the final half line:

> at their best,
> Sweetnesse, and wit they'are, but, Mummy, possest.

"The Blossom"

60. The evidence for my theory that the poem was written to Mrs. Herbert is complicated, and since this biographical ascription is not essential to my reading of the poem, it had better be discussed here, rather than in the analysis of the poem. "The Blossom" is grouped in the early editions and in a number of the manuscripts with "The Relic," "The Primrose," and "The Funeral." There is some evidence to connect the other poems in this group with Mrs. Herbert. In the 1635 edition "The Primrose" is subtitled "being at Montgomery Castle," though this ascription does not appear in the 1633 edition, nor in the manuscripts. "The Funeral" seems merely another performance on the situation which Donne treats in "The Relic," the lady's gift to him of a bracelet of her hair—in fact, it looks like a first try at the job which Donne does better in "The Relic." The strongest case for associating any of these poems with Mrs. Herbert can be made for "The Relic." In the first place, I think it is almost certain, as Grierson suggests, that line 17 of that poem—"Thou shalt be a Mary Magdalen"—involves a play on Mrs. Herbert's first name. There seems no reason, from the characterization of the lady which the poem presents, to canonize her specifically as the Magdalen unless this was actually her name. Donne is not given to naming particular saints in his religious conceits, nor is he given to such particularity in the detail of a conceit unless the detail has a basis in fact. Moreover, if this line is a play on the lady's actual name, that would account for the rather peculiar vagueness and deliberate evasiveness of the rest of this sentence: "and I / A something else thereby." By the same logic which would make Magdalen Herbert into St. Mary Magdalen, John Donne would be canonized as St. John. Caught up in the logic of his conceit, Donne charges on to make this point, hints at the possibility ("and I"), and then backs off in mock confusion from so immodest a suggestion. In the second place, "The Relic" is very similar to the last four stanzas of the verse letter "To Mrs. M. H." ("Made paper stay"), not only in the details of Donne's imaginative dramatization of his relationship with the lady but also in its relaxed, gaily playful tone. (See below n. 63.) As I have pointed out, this tonal effect is unusual in Donne's work: it is not at all characteristic of Donne's other poems to noble patronesses, nor of the rest of his love poetry.

My case for regarding "The Blossom" as a poem to Mrs. Herbert depends primarily on its similarity, in tone and in the literary dramatization of their friendship, to the verse letter to her and to "The

Relic." And the indications of the temper of Donne's relationship
with her in the passage which I cite from the funeral sermon suggest
that she might well have been the recipient of so merry and facetious
a poem. Grierson's theory that "The Funeral," "The Blossom," "The
Primrose," and "The Relic" form a single group of poems addressed
to Mrs. Herbert is less certain, but there are some grounds for it, and I
would enter it as a further but somewhat dubious piece of evidence
to support my theory about "The Blossom."

Some students of Donne's poetry have agreed with Grierson's view
that "The Blossom" was written to Mrs. Herbert. Garrod, however,
who seems to read some rather playful poems with a heavy literalness,
holds out sternly for scientific proof: "There is nothing in anything
which Donne certainly wrote to her that suggests a relation 'romantic' or 'lover-like'; and to connect her with *any* of the *Songs and
Sonnets* seems speculative and idle." And Gosse demonstrates the critical danger of leaning too heavily on biographical conjecture—as
well as the danger of lacking a sense of humor—by reading the poem
solemnly as evidence for his theory that Donne once had an unhappy
love affair with a married woman. He sees the poem as a sad document about Donne's "great criminal liaison," a poignant cry from
Donne's unlocked heart—and something of a lesson to us all. Finally,
Pierre Leguois, in *Donne the Craftsman* (Appendix B) argues at some
length that none of this group of four poems was written to Mrs.
Herbert. He feels that Donne would not have addressed the "coarse
innuendo" of line 31 of "The Blossom" ("Practise may make her
know some other part") to a gentlewoman of Mrs. Herbert's "stainless character." Maybe—but Renaissance standards of propriety were
different from those of the twentieth century, and coarseness, in any
case, derives less from what is said than from the tone of saying it.
Moreover, though Donne greatly admired Mrs. Herbert as a gentlewoman of stainless character, he enjoyed her also as a merry lady who
loved "facetiousness and sharpness of wit." His own estimate of her
suggests that she might have been able to take this piece of playful
bawdiness in her stride.

My reading of the poem does not depend in any fundamental way
on my belief that it was written to Mrs. Herbert, but the poem does
contain some local and apparently personal details which need accounting for, and they can be accounted for very plausibly on these
grounds.

61. Walton gives a characteristically rosy account of the friendship in
"The Life of Mr. George Herbert" (*Lives* [New York, 1893], pp.
250-2) :

The rest of her character may be read in [Donne's] printed poems,
in that elegy which bears the name of the "Autumnal Beauty." For
both he and she were then past the meridian of man's life.

This amity, begun at this time and place [Oxford], was not an
amity that polluted their souls; but an amity made up of a chain
of suitable inclinations and virtues; an amity like that of St. Chrys-
ostom's to his dear and virtuous Olympias; whom in his letters,
he calls his saint; or an amity, indeed more like that of St. Hierom
to his Paula; whose affection to her was such that he turned poet
in his old age, and then made her epitaph; "wishing all his body
were turned into tongues, that he might declare her just praises to
posterity." And this amity betwixt her and Mr. Donne was begun
in a happy time for him, he being then near to the fortieth year
of his age (which was some years before he entered into sacred orders): a time when his necessities needed a daily supply for the
support of his wife, seven children, and a family: and in this time
she proved one of his most bountiful benefactors; and he as grate-
ful an acknowledger of it.

62. *Works, 6, 270.*

63. Of the three poems which clearly develop this situation of an imaginary courtship—"The Relic," "The Blossom," and "Mad paper
stay"—"Mad paper stay" is the most delicate and oblique in its
handling of these bawdy innuendoes. But in the conclusion of the
poem (lines 36–52) Donne dramatizes himself as a suitor who is jealous
of Mrs. Herbert's other lovers. He suggests that, though she still remains faithful to her husband, her fidelity is precarious, and that
some of her other lovers may have tempted her more successfully than
he has been able to do. He wonders whether, as she reads *their*
love letters, she hides them from her waiting woman and kisses the sig-
natures, and whether, at these times, she does not pine to be free of her
husband ("Mark if . . . she grieves she's not her own") and "chide
the doctrine that denies Freewill"—with a pun on the Renaissance
ambiguity of both "free" (= licentious) and "will" (= sexual desire).

"The Relic" pushes these bawdy implications further, in the comic
imaginative obbligato which plays against its basic theme of serious
and idealistic devotion:

> Difference of sex no more we knew,
> Than our Guardian Angels do;
>   Coming and going, we

> Perchance might kiss, but not between those meals;
> Our hands ne'er touched the seals,
> Which Nature, injured by late law, sets free . . .

"Seals" here, is, in the first place, a euphemism for the genitals. (See n. 16, above.) The last line alludes to the theory that the State of Nature was one of "community," in which lovers enjoyed complete sexual freedom, until this state was "injured" by the "late law" of civilized society, which established the moral codes that inhibit free love. But "seals" seems a rather arbitrary and pointless image here, if the word carries no other meaning than its sexual reference. And "late" seems a peculiar word to apply to a kind of law which was established in the prehistoric dawn of civilization. Those two words indicate that Donne is playfully applying the general doctrine of man's unfortunate decline from the natural condition of sexual freedom to the specific personal situation of Mrs. Herbert's recent marriage to Sir John Danvers. In general terms, the law which society established was the law of private property, which restricted the natural, communal possession of women and made the wife the property of her husband; and that law has recently operated, with unfortunate results, in Mrs. Herbert's "late" marriage. Donne and the lady, however, have bowed to the law: "seals" refers also to the seals on the marriage contract, which neither of them has violated. But Donne suggests that obedience to society's law, on her part at least, has required some effort. The word "Nature" carries, in this context, a similarly specific as well as a general reference: it refers to Mrs. Herbert's natural sexual impulses, which were "free" (= licentious) until her nature was "injured" by the recently imposed restrictions of that marriage contract. Donne's play with her name Magdalen (essentially on grounds of the pure spirituality of her love for him) carries also, I think, a playful suggestion of her sexual promiscuity before she reformed and became a high-minded married woman. And the cracks at women elsewhere in the poem ("For graves have learned that woman-head / To be to more than one a bed") carry the same suggestions that at heart she is like all the rest.

In "The Blossom" the bawdy innuendo of the other two poems is simply pushed a step further, to broad and hearty comedy, and the essential purity and probity of Donne's relationship with the lady— which is suggested by the poem's implicit statement that their love will never be anything other than a union of souls—is so taken for granted that it can be shoved into the background and treated comically.

64. This is clear from lines 27–8, where the heart is described as "think-ing" and where a "naked" heart (without the clothing of the body) is compared to a "ghost"—i.e., a disembodied soul. In Renaissance love poetry "heart" is often roughly synonymous with "soul," or "mind." This identification derives from the doctrine that the heart was the seat of the soul and thus of the rational faculties. In a few of his poems Donne follows the Aristotelian tradition which placed the seat of the soul in the brain ("The Funeral," "The Progress of the Soul"). But most of his love poems draw on another theory, derived from Plato and Galenist medicine, which located the soul in the heart (cf. Holy Sonnet 13: "Mark in my heart, O soul, where thou dost dwell"). For other passages where "heart" is clearly a synonym for "soul" see "The First Anniversary," 174 and 186; "The Legacy," 10–20; and "Lovers' Infiniteness," 27–30.

65. Donne puns here on "siege" in the sense of "seat" to splice this con-ceit with his image of a nesting bird's bowing the stiff branches of the tree.

66. Hazlitt responded enthusiastically to the romantic quality of the opening stanza, but he thought Donne's tasteless concern for "analyt-ical distinctions" wrecked the poem in the later stanzas. He described the poem as "beautiful and impassioned reflections losing themselves in obscure and difficult applications . . . , a lame and impotent con-clusion from so delightful a beginning." ("Lectures on the English Comic Writers," in *Collected Works,* ed. Waller and Glover [London, 1903], *8,* 51–2.) The whole passage is a neat illustration of the differ-ence between the tastes of the seventeenth century and those of the Romantic movement.

67. The modern sense of "heart" obviously overlaps the meaning of "soul" at this point.

68. I think this is the primary meaning of lines 26–7. Donne is using "show" in its technical meaning as a philosophic term to refer to the "accidents" of matter, as distinguished from the "substance" of spirit. But the line carries the further suggestion of a love which is frank and intellectually honest ("naked thinking heart") and not inclined to false display ("show").

69. The particularity of "twenty days hence" may be simply another de-vice of concreteness to support the effect of practical factuality which characterizes Donne's technique in these stanzas. But Donne is usually not so specific without good reason, and it is possible that the specifica-

tion of a twenty-day interval before the soul will rejoin him in London has a factual basis in the social situation from which the poem derives. If the lady had planned to come to London after twenty days, and if she and Donne had planned to meet again at this time, then she would naturally bring his soul along on the trip and could allow him to reclaim it when they met in the city. The conceit is an entertaining one, and it would fit in perfectly with the zany fun of the rest of the poem.

70. See, e.g., "The Damp," where Donne uses a poetic strategy similar to that of "The Blossom." In that poem the rough bawdiness of the last four lines makes the courtly artifice of the rest of the poem seem merely ridiculous.

CHAPTER 2: "THE GOOD-MORROW"

1. Grierson points out Donne's debt to this genre in his notes to "Break of Day" and suggests that Donne's handling of the form derived also from the thirteenth elegy in the first book of the *Amores* (*The Poems of John Donne, 2, 13, 22*). Some of the details of "The Sun Rising" seem to have been suggested by Ovid's poem.

2. "Good-Morrow" was evidently a conventional title for an aubade, a dawn song. It appears as one of the stock titles which Gascoigne gives to his series of experiments in various established genres in *A Hundreth Sundrie Flowres*. The title there—"Gascoigne's Good Morrow"—is applied to a religious poem, and the poem is paired with an exercise in another standard genre—"Gascoigne's Good Night."

3. Cf., e.g., the tone of dawn love scenes in *Romeo and Juliet,* III, v; and in *Paradise Lost,* Book V, 18 ff.

4. The poem exists in two versions and was apparently revised by Donne. I am using the text given by Grierson and by Hayward, which is probably the revised version. In the other version lines 3–4 read:

> But suck'd on childish pleasures seelily?
> Or slumbred we in the seven sleepers den?

Donne's changes in these lines seem to have been made chiefly for a tonal purpose: he evidently wanted to sustain the effect of vigor and colloquial vividness which is established by lines 1–2 through "T'was so" in line 5. The only other significant variations between the two texts are the use of "fitter" instead of "better" in line 17, and the variant reading of line 21: "Love just alike in all, none of these loves can die."

5. "The Seven Sleepers' den" is a reference to the legend of the seven young men of Ephesus who hid in a cave to escape the persecution of the Christians by Decius and remained asleep there for over two hundred years.

6. Sir Edmund Gosse missed the turn and was misled throughout the poem: "In these foppish, heartless lyrics Donne is most interesting when most frankly sensual. 'The Good-Morrow' is the perfectly contented and serene record of an illicit, and doubtless of an ephemeral, adventure." (*The Life and Letters of John Donne* [New York, Dodd Mead, 1899], *1*, 65.) Gosse obviously did not read the poem closely all the way through, but his wrong impression of it is, I think, exactly the response which Donne was working for in the opening lines.

7. "But this" = except for this.

8. For the personal use of the word, in the sense of "a beauty," see "Farewell to Love," 35; Elegy 17, line 24; and Elegy 9, lines 1–3. Donne's use of the word to refer to beauty in general is parallel: it applies to beauty which is specifically physical—cf. "Heroical Epistle," 30; Elegy 18, line 90; "A Valediction: Of the Book," 36.

9. Cf. "Song" ("Sweetest love"), stanza 2; "Heroical Epistle," 6; Satire 1, line 38; "Farewell to Love," 30; Elegy 16, line 2. And note the moralistic distinction implied by *"good desire"* in the "Epithalamion" for the Earl of Somerset, 32.

10. For Donne's use of the word in a specifically sexual sense see "Farewell to Love," 23; and "Heroical Epistle," 36. And compare the puns on this meaning of the word in Marvell, "The Garden," 41; and Middelton, *The Changeling*, II, ii, 151, and III, iii, 5.

11. Donne engages in a similar semantic maneuvering with the word as a central literary effect in "Love's Usury." And he uses a different but equally proscriptive meaning of "love" (= lust) as the basis for playing a game of intellectual tag with his reader throughout the first 38 lines of Elegy 18. This intellectual juggling with different meanings of "love" was a common literary device in Renaissance love poetry. See, e.g., Shakespeare's Sonnet 116: "Love is not love which alters when it alteration finds"; and "Hero and Leander," 176: "Whoever loved, that loved not at first sight." This kind of play on a specialized

meaning of the word clearly derives from the Renaissance philosophic debate about the essential nature of love. That climate of ideas accustomed readers of Donne's age to lines of thought which insisted that only *this* sort of erotic experience was true love, and that other varieties of love were not really "love," and it made them alert to the use of the word in certain limited, dogmatic meanings. A writer of love poetry could exploit this alertness by playing on different meanings of the word as a literary device to dramatize the specific conception of love which he was presenting. Donne's juggling with the word in "The Good-Morrow," then, is an effect which his contemporaries would have caught more readily than modern readers, since they would probably have been more inclined to ask, as they read a love poem, "Just what does this man mean by the word 'love' in this poem?"

12. I suspect that Donne also has in mind the religious implications of the reference to the Seven Sleepers. In the "A Valediction: Forbidding Mourning," and in other love poems which deal with a love of this kind, Donne treats spiritualized love as a religious mystery and the lovers as religious initiates, in contrast to the "laity" (ordinary sensual lovers). (See, e.g., "The Canonization," "The Undertaking," "The Ecstasy.") The rest of "The Good-Morrow" does not develop this identification of love with religious devotion, but the parallel between love and religion is so habitual an imaginative association with Donne that it seems probable that he has it in mind here. If so, the image of Seven Sleepers implies that the lovers belong to the small band of devotees to the true faith of an essentially spiritual love and that they have not been practitioners of their belief during their earlier love affairs.

13. Cf. *Hamlet,* III, ii, 119–23: "Lady, shall I lie in your lap? . . . Do you think I meant country matters?" See also Donne's verse letter "To the Countess of Bedford" ("Madame, you have refined me"), 50: "On these [her physical charms as distinguished from the beauty of her soul] I cast a lay and country eye"; and the verse letter "To Sir Henry Wotton" ("Sir, more than kisses"), 25–32, where Donne refers to lust as the vice "several to" the country and describes the country as a place where "men become beasts."

Donne's revision in this line of "The Good-Morrow"—from "suck'd on childish pleasures seelily" to "sucked on country pleasures childishly"—was probably made to introduce an ambiguity which would support the double-take effect that he was working for in the opening lines.

14. Compare *Troilus and Cressida*, V, ii, 109 ff.:

> Ah, poor our sex! This fault in us I find,
> The error of our eye directs our mind.
> What error leads must err. Oh, then conclude
> Minds swayed by eyes are full of turpitude.

In these lines Shakespeare puns on "error" = wandering.

15. Donne uses the word "controls" with a strongly dynamic connotation, to imply the action of an authority which masters and subjugates. Cf. "A Hymn to Christ, at the Author's Last Going into Germany," 17; and "The Ecstasy," 44. This usage was general in Renaissance English.

16. This line is intelligible enough without philosophic commentary, but I think it had for Donne a precise philosophic basis in the concept of the transforming power of love, which is one of the commonplaces of Renaissance Platonism. Donne often refers to this concept—see, e.g., "The Ecstasy," 23; and "Hymn to God, My God, in My Sickness," 6.

  Donne plays in this line on an ambiguity of the word "room" in Renaissance English. He normally uses the word in the more general sense of "place," and that meaning is implied here by the parallel between "room" and "every where," since "where" in Renaissance usage is a noun meaning "place." (For the same ambiguity on "room" see "The Canonization," 32; "Elegy upon Mrs. Boulstred," 37–8; and also, I believe, "Hymn to God, My God, in My Sickness," 1.)

17. The texts of Grierson and of other modern editors follow the early editions in reading "other" rather than "others." "Other" in the plural sense is acceptable Renaissance usage, but I have not noticed this usage elsewhere in Donne's work. And "others" is the normal reading in the manuscripts.

18. Donne is playing in this line on two meanings of the word "world." His imagination normally works in terms of medieval geography, which divided the earth into two hemispheres—a hemisphere of water and a hemisphere of land. The hemisphere of land, which was made up of the three continents of Europe, Africa, and Asia, comprised the entire habitable world. Donne often equates these three continents with "the world"—see "A Valediction: Of Weeping," 10–13; "Hymn to God, My God, in My Sickness," 16–20; and "To the Countess of Bedford" ("T'have written then"), 67. I think, then, that the first

"world" in line 13 refers to the New World, and the second "world" to the Old World of the three continents.

19. The logical basis for this imaginative equation is made clear by the further development of the conceit in stanza 3. Donne is equating a love based solely on desire to possess a woman's body with a desire to possess the earth, which is made up of matter. But I think the "sea-discoverers" image was probably suggested to Donne by the stock Petrarchan conceit which equated the physical beauties of the mistress with the treasures of the Indies discovered by the Renaissance voyagers. (See the discussion in Chapter 1 of Donne's use of this metaphor in Elegy 19.) The exploration metaphor thus would have had for Donne an association with conventional love poetry and with the preoccupations of ordinary lovers.

20. This implication is suggested by lines 9–10 and is developed more fully in stanza 3. The feverish restlessness of lust was a commonplace of Platonic doctrine, and the Platonic reference of Donne's thought in this poem would function to sharpen this suggestion of the image.

21. In Renaissance usage "possess" often has much stronger connotations than in modern English: it implies absolute mastery. In Donne's time the word still retained its metaphoric connection with demonic possession. (Cf. *Much Ado about Nothing*, III, iii, 163–4.) And I think the implications of the map reference in line 13 are related to the distinction between "possessed," "have gone," and "have shown." A map has a specialized significance for Donne's imagination as a metaphor for something which offers only limited and imperfect knowledge. (See below, Chapter 4, n. 11.) I believe, therefore, that Donne is implying that the map readers are even further removed from complete "possession" of a world than the sea-discoverers.

22. This detail of the analogy derives from Donne's habitual visualization of the earth as sharply divided into two hemispheres. Compare Sermon 66: "If you look upon this world in a map, you find two hemispheres, two half worlds. . . . And as of those two hemispheres of the world, the first hath been known long before, but the other (that of America, which is richer in treasure) God reserved for later discoveries." (*Works, 3,* 175.)

23. In *Troilus and Cressida* (III, iii, 100 ff.) Achilles expounds a similar theory of sight, and Ulysses replies:

> I do not strain at the position,
> It is familiar.

24. Cf., e.g., "The First Anniversary," 316: "as to our eyes, the forms
from objects flow"; and "The Second Anniversary," 291–2. And see
the distinction in Sermon 154 between the immediate knowledge of
angels and the mediate knowledge of men, which is based on sense
experience: "Neither do the angels know *per species,* by those result-
ances and species which rise from the object, and pass through the
sense to the understanding." (*Works, 6,* 183.) See also, however, Sermon 28, where Donne refers to the eyebeams and the phantasms as
belonging to contrasting theories of sight: "No man knows so, as
that strong arguments may not be brought on the other side, how he
sees, whether by reception of species from without, or by emission of
beams from within." (*Works, 1,* 567.) In *Pseudodoxia Epidemica*
Browne discusses the concepts of phantasms and of eyebeams as alternative hypotheses of sight. He refers to Aristotle and others "who
hold that sight is made by Reception, and not by extramission; by
receiving the rays of the object into the eye, and not by sending any
out," and cites Pythagoras, Plato, Galen, and Euclid as proponents
of the theory of "extramission." (*Works,* Bohn Library [London,
1852], *1,* 334–5.) The theory existed in variant forms, and my summary is based on the doctrine that Donne normally works with,
which is actually a combination of two separate theories of sight.

25. Cf. "The Canonization," 40–1; and "The Ecstasy," 7–12:

> Our eye-beams twisted, and did thread
> Our eyes, upon one double string . . .
>
> .   .   .
>
> And pictures in our eyes to get
> Was all our propagation.

Much of Renaissance love poetry shows a similar sense of the concreteness of the eyebeams, the image in the eye, and the image in
the heart. See also Browne, *Pseudodoxia Epidemica:* "The visible
species of things strike not our senses immaterially, but streaming in
corporeal rays do carry with them the qualities of the object from
whence they flow, and the medium through which they pass" (p. 256).
And compare Aquinas, *Summa Theologica,* Q. 12, Art. 2: "For vision is made actual only when the thing seen is in a certain way in
the seer. Now in corporeal things it is clear that the thing seen cannot be by its essence in the seer, but only by its likeness; as the likeness of the stone is in the eye, whereby the vision is made actual,
whereas the substance of the stone is not there."

26. My summary of the theory is based on the exposition of the physiology of love in Bembo's speech on Platonic Love in Book 4 of *The Book of the Courtier* and on Donne's references to the same theory in "The Ecstasy."

27. Cf. Marvell, "To His Coy Mistress," 35–6:

> And while thy willing soul transpires
> At every pore through instant fires. . . .

28. The notion that love shows itself in the face is common in Renaissance love poetry. Cf. "Hero and Leander," sestiad 2, 132: "Affection by the countenance is descried"; and the sonnet of Petrarch's translated by Wyatt:

> The long love that in my thought doth harbor,
> And in my heart doth keep his residence,
> Into my face presseth with bold pretense,
> And there encampeth, spreading his banner.

29. The "true plain hearts" are the "waking souls" of line 8. For Donne's use of "heart" as a synonym for "soul" see Chapter 1, n. 64.

30. I think Donne's comparison of spiritualized love to a celestial sphere probably carried, in his own mind, further philosophic connotations from his habitual association of the spheres with the symbol of the circle. This symbol, which had acquired a rich significance from Aristotelian metaphysics and from scholastic theology, appealed strongly to Donne's imagination: he used it many times in his sermons and several times in his verse. (Cf., e.g., the final stanza of "A Valediction: Forbidding Mourning" and lines 1–16 of the elegy on the death of Prince Henry.) In "The Good-Morrow" the religious and cosmological connotations of the symbol of the circle lie only in the penumbra of the suggestions of the image of the celestial sphere, but they surround that image with a further aura of implication—a suggestion that this love is something which is perfect, entirely self-contained, serene, and permanent, something which belongs to the philosophic category of spirit and is beyond the category of earthly things.

31. Donne uses similar conceits in "Love's Growth" and in Elegy 18, lines 25 ff. See also "The Dissolution," where he analogizes lust to the four elements. But the parallels with the "Valediction" are so close as to suggest that that poem may be a conscious reworking, at a later date, of some of the materials of "The Good-Morrow."

32. "Sharp North" suggests, I believe, more than the mere physical discomforts of a hard winter. To the Renaissance mind the change of seasons on the earth was a consequence of the Fall and therefore a symbol of the fleshly corruption and imperfection of man's life on earth. Cf. *As You Like It,* II, i, 5–11:

> Here feel we but the penalty of Adam,
> The season's difference: as the icy fang
> And churlish chiding of the winter's wind,
> Which, when it bites and blows upon my body
> Even till I shrink with cold, I smile, and say
> "This is no flattery; these are counsellors
> That feelingly persuade me what I am."

The use of "West" as an image for death recurs throughout Donne's work. See "Hymn to God, My God, in My Sickness," 9–15, and the parallels to that passage which Grierson cites in his notes to the poem.

33. Cf. "The Second Anniversary," 135–40, where Donne refers to the "even constitution" which preserves the sun from "disuniting" and decay. In this line of "The Good-Morrow" Donne plays on the ambiguity of the word "equally" in Renaissance English. Here it means (a) "of identical, or equivalent, components," and (b) "evenly, temperately." Donne often uses the word "equal" to mean "temperate"— see "The Progress of the Soul," 424; Elegy 8, line 35; and "To the Countess of Huntingdon" ("That unripe side of the earth"), 117–19. This second meaning of the word suggests, then, the peace and emotional stability of the love affair.

34. Cf. "The Ecstasy," 45–8:

> We then, who are this new soul, know,
> Of what we are composed, and made,
> For, th'atomies of which we grow,
> Are souls, whom no change can invade.

35. "Our two loves" in line 19 evidently means "our two amorous souls." In his poems which deal with an essentially spiritual love Donne sometimes uses "love" as synonymous with "soul." Cf. "Air and Angels," 7 and 25; and "The Anniversary," 17: "Souls where nothing dwells but love."

Donne offers in these lines the same alternative hypotheses to account for the psychological phenomena of spiritual love which he

presents in "A Valediction: Forbidding Mourning," 21–8. The hesi-
tation between these two theories in "The Good-Morrow" is evidently
the doctrinal basis for Donne's use of the two different microcosm
analogies, which present the lovers, first, as two separate worlds and,
later, as joined into a single world.

36. Cf. "A Lecture upon the Shadow," 19: "If our loves faint, and west-
wardly decline."

37. This implication of the metaphor of a sphere is common in Renaissance literature. Cf., e.g., Claudius' speech in *Hamlet* about his love
for Gertrude (IV, vii, 14–16):

> She's so conjunctive to my life and soul
> That, as the star moves not but in his sphere,
> I could not but by her.

38. See Jonson's statement to Drummond that "Donne said to him he
wrote that Epitaph on Prince Henry . . . to match Sir Ed. Herbert
in obscureness" (*Conversations,* #7).

39. The only external evidence which connects any of these poems with
Anne More is Walton's testimony, in his *Life of Dr. John Donne,* that
Donne wrote "A Valediction: Forbidding Mourning" to his wife
in 1612, when he was about to leave her to go abroad on a diplomatic
mission. Walton was not the most scientific of biographers, but I see
no reason, from the content of the poem itself, to doubt his testimony.
And "The Ecstasy," "The Canonization," and "The Good-Morrow"
seem to deal with the same love affair on which the "Valediction" is
based. All four of these works are poems of intense and wholehearted
emotional commitment; they all insist on the uniqueness of the love,
both in contrast to the love affairs of other men and in contrast to
Donne's other experiences of love; and they all present an identical
theoretical analysis of the nature of the love to justify Donne's contention that it is exceptional or unique in kind. Moreover, all of them
except "The Ecstasy" are explicit in their expression of attitudes of
withdrawal from the world and renunciation of the concerns of ordinary men. These poems demonstrate such an internal consistency
in their treatment of the love affair, and they express attitudes which
conform so closely to those which we would expect Donne to have had
as a result of the circumstances of his marriage—and which we know
from his letters that he actually did have—that it seems to me virtually certain that they were all based on Donne's love for Anne
More.

CHAPTER 3: "THE CANONIZATION"

1. This poem has recently been analyzed in detail by Cleanth Brooks, in *The Well-Wrought Urn,* and more briefly by Leonard Unger and by Doniphan Louthan. While I do not disagree essentially with their readings of it, I think it is a richer and more complex poem than their analyses suggest, and I hope that those who have read these other analyses will find it worth their time to go through "The Canonization" again.

2. I have emended Grierson's text of line 15 ("Adde one more to the plaguie Bill") to read "man" in place of "more." "Man" is the reading of a number of the best manuscripts, and the effect of both concreteness and extravagance of statement which it gives to the line is consistent with the technique of the rest of these opening stanzas.

3. Donne invariably uses the word "contemplate" with specific reference to religious contemplation. In this passage the theological implication of the word points to the conceit of the preceding line: it draws the standard Renaissance analogy between the king and God, and a further analogy between the king's act of impressing his face on a coin and God's act of impressing Form on matter in creating the world. (This second analogy is one of Donne's favorite conceits and appears throughout the sermons and frequently in the poems. See, e.g., "A Valediction: Of Weeping," lines 1–16.) The ironic force of these lines, then, comes from equating the pursuit either of advancement at court, or of money, with religious devotion, a devotion which leads one to seek God either through trying to see Him face to face in the Beatific Vision or through trying to see Him indirectly as revealed in created nature.

4. See Chapter 1, nn. 2 and 54. There is no question that this medical theory gave Donne many an uneasy moment—cf. "The First Anniversary," 105–10:

> For that first marriage was our funeral:
> One woman at one blow, then killed us all,
> And singly, one by one, they kill us now.
> We do delightfully our selves allow
> To that consumption; and profusely blind,
> We kill our selves to propagate our kind.

5. Cf. the reference in *Samson Agonistes* (673–5) to the "common rout" of men who "grow up and perish as the summer fly"; Othello's

description of the lust of Cassio and Desdemona, "as summer flies
are in the shambles, / That quicken e'en with blowing" (IV, ii, 66–7);
and King Lear's speech on lust:

> Die for adultery? No.
> The wren goes to't, and the small gilded fly
> Does lecher in my sight.
> Let copulation thrive.   (IV, vi, 113–16.)

6. Cf. Lyly, *Euphues and His England:* "she hath showed herself a
lamb in meekness when she had cause to be a lion in might, proved
a dove in favour when she was provoked to be an eagle in fierceness."
(*Complete Works*, ed. R. W. Bond [Oxford, 1902], 2, 208.) Crashaw
uses the antithesis in "The Flaming Heart" ("By all the Eagle in thee,
all the Dove") with the same mixture of sexual and religious implications which it carries in "The Canonization."

7. The particular "riddle" about the phoenix which Donne refers to
here is the problem of how it could propagate its kind when there was
only one phoenix in existence. The phoenix, therefore, according to
Renaissance natural history, must have embodied both sexual principles in one creature. The phrase "hath more wit" can be translated:
"makes more sense."

8. I think the word "us" in line 22 is also meant to imply that the
lovers' souls have been mysteriously united into a single new metaphysical entity. The syntactical awkwardness of phrasing in "we in
us" seems designed to throw an emphasis on the word "us" which
will call the reader's attention to the fact that Donne is using it in a
specialized meaning. I have referred earlier (Chapter 1, n. 24) to
Donne's characteristic trick of playing with specialized meanings of
the different cases of personal pronouns as a grammatical device to
dramatize his presentation of the philosophic doctrines of spiritualized love. I think Donne uses "us" in this line in the same sense as in
lines 51–4 of "The Ecstasy":

> They [our bodies] are ours, though they are not we, we are
>   The intelligences, they the sphere.
> We owe them thanks, because they thus,
>   Did us, to us, at first convey . . .

In this last line the two "us's" refer to the souls of each of the two
lovers. These souls have been "interinanimated" with one another
so that they have changed their metaphysical nature and each soul
has become a new collective self for each of the lovers: their souls

are therefore no longer "me" and "you," since each soul has now been changed into an "us."

9. Modern editors have differed over the proper punctuation for lines 24–5. Grierson punctuates as follows, connecting line 25 logically with lines 26–7 rather than with lines 23–4:

> The Phoenix ridle hath more wit
> By us, we two being one, are it.
> So to one neutrall thing both sexes fit,   25
> Wee dye and rise the same, and prove
> Mysterious by this love.

The seventeenth-century editions end both line 24 and line 25 with a period, but Grierson's punctuation has the support of some good manuscripts. I think, however, that line 25 belongs in sense with lines 22–4 rather than with lines 26–7, since it sums up the implication of both the eagle-dove reference and "the Phoenix riddle"— that of the mysterious union of two sexes. The sense of lines 23–5 seems to be: "Both sexes have fitted into one neutral thing so completely that we two have become the phoenix." The two following lines, then, define a further analogy between the lovers and the phoenix.

10. The jarring suggestions of lust in the sexual pun on "die" in "we die and rise the same" are enforced by the parallel with the phoenix's death by fire, which echoes the implications of the taper image in line 21.

11. Donne's emphasis on advancement through commercial enterprise in stanzas 1 and 2 suggests that "chronicle" does not refer to historical chronicles like Holinshed's but rather to the contemporary bourgeois chronicles which glorified the achievements of successful citizens. A passage in Nashe's *Pierce Penniless* (ed. Harrison [London, 1924], pp. 59–60) suggests that the contrast between the immortality afforded by this kind of chronicle and that afforded by "verse" may have been Renaissance commonplace:

> Gentles, it is not your lay chronographers, that write of nothing but of Mayors and Sheriffs and the dear year, and the great frost, that can endow your names with never dated glory. . . . It is better for a nobleman or gentleman to have his honour's story related, and his deeds emblazoned by a Poet, than a citizen.

12. "Hearse" is the term for the ornate carved canopy over an elaborate Renaissance tomb. The statement that a "legend" might be "unfit

for tombs and hearse" derives from the fact that the memorial poems which were a normal part of Renaissance funeral observances might either be carved on the tomb as an epitaph or hung on the hearse in tribute to the dead.

13. The antithesis between proving a "piece of chronicle" and building "pretty rooms" defines the submerged metaphor of lines 31–2: the chronicle is compared to an imposing building—the half-acre tomb—and "pretty rooms" evidently refers to small chapels or shrines. The word "room" carries a shadowy pun on its generalized meaning of "place," so that the conceit continues into the following lines in the antithetic pattern: chronicle = tomb/sonnet = urn.

14. The word "sonnet" here has its generalized Renaissance meaning of "love poem," as in the collective title for Donne's love poetry: "Songs and Sonnets."

15. This doctrine is not explicitly defined in the text of "The Canonization," which presents no explanation for the statement that in future days love will have declined into the "rage" of lust. But reference to the Decay of Nature was so common a convention of Renaissance funeral verse that I think there is little doubt that this idea lies behind the dogmatic statement of line 39. In the genres of both the epitaph and the funeral elegy the concept of the Decay of Nature was normally used, as Donne uses it here, to establish the conceit that the death of the person being mourned has removed from the world all beauty, or virtue, or artistic talent, so that Nature's decay will henceforth proceed unchecked. (Cf. Donne's use of this convention in "The First Anniversary.") Other Renaissance elegies indicate that an allusion to the Decay of Nature was so much an expected commonplace in verse of this kind that a poet could merely hint at the idea and rely on his reader to supply the doctrinal basis for the suggestion that, in the future, things would inevitably go from bad to worse. See, e.g., Jonson's "Epitaph on Elizabeth, L. H.," lines 5–6 and 11–12; and Carew's third "Epitaph on Lady Mary Villiers," which parallels Donne's conceit in "The Canonization":

> This hopeful beauty did create
> New life in Love's declining state.

The doctrine of the Decay of Nature flickers in and out of Donne's earlier poems, usually as the basis for a mere point of wit. It does not seem to have taken hold of Donne's imagination strongly until the early 1600's, shortly before he wrote the two Anniversaries.

16. Cf. Donne's use of the phrase "harmless [= sinless] lovers" in "The Relic," 22, in a proscriptive sense to define a Platonic relationship. In that passage the adjective is similarly emphatic.

17. See the analysis of the last stanza of "The Good-Morrow" in the preceding chapter for a discussion of the theory behind Donne's concern with the image in the eyeball in this passage.

18. Cf., e.g., Donne's use of the term in the elaborate Creation conceit which runs through the first two stanzas of "A Valediction: Of Weeping," where "All," in its specific application, refers to the earth but where the word carries also a connotative reference to the cosmos. When the word is used in this sense it is so frequently capitalized in the early editions of Donne's poetry and prose that I think the capitalization probably existed in Donne's manuscripts, and I have therefore added the capital in my text of this poem.

19. The Neo-Platonic doctrine of the Anima Mundi had a general currency in Renaissance England, and Donne often alludes to it. See, e.g., Satire 3, lines 35–9 (where "self" = soul), and "The First Anniversary" where it is the basis for the central conceit. Cf. Shakespeare's sonnets 107 and 146, and Jonson's reference to Shakespeare in his memorial verses as "Soul of the World."

20. "Contract" in line 40 is the reading of all the early editions, but "extract" is the normal reading in the manuscripts. I agree with Grierson and other modern editors in preferring "contract," since it parallels "epitomize" in line 43 and is allied in connotation to "drove." But "extract" certainly defines part of the sense of the line, and it may be that "contract" is a later change by Donne in the original reading of this line. At any rate, Donne often uses "contract" to carry the double implication of extracting and of concentrating the essence of something. Cf. the passage from the Sermons which Grierson cites in his note on these lines in "The Canonization."

21. See Spenser, "An Hymne in Honour of Beautie," 29–49. And compare the following passage from the Sermons: "And therefore he [St. Augustine], and others of the Fathers read that place . . . *Quod factum est, in ipso vita erat,* that is, in all their Expositions, whatsoever is made in time, was alive in God, before it was made, that is, in that eternal Idea and pattern which was in Him." (Quoted by Evelyn M. Simpson, *A Study of the Prose Works of John Donne* [Oxford, 1948], p. 55.)

22. The early editions and a few good manuscripts read "A pattern of *our* love." This reading at least defines a secondary implication of the word "pattern"—a model of behavior. In this sense the word has connotations which relate it specifically to the sainthood conceit, since, because of a linguistic confusion with "patron," "pattern" was used in the Renaissance as a specific term for a saint. (See *N.E.D.:* "pattern.") I suspect that Donne is aware of this connotation from his use of this word in the extended sainthood conceit at the end of "The Second Anniversary":

> Since His will is, that to posterity,
> Thou should'st for life, and death, a pattern be . . .
>
> (Lines 523–4.)

23. The image in these lines is parallel in doctrinal significance to the metaphor of the "glass" or "mirror" images in "The Canonization." The body is analogized to the entire physical world, the "Book of Nature," through which mortals may attain indirectly to an apprehension of the "mysteries" of soul, or metaphysical essence.

24. Donne expresses this contemporary commonplace in "The First Anniversary," 425–6:

> She that did thus much, and much more could do,
> But that our age was Iron, and rusty too . . .

25. I offer this burrowing into the private processes of mind behind the poem tentatively, as speculation. But I think there are additional reasons, beyond those given here, to support my theory that "The Canonization" derived from a seriously divided state of mind on Donne's part. See the further discussion of this poem in Chapter 5, pp. 172–5.

CHAPTER 4: "HYMN TO GOD, MY GOD, IN MY SICKNESS"

1. I think John Sparrow's arguments for the 1623 date (*Modern Language Review, 19,* 462–6) are very convincing. The close parallels which he cites between this poem and the *Devotions* seem to me significant, and I agree with his suggestion that "in My Sickness" looks like a title which Donne gave the poem later in order to connect it with the particular sickness that he had publicized in the *Devotions.* Helen Gardner reviews the problem of dating the poem in Appendix E of *John Donne: The Divine Poems* (Oxford, 1952) and casts a tentative vote for 1623.

2. Cf. "Obsequies to the Lord Harrington," 1–2:

> Fair soul, which wast, not only, as all souls be,
> Then when thou wast infused, harmony . . .

3. See, e.g., Browne's reference to the doctrine in the passage which I allude to on p. 99, where it appears in connection with the same general musical analogy which Donne is using in this stanza: "I will not say, with Plato, the soul is an harmony, but harmonical, and hath its nearest sympathy unto music." (*Religio Medici,* Pt. 2, Sec. 9.)

4. Cf. "The First Anniversary," 311–12, and Grierson's note; "A Hymn to Christ, at the Author's Last Going into Germany," 18; and the following passage from Sermon 9: ". . . that soul who, whatsoever string be strucken in her, base or treble, her high or low estate, is ever tuned toward God." (*Works, 1,* 177.)

5. Cf. Sermon 21: "Here [on earth] God does all in all; but here he does all by instruments; even in the infusing of faith he works by the ministry of the Gospel. But there [in heaven] he shall be all in all, do all in all immediately by himself." (*Works, 1,* 424.) The use of the word in this sense is frequent in Donne's sermons. See also the "Elegy upon . . . Prince Henry," 32–4; "A Valediction: Of the Book," 22; and the similar ambiguity on "organ" in "Upon the Translation of the Psalms," 16.

6. Lines 85–92 in "The Second Anniversary" provide the closest parallel; they look, in fact, like the embryonic form of this passage in the "Hymn":

> Think then, my soul, that death is but a groom,
> Which brings a taper to the outward room,
> Whence thou spiest first a little glimmering light,
> And after brings it nearer to thy sight:
> For such approaches doth heaven make in death.
> Think thy self labouring now with broken breath,
> And think those broken and soft notes to be
> Division, and thy happiest harmony.

For an earlier use of the image see Elegy 16, lines 43–6, where it seems to be developed out of a pun on the word "presence" (= throne-room) in the phrase "the presence of God."

7. Donne plays on the same ambiguity of the word in "The Good-Morrow," 11; "The Canonization," 32; and the "Elegy on Mrs. Boulstred," 37–8. For his use of the word in the more general meaning of "place" see "The Progress of the Soul," 70–7, and "The Second Anniversary," 251. All of these passages suggest the Aristotelian doc-

trine which probably underlies the reference to heaven as a "holy room" in the "Hymn." All created things have their proper "room," or place, in the cosmos, to which they tend by nature. The human soul, as Donne often points out, has such a place in heaven, but it occupies temporarily a "lower room" in the earthly body before it goes to its final, and proper, "upper room" in heaven. Compare Meditation 2 in the *Devotions:* "earth is the center of my body, heaven is the center of my soul: these two are the natural places of those two; but those go not to these two in an equal pace"; and Sermon 21, where Donne refers to heaven as "our sphere and that which we are fain to call our place." (*Works, 3, 500; 1, 423.*)

8. Line 10. See also lines 433–4:

> But those rich joys, which did possess her heart,
> Of which she's now partaker, and a part.

And cf. Sermon 72: "that great marriage feast which is the kingdom of heaven, where whosoever is a dish is a guest too; whosoever is served in at the table sits at the table . . ." (*Works, 3, 304.*)

9. Cf. the following passages from Paracelsus' medical tracts (*Selected Writings,* ed. Jolande Jacobi [New York, 1951], pp. 144, 147):

> [Some physicians] would rather harm a patient and even kill him than grant a colleague his meed of praise. From this, everyone can judge why a man has become a physician: not out of love for the patient, which should be the physician's first virtue, but for the sake of money.

> Now by what manner on earth can greater love be shown a neighbour, than when a man motivated by true love discovers the curative virtues of remedies, in order to avert the great sufferings, the diseases, and the death that threatens his neighbour?

10. Cf. "The Ecstasy," 23: "And by good love were grown all mind"; "A Valediction: Forbidding Mourning," 17–19; the statement that "we are made such by love" and "prove mysterious by this love" in "The Canonization"; and the statement in "The Good-Morrow" that love "makes one little room, an every where."

11. See, e.g., Satire 4, lines 1–4:

> My sin
> Indeed is great but I have been in
> A Purgatory, such as feared Hell is
> A recreation to, and scarce map of this.

(Here "scarce" = scant, inadequate.) There is a similar use of the metaphor ("strict map") in line 8 of the verse letter "To Mr. T. W." ("At once, from hence"). And compare the opening of the fourth Meditation in the *Devotions:* "It is too little to call man a little world; except God, man is diminutive to nothing. . . . And if those pieces were extended, and stretched out in man, as they are in the world, man would be the giant, and the world the dwarf, the world but the map, and the man the world." In this passage Donne is paradoxically inverting the normal concept, making man the macrocosm and the world the microcosm, but the significance of the passage for my purpose is that it treats a map as a diminished and inadequate representation of the world.

This special suggestion of the metaphor of a map was common in Renaissance literature and is not peculiar to Donne. It derives from the fact that the man of the Renaissance usually looked to maps as a way of satisfying his curiosity about the new lands discovered by the voyagers, that the maps he read were partly pictorial and representational, and that they were notoriously inaccurate and incomplete. His experience with maps, therefore, was likely to suggest the particular implications which the image of the map has in this poem. Compare Daniel, *A Defence of Rhyme:*

> Nor must we think, viewing the superficial figure of a region in a map, that we know strait the fashion and place as it is. Or reading an history (which is but a map of men, and doth no otherwise acquaint us with the true substance of circumstances than a superficial card doth the seaman with a coast never seen, which always proves other to the eye than the imagination forecast it), that presently we know all the world, and can distinctly judge of times, men, and manners, just as they were. (*Elizabethan Critical Essays*, ed. G. Smith [Oxford, 1904], 2, 370.)

12. Since Donne equates the passage through the narrow and arduous "strait" with the sufferings of death, which he presents as the "door" into immortal life, I suspect that the phrase "strait is the gate and narrow is the way which leadeth unto life" was hovering in his mind as he evolved this conceit.

13. See Satire 3, lines 21–2, where Donne refers to the Northwest Passage (Anyan, or Bering Strait) and to the Northeast Passage (the passage around the north of Europe) as the "frozen North discoveries." The meaning of these lines in the Satire is made clear by the parallel passage in lines 111–13 of the "Epithalamion" for the Earl of Somerset.

14. This detail of the conceit, which implies that the current in the Straits of Magellan sets only westerly, is based on navigational data in contemporary travel literature. Compare the following passage from the account written by a member of Drake's expedition through the straits in 1577–79: "In this strait we found the sea to have no such current as some do imagine (following the course of the Primum Mobile from East to West) but to ebb and flow ordinarily as upon other coasts." (*Hakluyt's Voyages* [Everyman edition], *8*, 95.)

15. The poem is not explicit on the basis for the contrast between the reaction of the physicians and of Donne himself, but the syntax of the passage implies this distinction ("Whilst my physicians . . . I joy"), and some inference is necessary. I have expanded the implications of these lines on the basis of the suggestions of the contrast between the geographer and the explorer in the exploration metaphor and of the special significance which Donne assigns to a map. I think the doctrinal basis for the contrast is probably the conventional distinction, which Donne often alludes to, between the limited knowledge afforded by reason (= science) and the full understanding which comes from faith. To Donne the doctrine of the resurrection "is not a conclusion out of natural reason but an article of supernatural faith" (*Works, 1,* 363). The contrast in "The Good-Morrow" between the "sea-discoverers" who have actually "gone" to new worlds, and the "others" who have merely been "shown" new worlds by "maps" parallels the suggestions of this passage in the "Hymn": it implies a difference between the scanty knowledge of the map readers and the fuller knowledge of the explorers.

16. *Lives,* p. 65. The general connotations of this West-East imagery to Donne appear from the concluding lines of the epitaph: *Hic licet in occiduo cinere aspicit eum cuius nomen est Oriens.* ("Here, though in falling ashes, he looks unto him whose name is *Oriens.*") Donne puns here on two meanings of *occiduo*—(a) falling, and (b) western —so that the ambiguity of this word parallels the ambiguity of *Oriens* = (a) rising, and (b) east.

17. Compare Donne's own expansion of this conceit in the passage from a sermon which Grierson cites in his notes to this poem. The last two stanzas make clear that Donne's concern in the poem is that his soul be received into heaven immediately after the death of his body. The word "resurrection" in line 15 refers, therefore, to the "resurrection of the soul by grace" (*Works, 3,* 389) rather than to the resurrection of the body at the Last Judgment. In Sermon 17

Donne argues the technical theological accuracy of this usage of "res-urrection" and cites patristic authority for it. I have used the word in this sense throughout my discussion of the poem.

18. Cf., e.g., Hamlet's "undiscovered country, from whose bourn no traveller returns," and the final speech of Roger Mortimer in Mar-lowe's *Edward II:*

> weep not for Mortimer,
> That scorns the world, and, as a traveller,
> Goes to discover countries yet unknown.   (V, vi, 63–5.)

19. See Helen Gardner, op. cit., p. 108.

20. This doctrine would have been in no way recondite to the devout Renaissance reader. He would have found it most readily in the gene-alogical tables of the descendants of Adam prefixed to the 1611 folio of the King James Bible.

21. If a modern reader finds it strange that Donne could be aware of the discovery of America in stanzas 2 and 3 of this poem and oblivious to it in stanza 4, he might examine "The First Anniversary" and Med-itation 21 in the *Devotions*. In both of those works Donne draws on the theories of Copernican astronomy, but the general pattern of the astronomical imagery and thought is Ptolemaic. This imaginative combination of intellectually inconsistent doctrines is typical not only of Donne's imagination but of seventeenth-century thought in gen-eral. It is one of the symptoms of a crisis period in intellectual history, when the elaborate logical structure of the medieval synthesis was crumbling under the impact of new discoveries and new ways of thinking. The logical patterns of the old world view remained, for Donne and his contemporaries, as ingrown habits of imaginative as-sociation, and they appear as patterns of metaphor even in poems which deal with the newly discovered facts that have made those patterns logically untenable. The concepts of medieval geography often show up as fossils in the literary imagination of later Renais-sance poets. See, for instance, "To His Coy Mistress," 5–7, where Marvell expands his reference to the "world" in line 1 by alluding to the traditional eastern limit of the hemisphere of land on the Ganges, and to the western limit in the British Isles ("Humber"). And Milton, who was eagerly interested in new geographical discoveries, habitu-ally thinks of the morning, precisely as Dante did, as beginning "on th' Indian steep" (*Comus*, 139), i.e., at the eastern boundary of the hemisphere of land.

22. See the verse letter "To the Countess of Bedford" ("T'have written then"), 67, where Donne speaks of the new geographical discoveries as having added "Virginia" (the new continent of America) to "the world" (i.e., the three continents); and the second stanza of "A Valediction: Of Weeping," where the act of a cartographer who inscribes Europe, Africa, and Asia on a globe is compared to God's creation of the world (making "All" from "nothing," *ex nihilo*). See above on "The Good-Morrow," Chapter 2, n. 18.

23. Grierson points out in his notes to this poem that "the Eastern riches" would mean, to a Renaissance reader, Cathay and the Indies (i.e., Asia) and that "the Pacific Sea" refers not to the entire Pacific Ocean but to the South Pacific, the *Mare Pacificum,* as it is usually labeled on Renaissance maps. This was the name that Magellan gave to the ocean which he entered after passing through the Straits of Magellan. The association of the Mare Pacificum with Africa seems a little arbitrary, but the schematic pattern of Donne's conceit of the three continents and the three straits indicates that he is thinking of "the Pacific Sea" as the waters which lead the voyager to the coast of Africa. For the association of Jerusalem, the Southern Ocean, and the East with the Earthly Paradise, see Helen Gardner's commentary cited in n. 19 above.

24. Cf. the passage from the Sermons referred to in n. 17: "Still thy prospect is the East, still thy climate is Heaven, still thy haven is Jerusalem."

25. Cf. the verse letter "To Mr. S. B.," 1–3, where Donne equates India with "Paradise." See also the verse letter "To Mr. R. W." ("If, as mine is"), 27–8, where he analogizes the opulence of India to the omneity of God.

26. Cf. Elegy 19, line 35, and "The Second Anniversary," 485 ff. Donne frequently uses the collective riches of the earth as an image, and he normally sums up the suggestion of the image by the word "All."

27. Donne seems to regard this myth as a traditional concept. He refers to it in "The Progress of the Soul," stanza 8, as something which "devout and sharp men fitly guess." But Helen Gardner, who has tried to locate Donne's source, can find no authority, in either the patristic writings or Renaissance commentary, for a myth that the Cross stood on the same spot as the Forbidden Tree (op. cit., pp. 135–7). Don Cameron Allen has suggested that Donne has combined two other legends which analogized Eden and Calvary. ("John Donne's

'Paradise and Calvary'," *Modern Language Notes, 60,* 398–400.) I have no solution to the problem of where Donne picked up this belief, but I think the passage in the "Hymn" indicates that he does think that the Cross and Adam's Tree may have stood either on the same spot or in the same geographical locality ("place"), and also that he regards the myth as not just his own speculation but rather a tradition which other men have believed ("we think").

28. For a similar treatment of the analogies between the Fall and the Redemption (involving, in this case, a parallel between two trees, two gardens, and two men) see Giles Fletcher, "Christ's Triumph over Death," 97–120. I am citing Fletcher's poem not as a source but rather as a parallel manifestation of the medieval-Renaissance literary tradition in which Donne is working.

29. I think Donne must have been aware that each of the opposed terms of his antithesis carries in itself connotations of both death and immortality, but I hesitate to complicate the poem further at this point.

30. The reference in line 24 is to God's decree of punishment to Adam after the Fall: "In the sweat of thy face shalt thou eat bread, till thou return unto the ground . . . , for dust thou art, and unto dust shalt thou return" (Genesis. iii. 19).

31. Donne seems to use "surround" in the specialized meaning of "drown," or at least with some connotation of destruction. Cf. "Twicknam Garden," 1: "Blasted with sighs, and surrounded with tears." See also Sermon 52, where Donne discusses David's penitential tears: David "watered his bed, dissolved his bed, made his bed to swim, surrounded his bed with tears"; "it drowned his bed, surrounded his bed, it dissolved, it macerated, it melted his bed with the brine." (*Works, 2,* 453, 461.)

32. The significance of these Eden-Calvary analogies to the medieval and Renaissance mind is explicitly stated in the church hymn of Venantius Fortunatus, "Pange lingua gloriosi":

> When he fell on death by tasting
> Fruit of the forbidden tree,
> Then another tree was chosen
> Which the world from death should free.
> Thus the scheme of our salvation
> Was of old in order laid. . . .

(Quoted by Rosemond Tuve, "On Herbert's 'Sacrifice,'" *Kenyon Review, 12,* 67.)

33. I think Donne is using the accusative case of the personal pronoun here in his characteristic specialized meaning to refer to the soul, a man's metaphysical identity, as distinguished from the body ("mine"). (See above, Chapter 1, n. 24, and Chapter 3, n. 8.) It is evident throughout the poem that Donne thinks of the soul as a sharply discrete part of the human organism—see, e.g., line 28, where he speaks of preaching his sermons not "to others," but rather "to others' souls." This conception comes particularly clear when he is dealing with death, since he thinks of death specifically as the event which releases the soul from the body.

34. Thorns, like sweat, were a symbol in Christian thought for the punishment for Original Sin—because of Genesis. iii. 17–8: "Cursed is the ground for thy sake . . . thorns and thistles shall it bring forth to thee." And patristic exegesis had assigned this symbolic significance to Christ's crown of thorns on the basis of The Song of Solomon. iii. 11. In his funeral sermon for James I Donne develops these implications in the antithesis between the crown of thorns and the heavenly crown. He cites the patristic authorities who saw in the crown of thorns a symbol for Christ's "infirm, his human nature," and continues: "You know the curse of the earth, *Thorns and thistles shall it bring forth unto thee;* it did so to our Solomon here, it brought forth thorns to Christ, and he made a crown of those thorns, not only for himself, but for us too." (*Works, 5,* 8–9.)

35. See Mark. xv. 17: "And they clothed him with purple, and platted a crown of thorns, and put it about his head." Since "sweat" and "thorns" both carry a reference to the specific physical symptoms of Donne's sickness, I think Donne probably intended "in his purple wrapped" to have a similar concrete reference: an allusion to the fever flush of the illness.

36. Lines 28–9 echo—I think intentionally—the words of St. Paul in 1 Corinthians. ix. 27; and the quotations from St. Paul in the preceding stanza function to enforce this reference. Compare Expostulation 3 ("The Patient Takes His Bed") in the *Devotions:* "But the apostle's fear takes hold of me *that when I have preached to others, I myself should be a castaway* . . . : and therefore am I cast down, that I might not be cast away." Donne's tendency to identify himself imaginatively with St. Paul, as with St. Augustine, is evident from many passages in the sermons. He took holy orders just before the festival of the Conversion of St. Paul, and he was Dean of St. Paul's at the time when this poem was written.

37. I have conjecturally emended the text here. I think "therefor" is the word Donne intended, rather than "therefore," or "therfore," which are the readings of the single manuscript, of the early editions, and of Walton's variant text. "Therefore that" is not clearly wrong, but it makes poorer sense, since neither this line in the poem nor the original biblical text is a statement of a logical conclusion. And "therefor that" (= in order that) is acceptable Renaissance idiom. The vagaries of Renaissance spelling would obscure the distinction between the two words. Compare Donne's use of the same phrase in the closely parallel passage in Sermon 44: "But the fall which we consider in the text . . . is a medicinal falling, a falling under God's hand, but such a falling under his hand, as that he takes not off his hand from him that is fallen, but throws him down therefore that he may raise him." (*Works*, 2, 304.) In this passage "therefore" is clearly a variant spelling of "therefor."

38. In the Authorized Version: "the Lord raiseth them that are bowed down." The discrepancy between the wording of the text in the poem and in the Authorized Version ("throws down" instead of "bowed down") is accounted for by the fact that Donne habitually translates from the Vulgate instead of quoting from the King James Bible. The Vulgate reads: "Dominus erigit elisos."

39. See the verse letter "To the Countess of Huntingdon" ("That unripe side of earth"), 28, where Donne plays with the same ambiguity on "throw down" in a sexual context: "I may be raised by love, but not thrown down." And compare the play on "cast down," to refer to Donne's lying in his sickbed, in the passage from the *Devotions* cited in n. 36 above.

40. Joan Bennett's essay in *Four Metaphysical Poets* is the most perceptive and skillful attempt which I have seen to define the distinctive quality and special effectiveness of Donne's metrics.

41. The "-tion" suffix in "resurrection" is disyllabic.

42. Cf. "A Hymn to God the Father," 17; Elegy 10, line 13; Elegy 16, line 37 (the variant reading which Grierson gives in his notes: "Will quickly know thee, and know thee, alas!"); "The Progress of the Soul," 55; and the plays on "love" and "worlds" in lines 10 and 13 of "The Good-Morrow," and on "well" in line 33 of "The Canonization."

43. Modern pronunciation obscures Donne's rhythmic effect in this line. The accents indicate his scansion. I have retained the seventeenth-

century spelling "Gibraltare" because it points to the Renaissance pronunciation of the name. Compare *Tamburlaine, Part I,* III, iii, 253–6, where Tamburlaine speaks of the ships that

> Sailing along the oriental sea
> Have fetch'd about the Indian continent,
> Even from Persepolis to Mexico
> And thénce untò the stráits of Júbaltér.

The pronunciation Mágellán evidently derives from a preliminary stage in Anglicizing the name from its Spanish form Magallañes, a form which sometimes appears in English Renaissance writings.

CHAPTER 5: SOME CONCLUSIONS

1. "The Metaphysical Poets," in *Selected Essays, 1917–1932* (New York, Harcourt Brace, 1932), pp. 247–8.

2. *Four Metaphysical Poets* (Cambridge, Cambridge University Press, 1934), p. 14.

3. The reference is to the gingerbread figures sold at Renaissance fairs.

4. "An Elegy upon the Death of Dr. Donne," 63–6.

5. *Religio Medici,* Pt. 1, Sec. 32.

6. As "melodious" suggests, the word "noise" had no jarring implications here for the Renaissance reader. It refers to an orchestra, or a band of musicians.

7. The phrase is from Donne's third Holy Sonnet.

8. Stanzas 8, 21, and 24.

9. "Whispers of Immortality," in *Complete Poems and Plays of T. S. Eliot* (New York, Harcourt Brace, 1952), p. 32. Quoted by permission of the publisher.

10. *Works, 6,* 68.

11. *Religio Medici,* Pt. 1, Secs. 38 and 40.

12. *Works, 4,* 231.

13. Stanza 15.

14. *Religio Medici,* Pt. 2, Sec. 6.

15. Ibid., Pt. 1, Sec. 9.

16. "To the Countess of Bedford: On New-Year's Day," 38.

17. J. W. N. Sullivan, *The Limitations of Science* (New York, New American Library of World Literature, 1941), p. 1.

18. This quality in Donne's imaginative actualization of the spiritual union of lovers shows more clearly in "A Valediction: Forbidding Mourning," which presents the same alternative hypotheses about this union which we see in "The Good-Morrow." It appears in the startling concreteness of the conceit of the compass and also in some of the terms which Donne uses to describe the spiritual interaction of the two souls: "expansion," "leans," "moves," and "draws." (I agree with Hayward in preferring the reading "draws" in line 35 to "makes" in Grierson's text of the poem.)

19. *Religio Medici*, Pt. 2, Sec. 5:

> There are three most mystical unions: two natures in one person; three persons in one nature; one soul in two bodies; for though indeed they be really divided, yet they are so united, as they seem but one and make rather a duality than two distinct souls.

In this passage (which refers to masculine love-friendship), Browne accepts the theory of the conjunction of lovers' souls as factually true, as a concept of the same order of validity as the doctrines of the Trinity and of Christ's Dual Will. But by describing this union as "mystical" he implies that the doctrine is repugnant to common sense and that it is something which cannot be thought of in terms of the scientific principles which normally govern the natural world.

20. A. N. Whitehead, *Science and the Modern World* (New York, Macmillan, 1941), p. 3.

21. *Novum Organum*, Book 1, Aphorism 112.

22. Cf. Milton's defense of the imaginative vocabulary of myth in *Comus*, 513–19:

> 'tis not vain or fabulous,
> (Though so esteemed by shallow ignorance)
> What the sage Poets, taught by th' heav'nly Muse,
> Storied of old in high immortal verse
> Of dire Chimeras and enchanted Isles,
> And rifted Rocks whose entrance leads to hell,
> For such there be, but unbelief is blind.

23. *Autobiography* (New York, Macmillan, 1938), p. 188.

24. "To a Young Beauty," in *Collected Poems* (New York, Macmillan, 1951), p. 138. Quoted by permission of the publisher.

25. These statements occur in Cummings' prefaces to *Is 5* (New York, Liveright, 1926) and to his *Collected Poems* (New York, Harcourt Brace, 1938).

26. Stanza 7.

27. *Conversations*, #8.

28. The passage on Queen Elizabeth in "Ignatius His Conclave" (Hayward, pp. 401–3) gives her a more favorable treatment, since she is presented there as one of the strong defenders of the Protestant Reformation against the machinations of the Jesuits. The difference between this passage and the one in "The Progress of the Soul" can be explained, I think, by the rather strained anti-Catholic pose which Donne adopts in "Ignatius His Conclave" and by the evidence that in this satire, written in 1610, Donne is concerned to please James I. But, beneath its surface approbation of Elizabeth, the passage gives a far from flattering picture of her feminine vacillations and follies, and its latent implications are not very different from those of the lines in "The Progress of the Soul."

29. "Musophilus," 239–51.

30. Cf. the reference in Elegy 18, line 16, to the new fashions in love poetry as the result of "our new nature (use)"—with a pun on "use" = (a) fashion, and (b) sexual intercourse—and the jibes at the Petrarchan attitudes as the consequence merely of "use" and "that vice-nature, custom" in "The Flea" and "Love's Deity."

31. "Fate" carries the ironic suggestion of expediency here. It refers to the theological concept of Fate as a subdeity, "God's Lieutenant," to whom God has entrusted the management of purely worldly affairs.

32. See Grierson, *2*, 104.

33. "All Souls' Night," *Collected Poems*, p. 224.

34. *Religio Medici*, Pt. 2, Sec. 11.

35. See "Per Amica Silentia Lunae," in *Essays* (London, 1924), pp. 489–90. Yeats's analysis in *A Vision* (New York, Macmillan, 1938) of the kind of temperament which he saw in Landor defines more fully the

implications of his analogy between Landor and Donne. Landor, as a typical man of Phase Seventeen in Yeats' System, had a literary Mask which sought personal "simplification through intensity." Faced with mental images which continually "flow, change, flutter, cry out," the mind of a man of this character "must synthesize in vain, drawing with its compass-point a line that shall but represent the outline of a bursting pod. The being has for its supreme aim . . . to hide from itself and others this separation and disorder. . . . When true to [historical] phase, the intellect must turn all its synthetic power to this task." (P. 141.)

36. *Autobiography,* pp. 235, 149.

37. Quoted by E. M. W. Tillyard, *Studies in Milton* (New York, 1951), p. 108.

38. Gosse, *1,* 214.

39. Cf. the passage in a letter to George Gerrard (Gosse, *1,* 303–4) in which Donne winces at the criticism of his two Anniversaries, the only poems, except for his commendatory verses on *Coryat's Crudities,* which were published during his lifetime:

> of my *Anniversaries,* the fault that I acknowledge in myself is to have descended to print anything in verse, which though it have excuse even in our times by men who profess and practice much gravity, yet I confess I wonder how I declined to it, and do not pardon myself.

40. This question of the extent to which Donne's poetry can be considered essentially metaphysical, in the common sense of that term, has been discussed by James Smith in an excellent article, "On Metaphysical Poetry" *(Scrutiny, 2,* 222–39). His approach to the problem involves a somewhat different issue from the one which I am investigating. He believes that the metaphysical concepts in Donne's work have a rather different origin, and a different literary purpose, from the metaphysical concepts in the work of poets like Dante and Lucretius, both of whom wrote as the disciples of certain philosophic masters and who were therefore convinced of the truth of the philosophic ideas which they employed in their work and concerned that their readers should accept these concepts as sound doctrine. Smith argues that the metaphysics in Donne's poetry derives from another cast of mind. He believes that Donne wrote as a man who was himself disposed to original metaphysical speculation, a speculation which involved the exploration of traditional philosophic doctrines

and the imaginative application of these doctrines to his personal experience, but that he was more concerned to view his experience against the background of the essential questions of metaphysics than he was to assert the truth of any one system of answers to these questions. I believe that this view of the kind of speculative impulse which lies behind Donne's poetry is essentially correct, but I think that the question of the extent to which Donne thought of the metaphysical concepts which he employed as sound doctrine is worth investigating further, both because it raises an important interpretive problem for the reader of Donne's work, and because I am interested in exploring the personal psychological motivations behind Donne's imaginative preoccupation with metaphysical ideas.

41. "Donne in Our Time," in *A Garland for John Donne,* ed. Theodore Spencer (Cambridge, Harvard University Press, 1931), pp. 11–12.

42. *Four Metaphysical Poets,* pp. 11 and 2.

43. I am assuming here that Walton's date of 1612 for the "Valediction" is accurate. "The First Anniversary" was written for the first anniversary of Elizabeth Drury's death and published in 1611. It could not have been composed earlier than 1610, the year of her death.

44. The implication of "The First Anniversary," more precisely stated, is that the Ptolemaic astronomy was once essentially correct, but that the Decay of Nature has so changed the heavens from "their spherical, their round proportion embracing All" that the Ptolemaic astronomy now seems very dubious as an account of the present degenerated condition of the universe, and the "new Philosophy" appears to be the more accurate description.

45. "At a Vacation Exercise," 19–20. Some scholars have questioned whether this passage refers to the Metaphysical Poets on the grounds that the word "late" seems to allude to a style which had been popular in the recent past rather than to poetic fashions which were current at the time when Milton was writing (1627). But the use of the present tense—"which *takes* our late fantastics with delight"—indicates that Milton is speaking of contemporary poetic affectations. I read "our late fantastics," then, as a colloquial phrase meaning "those who have been writing lately"—i.e., in these days—and, except for the Metaphysical tradition, I can think of no flashy and extravagant poetic style which was a "new-fangled" fashion among poets of the 1620's.

46. I am quoting from Stephen Dedalus' definition of his aesthetic theory in *A Portrait of the Artist as a Young Man* (New York, Modern

Library, 1928), p. 241. This theory forms the basis for Joyce's own artistic practice in *Ulysses* and also, as far as I can determine, in *Finnegans Wake*.

47. I am indebted to Mr. Ellsworth Mason for this quotation. It occurs in an unpublished letter from Joyce to Harriet Shaw Weaver.

48. Cowley, "Ode to the Royal Society," 151.

Index: Works by Donne Discussed

A

[